A Gallant Grenadier

F. S. Brereton

[ZHINGOORA BOOKS]

Chapter One.

Philip Western.

"You positively annoy me, Joseph, and make me feel more angry than I care to admit. The matter is a serious one, and I am deeply distressed. After thirteen years of the most careful bringing-up there is complete and absolute failure. It is a miserable reward. And then, to make matters worse, you laugh at me, and egg the lad on to even greater crimes!"

"Fiddlesticks, sir! Humbug! A miserable reward indeed!" was the spirited answer. "No one but yourself would admit it. He is a fine lad, though a little wild I will own; but for all that a generous, good-hearted boy. Let him alone! Don't worry him with all these goody-goody ideas. There is plenty of time for him to settle down, and meanwhile he will come to no harm, and, I'll be bound, will bring no discredit on you." The speaker shook his head knowingly, and helped himself to a large pinch of snuff.

"How can you argue like that, Joseph, when you know what the lad has done?" the former speaker replied with much sternness. "I hold practical joking to be at any time disgraceful, but when one's adopted son is one of three who actually laid a booby-trap for the mayor of this town in broad daylight, and made him a laughing-stock for all, then discreditable is the least one can say of it. It is positively scandalous."

"Nonsense, Edward! Barrington deserved all he got. He is an odious man, and the fright those youngsters gave him will teach him to mind his own business in future, and not meddle with other people's affairs. Serve him right, I say! Just because a lad breaks one of his windows with a catapult, and by pure accident, he gets the following half-holiday stopped for the whole school. If he hadn't blustered so much, and looked so fierce, I've no doubt the culprit would have given himself up; but he was afraid of the consequences, and most naturally, too. Ha, ha, ha! It was funny! I saw his worship immediately after he had fallen a victim to the joke. He was quivering with mingled fear and rage, and the laughter of the by-standers did not help to soothe him."

Joseph threw himself violently back in his chair, causing it to creak in an alarming manner and almost overturn, and gave vent to roars of laughter, followed by chuckles of intense amusement, produced in such deep tones that they seemed to come from the smart Wellingtons he wore. He was a stout, comfortable-looking man of middle height, with a round, clean-shaven face, which, now that he was laughing, was as red as fire and wrinkled in all directions. He had a shiny head, almost devoid of hair, and a double chin which half hid the wide collar and large bow he wore, while smartly-cut trousers and coat, a wide expanse of shirt front, and a double-breasted waistcoat, which seemed almost too small to reach across his massive chest and "corporation", completed an appearance which made Joe Sweetman remarkable. He looked a gentleman all over, and his merry laugh and jovial manner made one certain at once that he was a general favourite.

Opposite him, seated in an uncomfortable armchair, and hugging one knee with his bony hands, was a big, gaunt man, whose heavy face and dull leaden-looking eyes seemed never to have lightened with a smile. A square chin, set off by long Dundreary whiskers, and knitted brows showed him to be a man of fixed purpose; one who, having made up his mind upon a subject of any importance, would adhere to his decision with exasperating stubbornness, refusing to be persuaded by any argument, and holding firmly to his convictions, though their falseness was apparent to everyone but himself.

A hard, bigoted man was Edward Western, and even good-natured Joe Sweetman was often within an ace of losing his temper when conversing with him. An educated man, and in his younger days an officer in a line regiment, Edward had suddenly taken it into his head that a soldier's life was not the calling he should follow. Once convinced of this he sent in his papers, and now for years had acted as the vicar of Riddington, a town of some importance in Hampshire. A wife, holding somewhat similar views to his own, and an adopted son of sixteen completed his family, while Joe Sweetman, his brother-in-law, was so constantly at the house that he might be said to form one of the establishment.

The one great aim and object of Edward Western's life was that his adopted son, Philip, should follow in his footsteps, and one day fill his place as vicar of the town. Fortune had decreed that he should be childless, and at first this had not been a matter for regret. But for many years the vicar of Riddington had declared to all his parishioners, when lecturing to them and advising them as to the training of their children, that by careful education they could make them what they wished. "Neglect your offspring," he would say solemnly, shaking a warning finger at his audience, "and they will become the evil-doers of the future. They will disgrace you, and even make you almost long to disown them. But with diligence, with never-ceasing care, you will instil into their minds all that is good, and will train them to follow that profession which you have decided they shall enter. There should be no need to worry yourselves in the future as to what your sons should be. Choose now, while they are infants, and bring them up according to your wishes."

This was all, undoubtedly, very true and excellent advice to give, but Mr Western went further. "There is no such thing as 'breeding' and 'noble blood'," he would declare. "Take a lad from the gutter, and I will engage that by using towards him the same amount of care as is devoted to the child of gentlefolks, you will make him a gentleman."

So strongly did he feel upon the subject that, after mature consideration, he decided to prove the truth of his sayings to all in the parish. To decide was to act. In spite of Joe Sweetman's remonstrances he inserted an advertisement in the papers, in which it was set forth that a certain clergyman, living in a country town, was anxious to adopt a son.

No difficulty was thrown in his way. An answer reached him by return of post, stating that a widow with many children would be glad to dispose of one of them if a good home were offered. A hurried visit and a few questions satisfied the vicar that the woman was truthful, and that to relieve her of a child would be an act of charity. A few guineas were handed to the widow, and Phil Reach, a fair-haired, blue-eyed boy of two, was hugged in his mother's arms, smothered with kisses and big tears, and finally, wondering no doubt what all the commotion meant, was handed over to Mr Western.

He was an interesting little mite too, always happy and bright, and ever ready for a romp. And to do them justice, Mr Western and his wife proved a devoted father and mother to their adopted son. They lived for him, and never for a single moment forgot what was the object of their lives.

When the child was four years old his training commenced, and from that day it had proceeded unceasingly. Had his days been made bright and joyous, success might have attended the efforts of the worthy vicar and his wife; but Phil Western—as he was now called—seldom knew what it was to be really happy. Living with an eccentric couple, whose austerity would have tried an adult, and deprived of playmates, he soon began to mope and pine. So much so, that at last the doctor ordered home lessons to be given up, and after a good deal of persuasion his adopted parents were prevailed upon to send him to the local school. What a change it was! From sorrow to sunlight. Phil rapidly picked up his health, and before long had hosts of friends. But at home the old life still continued. The training was never for one moment forgotten, and if only the desired end had been attained, Phil would have developed into one of those abnormally good boys who never do wrong, and whose lives are a pattern to all others. But, unfortunately, this was not the case.

Phil, indeed, grew up to be scarcely the studious and sober-minded lad his adoptive parents had hoped to see. Bottled up by the strictness of life at home, his spirits simply boiled over when once he left the house, and at school his masters knew him as a mischievous but good-hearted youngster, whose courage and lively nature often led him into doing stupid things, for which he was afterwards full of regret. There was not a prank played of which he was not the ringleader, and any batch of culprits mustered outside the doctor's study, waiting for punishment, was certain to number him in its ranks. And yet he was not a bad boy.

"He is simply incorrigible. I can do nothing with him, and you must take him away at the end of the term," the worthy doctor had said when discussing with Mr Western the affair of the booby-trap laid for the mayor. "I shall be sorry to lose the lad, for he is upright and truthful, and has done much for the school in the way of sports and athletics. But he is never out of mischief, and the example he sets is simply destroying the discipline of the school. Be advised by me, Western, and send him away. He is by no means dull at his work, and at a school where there is more opportunity of controlling him, and where he will be separated from his present companions in mischief, he will do well, I feel sure, and be a credit to you."

But no amount of reasoning could convince Phil's father that his son was all that the Doctor had said.

"He has disgraced me," he said bitterly to Joe Sweetman, "and all our care has been thrown away. I hoped that he would grow up a quiet and well-behaved young fellow; but he is never out of mischief, so much so that I am now obliged to send him to a boarding-school, an institution of which I have the greatest dislike. And I suppose he will soon be sent away from there. I really am more than grieved, and how I shall dare to meet his worship the mayor, after what has occurred, I do not know!"

"Bother the mayor! He's a prig, and got what he deserved!" Joe answered, with a sniff and a snap of his fingers. "Send Phil away and I'll swear he'll be thankful to you. Of course I know it was foolish and very wrong of those young monkeys to play their tricks on old Barrington, but then you yourself know what an unpopular man he is. Did he not try to put an end to the annual procession of the Riddington boys through the town, on the plea that they made too much noise? That put the youngsters' backs up; and then he must needs force his way into the school and demand that the lad who broke his miserable window should be caned, and in the event of his not being found that the whole school should lose a holiday. A pig of a fellow, sir, and I'm glad Phil and his pals paid him out."

This indignant outburst, and the roar of laughter which followed on Joe's remembering the unhappy mayor's fright, roused Edward Western's ire. He sat rigidly in his chair, staring blankly before him, with a fixed expression of annoyance on his face.

"I cannot compel him to follow the profession I have chosen for him," he said sternly, "but let him disgrace me again and I will pack him off to London and there find a position for him as a clerk, where he will be tied to his desk, and where he will have fewer opportunities of doing wrong."

"Pooh! pooh! You're too hard on Phil by a long way," exclaimed Joe Sweetman earnestly, springing from his chair and pacing up and down the room. "Give him a chance. Every dog must have his day, you know. Let him get rid of some of his wild spirits, and then perhaps he will be quite ready to fall in with your wishes. You accuse me of constantly egging the lad on. I deny that charge, Edward, and I do most sincerely wish that you could see the facts as they are. Perhaps I should not speak, for he is your protégé, not mine; but, just for a moment look squarely at the facts. Does the lad lead a happy life in his home? I tell you that he does not. He has comfort and plenty of good food, but the house is not brightened for the boy, and once within its walls he has learnt to subdue and cloak a naturally sunny nature simply because gay laughter and light-hearted chatter are disapproved of. Can you wonder, then, that he is inclined to run riot outside? His high spirits get the better of him, and he is ready for any fun—fun, mark you, Edward, on which you and I might look and never feel ashamed—for, mischievous though he is, he has a healthy mind."

M 845

AT BAY

Joe tossed his head in the air, thrust his fat hands beneath the tails of his coat, and leaned against the mantel-piece, staring hard at Mr Western. "Come," he continued, with an easy laugh, "think better of it, Edward. Pack the lad off to school, and leave him more to himself. He'll go straight, I'll wager anything upon it."

"Thank you, Joseph! I do not bet," Mr Western replied. "But I will do as you say. Philip shall go away, and his future must depend upon himself. Not all the arguments in the world will persuade me that there is any truth in the saying that it is good for young fellows to sow their wild oats before settling down to the serious business of life. Now let us go into the garden."

Mr Western rose slowly from his chair, and, opening a large glass door, stepped on to a verandah which surrounded his house and formed a most charming spot in which to sit during the heat of a summer's day. Joe followed him, still chuckling at the memory of the mayor's discomfiture, and together they stood looking out across the well-kept garden, with its beds of bright-coloured flowers, its splashing fountain, and its walls lined by rows of carefully-pruned trees. It was a scene which differed greatly from the monotony and lack of joyousness which marked Phil Western's daily life at home.

Within the house all was dull and sombre. Scarcely a laugh or a smile brightened his existence. Stern and full of earnestness, his adoptive parents gave themselves up to their work, the religious education of the parishioners and the careful bringing-up of their son. Outside there was a landscape teeming with life and movement; a town of some size in the hollow below, its streets filled with country folk who had come in to attend the market, and across the haze caused by the smoke rising lazily from the chimneys, a huge vista of green trees and fields, broken here and there by a wide silvery streak which marked the course of the river, twisting and twining, now hidden by the foliage, and again running through the open fields, flashing in the brilliant sun, and bearing upon its smooth surface a host of tiny boats filled with townspeople out for an afternoon's enjoyment.

A hundred yards or more beyond the outskirts of Riddington was a large, red-brick building, almost smothered in creeper, and bearing in its centre a tall tower from the four sides of which the face of a clock looked out. It was Riddington High School, and the hands of the clock were pointing close to the hour of four. A moment later there was a loud "whirr", and then the first stroke of the hour, followed almost instantly by a hubbub in the building below. Hundreds of shrill voices seemed to have been let loose, and after them the owners; for from all sides of the school lads appeared, rushing out in mad haste, some hatless, others jamming their hats upon their heads, and all in the same condition of desperate hurry. A minute later they had streamed across the playground and were racing towards the river, to a spot where an old waterman stood guard over some dozen boats. Charging down the hill the mob of excited lads swept the old man aside, laughed merrily at his expostulations, and in a twinkling were aboard and shoving off from the river-bank.

But not all the scholars of Riddington High School had joined in the excited rush. A tall, big-boned lad of some fifteen years, with hair which was almost red in colour, and a boyish, open face, strode from one of the doors accompanied by two others. Flinging his hat jauntily upon his head, Phil Western, for it was none other than he, walked across the asphalt which formed the playground of the school, and, putting his two forefingers in his mouth, produced a loud and prolonged whistle. Twice he repeated it, and after a minute's silence shouted "Rags! Rags! where are you?"

In the distance a series of short barks answered, and very soon a fox-terrier dog came racing across the grass.

"Ah, he's waiting all right for his master!" exclaimed Phil, with a short grunt of satisfaction. "Good dog!—the best in the whole of Riddington. Now, you fellows," he went on, after having greeted his canine friend with a pat, "what's the order for to-day? We're all agreed to give that old concern an airing. The last time the good people of this town had a chance of looking at it was in the year of the queen's coronation; and that was thirteen years ago. It's getting musty, and must certainly have an airing."

"That's exactly what we think, Phil," chimed in one of the other lads, a merry-looking youngster of fifteen. "Riddington started a state barge a hundred years ago, to take the mayor and councillors across the river to the church on great occasions. On other days they rowed over in ordinary boats or went by the bridge—when it wasn't washed away by the floods. Then a new stone bridge was built, and for a few years they kept up the old custom. But for a long while now it has fallen through—sunk into oblivion, as 'old Tommy' would say. It is clearly our duty to revive this extremely interesting—I may say this unique—old custom."

"Bah! Stop it!" exclaimed Phil, with a laugh, snatching his comrade's hat from his head and throwing it at his face. "Tell me what arrangements you have made."

"Simple. Simple as daylight, Phil. We saunter down to the river-side, and as soon as Peter looks the other way we enter the boat-house. Here's the key. It hangs over the pater's mantel-piece, where it has been for the last two years. He's keeper of the state barge and the bargemen's costumes."

"Splendid, Tommy! Splendid! We'll be off at once. Come on, you fellows. Here, Rags!"

Phil hurried off with his companions in mischief towards an old and somewhat dilapidated boat-house. The lad who had been addressed as Tommy slipped up to the door, and a few moments later all three entered and closed it behind them.

A match was produced and a small piece of candle lighted.

"This way, you fellows," cried Tommy, leading the way along a narrow shelf to the back of the house. Here there was a small room with a worm-eaten table and chairs and a heavy oak chest.

"It's no use doing things by halves, is it?" asked Tommy, with a broad grin on his face. "Here, in this old chest, are all the costumes, and if we don't make that old barge look as well as it ever did, I shall be astonished."

"You'll probably get licked, you mean," laughed Phil. "But, all the same, it's a splendid idea. We won't spoil the show for a ha'porth of tar. Let's see how these things fit."

Ten minutes later, had any councillor of Riddington had sufficient interest to pay a casual visit to the boat-house, he would have seen a sight which would certainly have given a rude shock to his nerves. For in the old and musty building stalked three figures gorgeously attired in costumes of red velvet, slashed in all directions with what had once been white, red stockings and big-bowed shoes, heavy chains of brass round their necks, and huge beef-eater hats upon their heads. Beneath the hats, where bearded faces should have been, were the merry countenances of three boys who were bent upon a piece of mischief.

"Look here, Phil, you boss this show," said Tommy shortly, looking at the other lad to see if he agreed. "We're ready. Give your orders and we'll get aboard."

"Right, Tommy! Help with this tarpaulin. That's right. Now jump inside, you fellows, and fish out the rowlocks, and see that a couple of oars are handy. The rudder is already there. Now we can start. Hop in there and take your places. I'll open the gates and push her out."

Waiting to see that all was ready, Phil pulled the bolt of the gates which closed the exit to the river, and threw them open. Then he guided the old state barge, all bedecked with gold and colours and curious devices, out into the river, giving a lusty push off, and springing in just at the last moment.

"Out oars!" he cried. "Tommy, what are you grinning at? Remember you are a bargeman."

"Beg pardon, sir. Sorry, I'm sure," replied the irrepressible Tommy, with a broad smile on his face. "I say, Phil, what a sight you do look in those togs! and sha'n't we catch it when they find out who we are? Old Barrington will be furious. He said he'd have our blood—or something like that—when we held him up the other day."

"Oh, bother Barrington! I know he said we were a disgrace to the town, and that he'd keep a special eye upon us in future," answered Phil, with a laugh. "But pull hard, you fellows. I'll run up past the town; there are lots of boats there that we'll go close to. Let's make 'em believe all's correct. Keep straight faces, and pass them as though nothing were wrong."

"My eye, what fun!" chuckled Tommy. "But, all right, Phil! we'll do as you say."

Slowly, and with a stately stroke, the two lads plied their oars, while Phil, looking almost double his real size in his strange costume, sat upright in the stern, the dog Rags by his side, and steered the barge straight up the centre of the river. Soon they were close to the boats, and not many minutes had passed before their presence caused a sensation.

"Blest if it bain't his wushup, the mayor!" cried a hulking countryman out for a day on the river. "Row along, boys, and let's get closer."

From every side cries and shouts of astonishment and pleasure resounded, and all pressed towards the centre. And through them all the old barge swept grandly on its way, while its bargemen and the steersman kept a rigid silence and hastily jerked down their caps to hide the giggles which would come in spite of all their efforts. On they swept, and soon a throng of boats was following in their wake, while others ahead lay on their oars and waited. Suddenly, as they approached one of these, Phil leant forward and, shading his eyes with his hand, stared at the occupants.

"Keep on, you fellows," he muttered. "There's a boat ahead of us with my pater and mater aboard, and I believe the mayor too. There'll be trouble now, I expect."

And this was exactly the case. It was a lovely day, and, persuaded by Joe Sweetman, Mr and Mrs Western had engaged a boat, and, happening to meet the mayor before embarking, had invited him to join the party. Even as the barge appeared in sight, Mr Western was apologising for his son's disgraceful behaviour, and telling the mayor what a disappointment Phil was to him.

"Why, as I live," exclaimed Joe Sweetman suddenly, "that's the old state barge! What is happening, Barrington?"

"State barge! Yes, so it is. What can it be doing out here?" the mayor, a fat-faced personage, replied. "I have not given my permission. We must see to this, Mr Western."

A moment later the barge slipped past, and in spite of Phil's efforts to conceal his identity he was recognised.

"It's that rascal Western!" exclaimed the mayor, getting red with anger. "Stop, sir! What do you mean? Are you stealing that barge?"

At the mayor's angry order Tommy and his companion ceased rowing, and, seeing that all was discovered, Phil swept his hat from his head and politely wished all "good afternoon."

Mr Barrington almost exploded with rage. "Take that barge back at once, you young rascal," he shouted. "I'll have you up for stealing. How dare you? Take it back at once!"

But meanwhile a crowd had gathered, and quickly understanding the joke, they laughed long and loudly and cheered the three boys. As for Joe Sweetman, he was convulsed, and this added not a little to the mayor's ill-temper.

Mr Western had not spoken a word. All the while he gazed sternly at Phil, as though he could not trust himself to speak, and he had landed at the steps and was on his way home before he opened his lips.

"The mayor is right," he said bitterly. "Philip is a disgrace, and I will not allow him to stay at home a single day longer than I can help. I know an excellent institution where boys of his character can be urged into obedience. He shall go there, and nothing shall persuade me to remove him till he has changed utterly and completely."

"What! You would send Phil to a school for backward and incorrigible boys?" exclaimed Joe Sweetman.

"Yes, that is exactly the class of institution I mean. I know of one close to London, and will send him there, so that he may be tamed into obedience."

"Then I tell you that you will do that boy a grievous wrong," cried Joe, roused to anger by Edward Western's words. "Only boys of vicious nature are sent to such schools. Of the backward ones I say nothing, for Phil's wits are as ready as any boy's, and he is decidedly not a dunce. Nor is he vicious, as you seem to think. For Heaven's sake look with a more open mind at the matter. Here is a merry, good-hearted lad whom, because he gets into mischief, you would pack off to a school for unruly boys. I hope you will not insist on sending him to this place, for, as I have said, he is not so bad as you think."

"Yes, I insist, Joseph, and no amount of argument will alter that decision."

"Ah, I wish I had the power to compel you to do so!" said Joe bitterly. "But perhaps it is all for the best. Such schools, no doubt, are much as the others, save that a boy starts as it were with a black mark against his name. Let us hope that the headmaster of the one in your thoughts will see at a glance what sort of a lad he has in reality to deal with, and treat him accordingly."

Chapter Two.

Old Bumble.

Mr Western was as good as his word, and within a week of his last escapade Phil was despatched to a certain school, situated in the outskirts of London, where only backward and incorrigible lads were received.

"I am thoroughly displeased and disappointed with you," said the vicar severely, as he lectured Phil just before his departure. "I lifted you from poverty, provided you with a home, and for years have devoted all my spare hours to you. You know what my wishes and hopes were. They are still the same. Disappoint me again, get into further disgrace, and I will disown you."

"I'll do my best to keep out of trouble," Phil answered, with a catch in his voice, for the lad was at heart fond of his home and of his guardians. "I will not promise to follow your wishes though. I don't know why it is, but I loathe the thought of being a clergyman. I love a free and open life; and besides, a clever man is required for the Church, and I am scarcely that. Still, father, I will try my best, and should I do anything wrong, it shall not be such as to cause you to feel any shame."

"Then we shall see, Philip. But remember my warning," answered the vicar.

That evening a cab stopped outside a big stone building in Highgate and deposited Phil and his baggage on the pavement.

For a moment he looked round in bewilderment, for this was the first time he had been in the neighbourhood of, or in fact, anywhere near, the great city; but a gruff "Five bob fare, please", and "that there's Ebden's School", recalled his wandering wits.

Phil paid the money, and then, remembering that he would require someone to help him with his baggage, asked the surly driver to get off his seat.

"Not if I knows it, young un," was the answer. "I've got me fare, and you've got to yer journey's end. So good-day to yer! Hope yer won't find it too precious warm in there. I passes by most every day and hears horrid yells a-coming from the 'ouse. Get up, won't yer!" and with a tug and a spiteful lash at his horse, this cheerful Jehu drove off with such a jerk that the dilapidated top hat he wore started backward, and, bounding from the box, was crushed beneath the wheels.

Phil, who had for the moment been somewhat taken aback by the man's ominous words, roared at the cabman's discomfiture and at the rage into which he promptly worked himself. Then, taking no notice of his growling, and seeing no one at hand to help him, he shouldered his box, pushed open the iron gate which formed the entrance of his new home, and mounted the steps. A double knock, sounding hollow and rumbling, was answered quickly by an individual who performed at once the duties of butler and general fatigue man of the school.

"Name, sir?" he asked politely.

"Western," answered Phil.

"Ah! you're the new boy, sir! Glad to see you. Let me help you with the box;" and in a twinkling Phil was relieved of his baggage.

Then he was ushered into a big room, where he waited, not without some feelings of uneasiness, for the appearance of the master.

"I wonder what he'll be like!" he thought. "I've heard of masters of his sort before. I wonder whether that cabby was rotting! Perhaps he wasn't, and perhaps I shall really be catching it hot. Never mind. I was happy at Haddington, and will be here too."

Phil was in the act of sketching for himself a big, heavy-looking man, with a hard unrelenting face, as his master, when there was a quick step outside, the door burst open, and a clean-shaven little gentleman, with a smiling, pleasant face, entered the room.

"By Jove! He's awfully like Uncle Joe, and would be just his image if he were a little fatter," Phil thought in an instant.

"Ah, Philip Western, the boy who has been in difficulties, I believe!" said the stranger, extending a hand and shaking Phil's heartily. "Glad to see you, my lad. Let me look at you. Yes—we shall be good friends, I hope." Then, murmuring to himself, he continued, "Larky—high-spirited—full of go, but no vice—no vice, I will swear. Yes, we shall be good friends."

Mr Ebden—for he it was—pushed Phil into the light and rapidly surveyed him, muttering audibly all the while.

"So you are a disappointment to your father!" he continued. "Come, tell me all about it, my lad. Let there be no secrets between us. Tell me the whole trouble; why you have come here, and in what manner you have proved such a deep worry to your people."

"I can't help it, sir," Phil blurted out. "I've done my level best to act as father wished, but somehow or other I am always in trouble. They said I was upsetting the discipline of the school, and that is one of the reasons for which I was sent away." Then he proceeded to describe what had happened, and how he had laid a booby-trap for the mayor, and afterwards played a prank with the town barge. Mr Ebden listened, and, much to Phil's relief, laughed heartily when he heard how he and his friends had afforded the townspeople of Riddington one more glance at an old-fashioned relic.

"That was a piece of pure, boyish mischief," he exclaimed, "and only deserved a lecture; but the other was bad. You ought to have been caned. You would have caught it severely here. However, from this day we start a new book. Turn over that fresh leaf which one so often hears about. I am your friend—remember that, Phil Western. You will meet with no harshness here. A piece of pure frolic I can enjoy; but anything else, any breach of discipline, shall meet with the punishment it deserves. But we will not talk of that. We shall be excellent friends, I feel sure. Now come with me and I will introduce you to your new school-fellows."

Mr Ebden led Phil along a passage and through another room into a garden, in which were some twenty boys.

"There they are," he said, giving him a push. "Go and make friends with them too."

Somewhat bewildered with the very pleasant greeting he had already received, and more than pleased with the difference between his forebodings and the reality, Phil walked forward and looked at the lads before him, wondering which one he should address first.

And they too stared hard at Phil, and summed him up in a moment. Here was a boy with a big loose frame that wanted some filling out, long legs and arms that looked as though a little exertion would push them far through his clothing, and a well-tanned and freckled face; not exactly good-looking, but distinctly pleasing, and possessing eyes which looked straight at you, and a mouth with a queer little line beneath it, which told that, though smiling now, it could become hard and stem on occasion. The whole, capped by close-cropped, almost reddish hair, made up an appearance which was taking.

"A decent chap. He must be a good fellow," was the half-muttered thought of the boys, the tallest of whom advanced and at once entered into conversation with Phil. The others joined in, and in a few minutes he was quite at his ease, and feeling more certain than ever that the change of schools was decidedly not for the worst.

Time proved that he was right, for there was no doubt that Mr Ebden had a wonderful power over his scholars. From the first he made friends of them, and endeavoured to keep them so. Indeed he seldom failed. A lad who had elsewhere been sullen and morose, and in many cases unmanageable, became under the new regime bright and laughing, and ready at all times to do his best to master his lessons. It was just the difference between the careless neglect and misunderstanding that had been his lot before, and the keen interest in all that concerned him that was shown in every word and act of his new ruler. A little kindness goes a long way with many an awkward, nervous boy, and Mr Ebden had proved this.

"Make a friend of him," he would say cheerily. "Forget sometimes that you are the master and he the boy. Coax him into trying by taking an interest in all he does, and you can make a convert anywhere."

He was right, as has been proved over and over again, for nowadays there is scarcely a school where the masters do not join heart and soul with the boys in their games, ay, and feel themselves the happier and the younger for it too?

Thus did Mr Ebden conquer the lads sent to him as a last resource.

Before a week had passed, Phil had become quite popular in the school, and his love of athletics helped him not a little. To these a fair proportion of the day was allotted, and as the school enclosure opened into a large and well-kept garden, which was the common property of the row of houses in which Mr Ebden's stood, there was plenty of opportunity for cricket. In the centre was a smooth stretch of lawn, with a carefully-laid pitch, and here Ebden's did battle with sundry neighbouring teams.

But it is not to be supposed that Phil and his comrades were always out of mischief. They were a high-spirited lot, and ever eager for adventure. Indeed, our hero had only been a year at his new home when he was once more in the deepest trouble. It happened in this way. The Highgate Wanderers had taken their departure in high dudgeon at the easy victory that Ebden's had scored over them, and Phil and his friends lay on the grass, full length, beneath the shade of a pleasant oak-tree. They were lolling idly and merely waiting for the hour to strike to go in and prepare for tea. Suddenly one of the number, a lad named Fat Bowen, pointed towards the farther end of the garden and exclaimed in a high-pitched voice, "Look, you chaps, there's old Bumble inspecting his statues again!"

All looked in the direction indicated, to see a stout old gentleman waddling slowly round an artificial lake, and halting at every other step to inspect and admire two statues which stood on pedestals placed in the centre of the water.

"Good Old Bumble!" cried Phil, with a laugh; "he spends his days in admiring that plaster Hercules. If you were close to him you would hear him muttering, 'Beautiful! Grand! Masterpieces! I will have two like these in my own garden'. Poor old boy! he's quite cracked on the subject. What would happen if they were to disappear?"

"There'd be a row, that's certain," answered Fred Wheeler, a particular friend of Phil's. "Yes, there'd be ructions, I expect. But what a joke it would be to take them away for a time!"

"Couldn't be done. Too heavy to move," answered Phil promptly. "But we might do something else," he added, nothing loth for a piece of mischief. "Now what could we do, you fellows?"

Various suggestions were offered, but none of them was practicable, and the hour striking a few moments later, the boys departed to the school and left the stout gentleman still gazing lovingly at his statues.

"Old Bumble", as he was generally, known to Ebden's boys, was a gentleman of the name of Workman, Mr Julius Workman, a wealthy merchant of the city of London, who owned vast property in the neighbourhood of Highgate, and, indeed, was landlord of the houses which formed the terrace in which the school stood. Consequently he was a man of some position; in fact in Mr Ebden's eyes he was one with whom it was well to be on the best of terms, and to treat with that amount of deference due to a man of consequence who holds one's fortune in his hands. To tell the truth, Mr Julius Workman was not altogether an agreeable person. Fat and ungainly, he was far from being the good-natured individual one might have expected. Increasing riches had not softened his nature, for he was grumpy and fussy, and apt to ride the high horse on every occasion. His tenants stood in awe of him, and, strange as it may seem, Mr Ebden, the strong-minded man, who could successfully rule a number of high-spirited boys, feared him more than all the rest. But there was good reason for this. For fifteen years Ebden's School had been in existence, and its increasing popularity had been a source of satisfaction to its head. Now to change the locality of the school and alter that paragraph in the advertisement which ran "at a charmingly-situated building, in the salubrious neighbourhood of Highgate" might have been to diminish the popularity of the school. Highgate was thought much of by fond parents, and more than one pupil had been sent to Ebden's in order that he might be in that part of London. Therefore it was of paramount importance that Mr Julius Workman should be kept in good-humour.

"Boys are nuisances, terrible nuisances," he had often remarked testily to Mr Ebden, "and 'pon my word those you have nearly worry me out of my life. There is no peace in the terrace. All day one can hear their chatter, and, out in the gardens behind, their shouts are simply unbearable. Be good enough to see that they are less noisy in future, please, for not only do they annoy me, but the neighbours complain, and I have no intention of allowing Silverdale Terrace to be depopulated on their account."

There was always a scarcely-veiled threat about the man's words. If he had put them into plainer sentences they would have run: "Your boys are nuisances, and if I am worried again, I will give you notice to leave."

"Bother the surly old chap!" Mr Ebden would exclaim under his breath, "he has me fairly on the hip. I am a good tenant and he knows it, but for all that I can never have a long lease of the house. Two years is as much as he will allow; if he were to give me notice to quit, I should have precious little time to look about me, and then—supposing I had to go elsewhere—what would become of the school? I should lose half my pupils and half my income at one blow."

Consequently Mr Ebden took care to conciliate the old man; but not so his pupils. Amongst those mischievous lads Mr Julius Workman was known as "old Bumble."

"Old Bumble" was voted a bore and a cantankerous Johnny, and each lad, finding that a shout annoyed him, took particular pains to lift his voice to the highest pitch whenever "Bumble" was in the vicinity.

Now the old gentleman was inordinately proud of the two plaster statues in the centre of the lake, and the lads at Ebden's knew it well. Often before had they thought of playing some practical joke at "Bumble's" expense, but never had they given it such deep consideration as upon this night. As they filed in to tea each was bothering his brains as to how a joke could be played upon him, and afterwards, as they sat at "prep." with their books in front of them, the glorious life and deeds of Caesar were forgotten in a vision of "Bumble" surveying his statues.

"Wheeler, what are you gazing at? Go on with your work, sir," Mr Ebden's voice suddenly rapped out.

Wheeler buried his head in his hands, and pretended to be very deep in his book. There was silence in the big room for a few minutes, and Mr Ebden once more bent over the letter with which he was occupied. A faint rustle in a far-off corner then attracted the attention of the boys, and, looking up, Phil watched a lad named Carrol spell off some words on his fingers.

"I've got it," they ran. "It's about Old Bumble's statues."

Then, as the lad's excitement increased, the message became unintelligible, and Phil sent back, "Can't make it out. Start again."

By this time all the boys were on the *qui vive* and staring hard at Carrol. But a sudden movement on Mr Ebden's part and a sharp "Go on with your work, boys!" disturbed them. Another attempt failed for the same reason, and then Carrol seemed to give it up altogether. But a few minutes later, keeping a wary eye upon the master, who was sitting at his desk in the centre of the room,

Carrol held up a slate upon which was written in large letters, "We'll tar and feather Old B.'s statues."

Instantly a suppressed giggle went round the room, and the lads looked at one another with eyes which clearly said: "By Jove! he's got it. What a joke it will be!"

That night, when Ebden's was supposed to be buried in profound sleep, a council of war was held in Phil's cubicle, at which the details of the plot were worked out.

"We're certain to catch it hot," Phil remarked, with a smile, as, dressed in a flimsy night-gown, he sat on the edge of his bed, and surveyed the three lads squatting on the floor in front of him. "Old Bumble will suspect us at once, and will do his best to find out which of us played the joke. But we'll do it, if only to show that we can. By Jove, I wonder what the old boy will do when he sees Hercules dressed like a hen? He'll simply blow up with rage, and I wouldn't miss the sight for worlds."

"There's safe to be a ruction," Wheeler broke in complacently, "and some of us will get a licking. But what does it matter? Ebden will talk at us till we feel as limp as rags, and then he'll cane us till we go as stiff as any poker. Then it will all be over, and we'll be as good friends as ever. It'll be a fine spree, and I vote we see about it to-morrow."

"I take a share in it at any rate," cried Carrol, looking round at the others to see if they agreed, for he was usually left in the background. "I invented the joke, remember that, you chaps."

"We're all four of us in it," Phil answered gaily; "and now how about the stuff? The feathers and the tar, I mean. Then we shall want a raft. I know we can buy some tar at Streaker's, and a call at the poultry shop will get us heaps of feathers. We'll manage that to-morrow, and dress our statue in the evening, between tea and prep."

The details of the prank to be played were quickly arranged, and soon Phil's companions slipped off like ghosts, and he tumbled into bed and fell into a deep sleep.

The following evening, after dusk had fallen, four figures, each carrying a long school-form, slipped out through the back gate of Ebden's, and stole down to the lake.

"Now for the raft," whispered Phil. "Place them alongside one another and lash them with the rope."

In a few minutes a raft was constructed, but to the disgust of all the lads it was so light and frail that it was not even sufficient to support one of them.

"We're done. Bother it!" exclaimed Carrol.

The others stood without a word, and stared at the raft in deep vexation.

"It's all right. I've got it, you chaps," Phil suddenly cried in tones of excitement and pleasure. "The lake's only a foot deep. We'll shove one form out, and then put another in front of it, and so on till we reach the statue. The bottom is made of stone, so there's no fear of toppling over or sinking in mud."

A half-suppressed shout of joy answered him, and all at once set to work to make the bridge. It was easier than they had hoped, and before very long, by means of two extra forms, Hercules was reached. Then began the work of tar-and-feathering, an act of vandalism for which each and every one of them deserved a good thrashing, done though it was as a piece of pure boyish mischief, and in all thoughtlessness.

At length it was finished, and with hands and faces smeared with tar, and feathers sticking to their clothes, Phil and his boon companions returned silently to the house, and having hastily washed themselves took their places in "prep." as though nothing had happened. But a scarcely-suppressed bubble of excitement and huge grins of amusement showed that all at Ebden's were conscious of the prank, save the worthy head himself, who, if he had only known, would there and then have gone out and done his best to clean the statue before the light of day disclosed it to Mr Julius Workman.

On the following afternoon a game of cricket was in progress, when a cry of "Here's old Bumble!" put a sudden stop to it, and the boys at once selected the nearest and best hiding-places from which to look on safely and observe all that happened.

Stalking pompously down the path leading from his own residence, Mr Julius Workman scarcely deigned to acknowledge the polite salute which two of the lads gave him. He walked—or rather waddled—along towards the lake, and, arrived there, sniffed, drew his snuff-box from a pocket in the tail of his coat, and helped himself to a liberal pinch. Then he drew out a highly-coloured silk handkerchief, and, holding it in one hand, was in the act of patting it to his nose, when his eye lit upon the statue. Unable to believe that what he saw was real, he wiped his glasses and stared again. Then his face assumed a livid hue, his cheeks puffed out, and for the moment he looked as though he were on the point of exploding, or of having an apoplectic fit.

"Tarred and feathered, as I live!" he shouted, dancing from foot to foot in his rage, and shaking his stick threateningly. "Some wretch has destroyed my statue, the most beautiful I ever saw. It is a piece of wickedness; yes, wickedness! and I will search Highgate—ay, and even the whole of London—to find the culprit."

For a moment he stopped for lack of breath, and behind their shelters Phil and his friends enjoyed the scene to their hearts' content.

"Ah, I know!" the old gentleman suddenly shouted; "it's one of those rascally boys. I know it. It must be their work. They shall pay for it, the young scamps, and so shall Ebden!" and, still shaking his stick, and in a towering rage, he went off to the school to interview its head.

"By George, the fat's in the fire now!" cried Wheeler, with a laugh which was not altogether cheerful. "Phil, there'll be an awful row. What shall we do?"

"Wait and see," answered Phil easily. "We've had our joke, and a good one it was, and perhaps we shall have to pay for it."

Meanwhile Mr Julius Workman had reached the school, and had asked for Mr Ebden. He was shown into the library, and there, as he waited and thought over the matter, his rage, instead of decreasing, grew even more violent, so that when the pleasant-faced little master entered, and in his cheery voice said, "Ah, Mr Workman! this is a pleasure I had not expected," the stout old gentleman was beyond himself, and could scarcely speak.

"Pleasure, sir! Pleasure!" he spluttered at last. "It's no pleasure to me, sir; let me tell you that. I have a serious complaint to make. What have you to say, sir?"

He stared at Mr Ebden as though the latter had had a hand in the prank.

"A complaint, Mr Workman? I don't understand," said Mr Ebden with astonishment.

"Yes, you do, sir; yes, you do," the irate old gentleman shouted rudely. "Why don't you look after your boys? I told you they were a nuisance, and now they've played a trick on me and ruined my statue of Hercules."

When Mr Ebden had heard the full details of the prank he too was extremely angry, or pretended to be so, and at once accompanied Mr Workman to inspect the ruined statue. Then, with a heavy frown on his usually pleasant face, he returned and summoned all the boys before him. Mr Julius Workman was also present, and glowered round at them as though he would like to do everyone some mischief.

"You've got to find out who did it, or there'll be trouble," he remarked significantly to Mr Ebden, as the latter was about to speak.

Now, the boys at Ebden's were, naturally, unaware of the peculiar reason their master had for keeping on good terms with "Old Bumble", but this remark struck them as peculiar, and Phil, thinking it over, and being a quick-witted lad, grasped its meaning, and determined at once to give himself up.

"I'm the biggest fellow here," he thought, looking round at his companions, "and though I'm not the eldest by some months, I'm usually the leader in these scrapes."

"Boys," said Mr Ebden severely, scrutinising each one of them in turn, and speaking slowly and distinctly, "a foolish and most objectionable prank has been played upon one of the statues in the gardens. Mr Workman declares that one of you is guilty. Is this so?"

"Of course it is," grunted "Old Bumble" angrily. "What's the good of asking if they did it? Of course they did!"

Mr Ebden took no notice of the interruption, but looked at his pupils, who stared guiltily at one another, knowing well that each had been a party to the plot, and yet waiting for one to give the lead before the others acknowledged.

Phil stepped forward in front of his comrades, and with upright head, and eyes fixed straight on Mr Ebden's, said:

"Yes, sir, it is so. I tarred and feathered the statue, and I'm sorry Old B—Mr Workman—is so angry."

"Old B! What did the scamp almost call me?" shouted Mr Workman, working himself into another rage. "You are a scamp, sir, and a disgrace to the school!"

"I am sorry, sir," Phil said again. "I did it for a joke only, and now I'll clean the statue if Mr Ebden will allow me."

But this was out of the question. The boys were dismissed, and a long conversation ensued between Mr Ebden and the irate old gentleman. After that work proceeded as usual, but, knowing that it was Mr Ebden's invariable rule to allow twenty-four hours to elapse before deciding upon the punishment for any serious offence, Phil did not permit his hopes to rise, or imagine that he was to get off easily.

And, as it turned out, he was right. After mature consideration Mr Ebden summoned the boys, and having read them a lecture, gave Phil the severest caning he had ever experienced in his life, all of which that high-spirited lad bore without so much as a whimper. Then he punished somewhat more mildly the three others who had helped in the prank, and who, not to be behindhand or allow one to suffer for the fault of all, had addressed a note to the headmaster the previous evening confessing their guilt.

"I cannot tell you how annoyed I am," said Mr Ebden in cold tones, which hurt his pupils far more than the cane. "You have aided and abetted one another in destroying a work of art, and you have deeply offended one with whom it was a matter of policy for me to be on good terms. Those four who did the actual tarring will have to pay for another statue out of their own pockets, and I shall communicate with their parents. Now you may go, and let there be no more of this foolishness."

Chapter Three.

Out into the World.

Letters did not travel so rapidly in the year 1850 as nowadays, and the fact that a week elapsed between the despatch of Mr Ebden's note and its receipt at the vicarage at Riddington was not a matter to lead to abuse of the postal authorities; for the town in which Mr Western lived was somewhat remote, and well away from the main line, and epistles which were addressed to its residents usually lay for a day or more at a post-office twenty miles away, from which they were removed at most twice a week. However, arrive the letter did at last, and Mr Western, gloomier and more severe if possible than ever, sat in his study reading it for the second time.

"Look at that," he said icily, tossing it across to Joe, who stood in his favourite position, leaning against the mantel-piece, with his hands beneath the tails of his coat.

"Humph! The young rascal!" Joe exclaimed with a chuckle, as soon as he had glanced through it. "Got himself into trouble, and his master too. Young donkey! Mischievous young donkey, that's what he is, Edward; and now he won't have a penny to bless himself with till his share of the statue is paid for." Then aside to himself he muttered as he helped himself to snuff: "Humph! Must send him a tip. A few shillings are always welcome to a school-boy."

Mr Western stared gloomily at the fire and kept silent for a minute or more. Then, bringing his hand down heavily upon the table, he exclaimed fretfully: "The boy worries me. What makes him wish to play these pranks? I have done my best, and so has your sister. He has had warning enough, and surely ought to keep out of these troubles. I believe he is wilfully mischievous, yes wilfully mischievous, and a bad boy at heart, and I will have no more to do with him. I will give him one more start, and leave him to make his way in the world as best he can. If he fails then he must look to himself, and thank himself alone for the trouble he has fallen into."

Joe started and looked uneasily at his brother-in-law.

"Nonsense, Edward! Nonsense!" he said sharply. "I cannot make you out; and, to be perfectly candid, you are as much a mystery to me as the lad seems to be to you. Cannot you understand that he is simply full of spirit, and though, no doubt, he is sorry afterwards for the pranks he plays, yet they are the result of thoughtlessness and an abundance of good health and animal spirits? Bless my life! where would England have been but for lads of his nature? A sunny, cheerful lad he is, and I tell you plainly you do him an injustice when you say he is bad at heart. Look at the letter again. Doesn't Mr Ebden admit that he owned up like a gentleman? What more do you want? Would you have the boy a girl?"

Joe snorted indignantly, and blew his nose so violently that Mr Western started. "The misunderstanding is not on my side," he retorted. "I who have watched him all these years should know; and it is you, Joseph, who have helped to ruin him. You have egged him on, and now, when he should be quiet and steady, he is simply unmanageable. But we will not wrangle about the matter. Philip shall leave Mr Ebden's house at the end of this term, and shall take a position as clerk in the office of a friend of mine. After that he must look to himself, for I will have no more to do with him."

"Then I tell you the lad will not submit to your proposal," Joe said hotly. "He is too free and easy to love one of your offices, and is not the one to sit down tamely and have his spirit broken by long hours of monotonous drudgery, paid for at a rate which would disgust the average workman. But I will say nothing to dissuade him, though, mark my words, he will disappoint you again; and then, if he is thrown on the world, I will look after him. It is not for me, Edward, to remind you of your responsibilities to Phil. You took him from the gutter, as I have often heard you say, and it is your duty to bear with him, however troublesome he may be. When he reaches man's age he will be well able to look to himself, but till then he is a boy, just as thoughtless and high-spirited as I was, and his pranks should not be treated as the deeds of a criminal.

"He got into mischief at Riddington High School, and you were asked to remove him, not only that the discipline of the school might not suffer, but also for the sake of the lad himself. By separating him from some high-spirited companions there was a better chance that they and he might settle down and become more sober, and the headmaster fully realised it. But why on that account you should send him to a school specially set aside for incorrigible lads passed my comprehension, and, as you will remember, did not meet with my approval. As a matter of fact Mr Ebden is a clever man, and took to leading and encouraging Phil instead of driving him. And now, merely because the foolish young fellow is dragged into another piece of mischief—innocent, clean-minded mischief, mind you—you would punish him severely, and possibly ruin his future by placing him in a position in which all his energies will be cramped, and from which he can scarcely hope to rise. I call it a short-sighted policy, and most unfair treatment of the boy."

Joe once more dipped into his snuff-box, blew his nose loudly, and then, seeing that his brother-in-law did not intend to reply, sniffed loudly and stumped out of the room. A month later, when the end of the term arrived, Phil did not return to Riddington for the holidays, but instead took his box to a dingy lodging in the heart of the city, and straightway set to work at his new duties.

Mr Western had written a cold and reproving letter to him, warning him that this was the last he could do for him; while Joe had sent him a few characteristic lines telling him to do his best, and never to forget that he had one good friend in the world.

Determined to get on well if possible, Phil was most assiduous in his duties at the office, and took pains to master the writing put before him. His employer he saw little of, but whenever they met he was greeted politely, so that he had no cause to find fault in that direction. But lack of friends and lack of outdoor exercise soon told upon him. He lost his healthy looks and became pale and listless, for in those days cycling was not in vogue, and it was seldom that a city clerk was able to shake the soot and dirt of the streets from him and get into the country.

"This won't do," thought Phil one evening as, chained to his desk on account of unusual business, he drove his pen till the figures were blurred and his fingers cramped. "If this is the life before me I had rather be a soldier or a sailor and earn my shilling a day, and a little adventure. Fellows have often told me that a steady young soldier is bound to rise, and if he works hard and has a little education, may even reach to commissioned rank. That takes years, of course, but supposing it took ten I should be better off than after spending the same time in this office. Larking has been here fifteen years, and look what he is!"

Phil raised his eyes from his work and stared thoughtfully at a bent and prematurely-aged man who sat on his right. "Yes, I'd sooner see the world and run the risk of losing my life in some far-off country than live to grow up like that," he mused pityingly. "At any rate I'll go and have a chat with Sergeant-major Williams."

The latter was a veteran of the Foot Guards, who had long ago earned a pension, and now lived with his wife on the same landing as Phil.

"Tired of your job, lad, are you?" he remarked, when Phil entered his room that night, saying that he had come for a chat and some advice. "Well, now, I'm not greatly surprised; though, mind you, there's many a poor starving chap as would only be too glad to step into your shoes. What chance has a youngster in the army, you ask? Every chance, sir; every chance. Look at me"—and the old soldier stood upright on the hearth-rug and threw out his chest, thereby showing the row of medals pinned to his waistcoat. "I was your age, my lad, when I first 'listed, and when I had got my uniform and stood on parade for the first time, trying to look as though I knew all about it, with my chest somewhere close to my back and my stomach showing well in front, why, the sergeant-major came along, and I thought to myself he must be the colonel, and miles and miles above me. I never guessed I'd reach his rank some day; but I did, sure enough, and steady, honest work, and being sober, was what lifted me there. But you've got education, and that's the pull. I had to teach myself, and a precious grind it was; but with you it's different, and if you only keep out of scrapes you're certain to go up."

"But I'm always in trouble and scrapes of one sort or another; at least I was at school!" exclaimed Phil.

"Yes, I dare say you was, and a precious baby you would be if you hadn't been; but that sort of thing don't go down in the army. Discipline's discipline, and so long as you remember that, and the fact that you're filling a man's place and are no longer a school-boy, you're all right. Play your larks in the barrack-room as much as you like, and no one will mind; but never give cheek back to a non-commissioned officer as orders you to stop. It's mighty trying at times, I know. Some young chap as has just been made a corporal gets beyond himself, and pitches into you. Grin and bear it is what you've got to do, and that's discipline, and it's minding that will help you to get on."

"Then you think I shall do well to enlist?" asked Phil.

"Do well? Of course you will. Why, I'd sooner pick rags than be at the work you're at," answered the sergeant-major. "How much do you earn a week, my lad, if it isn't a rude question?"

"Ten shillings, and extra if I'm kept overtime," said Phil.

"Then you'll be no worse off in the army," exclaimed the old soldier. "A shilling a day, less washing, and your extra messing, is what you'll have, and it won't be long before you're receiving corporal's pay. Now think it over, lad. I've no wish to persuade you; but if you decide to 'list for the army, I'll put you in the way of joining the finest regiment in the world."

Phil thanked the sergeant-major, and retired to bed, only to lie awake thinking the matter over. By the following morning he had quite made up his mind to be a soldier, and went in to see his friend.

"Look here, sir," the latter exclaimed, flourishing a morning paper, "you've made up your mind to leave that musty office and join the army, but you're barely seventeen yet, you say. Now, I've something to propose, and something to show you. Before you 'list try what it's like to rough it amongst rough men and earn your own living. Here's an advertisement asking for hands in a kind of private zoo. I know the show, and a friend of mine, an old soldier like myself, is office-man, and keeps the books. Take a job there for a few months and see how you like the life, and then, if roughing it suits you, join the army. Even then you'll be too young; but you're big and strong, and a few months won't make a great deal of difference."

"But I know nothing about animals," said Phil doubtfully. "I've ridden a horse occasionally, and always had a dog when possible. What does the advertisement say? Surely far more experience than I have had is wanted?"

"Here you are, sir. Read it, and judge for yourself. It's as fine an offer, and as good an opportunity for you to see what life is in the rough, as you could wish for."

Phil took the paper and read:

Wanted, a few hands in a large private menagerie. Applicants must be young and active, prepared to make themselves useful in any way, and must not object to travelling.

Then it concluded by giving the address, which was in the suburbs of London.

"Well, what do you make of it?" asked the old soldier, who had watched his face closely all the time.

"It certainly reads in a most inviting manner," Phil replied hesitatingly; "but still I scarcely think it would suit me, for I really have had no experience to teach me how to make myself useful. I should be a raw hand who was always in the way, and should be dismissed before a week had passed."

"You've no need to worry about that, I can assure you, sir," the sergeant-major answered encouragingly. "My friend will see that you have a fair chance given you, and I'll wager that a fortnight will set you on your feet and make you as knowing as those who've been working a year and longer with the firm. Mind you, though, I've scarcely more than an idea what is really required. Anyone can make himself useful if shown the way, but there must be a lot of work that's difficult and p'r'aps dangerous. One thing I've learnt from Timms, and that is, that animals has to be taken by road to various parties, and that means kind of camp or gipsy life at times. Now look you here, my lad. Just you go right off, read the 'vertisement again, and then think the matter over. It don't do to jump into these affairs, for you might find it a case of 'out of the frying-pan into the fire'. There's the place; top of the centre column. Come back this evening and tell me what you have decided on."

Phil did as the old soldier suggested. He took the paper to the office, and during the day thought the matter out, finally deciding to make the plunge and find out for himself what roughing it really meant.

"After all," he mused, as he absently traced lines and figures on the blotting-paper, "I shall be in just the position I might have occupied had not Father taken me from home. My mother was a poor widow, and long ago I should have had to earn my living and help to keep her too. I'll do it. I cannot put up with this office life. A few years later it might be different, but now it stifles me."

Many a wiseacre might shake his head at Phil's cogitations, and more emphatically still at his determination to abandon a certain livelihood for an extremely uncertain one. "Do not think of leaving the office," some would say, "till a better place offers itself'; or "Remain where you are till you are thoroughly acquainted with business life, and can command a higher salary." Certainly the majority would be strongly against his applying for the post proposed by the sergeant-major.

But deep in Phil's heart was a desire to show his adoptive parents that he had profited by their kindness, and was able to work his way up in the world. He knew that by leaving his present place he would give occasion for more disappointment; but then, after many a chat with others similarly situated, and being, for all his spirits, a thoughtful young fellow who looked to the future, he came to the conclusion that here he had no opportunity of rising. He knew that whenever a vacancy in some business house did occur there were plenty asking for it, and he knew, too, that without means at their disposal those who were selected had prospects none too brilliant. Many did rise undoubtedly from the office-stool to the armchair of the manager. But how many? Why should that good fortune come his way? No, in an office he felt like a canary in a cage; therefore he determined to forsake the life and seek one with more of the open air about it, and a spice of danger and hardship thrown in. Who could say that luck would not come his way? If it did, perhaps it would give him just that necessary heave which would enable him to set foot upon the first rung of the ladder which leads upward to honour and glory, and a position of standing in the world.

It was a brilliant prospect, and it must be admitted that Phil built many castles in the air. Yet for all that, once he had descended to *terra firma*, he plainly acknowledged to himself that plenty of hard work, plenty of rough and tumble, and no doubt a share of privation and hardship, must be faced before the height of his ambition could be reached.

"I've read the advertisement through," he said that evening, when once more seated in front of the sergeant-major, "and if you will introduce me to your friend I will apply for one of the vacant places. First of all, though, I should like to hear whether they will have me, and then I will give my present employer notice."

"Shake hands on it, lad! I'm glad you've decided, and I'll be hanged if you won't make a splendid workman, and one of these days as fine a soldier as ever stepped. Here's wishing you the best of luck. Now we'll go off to Timms right away and see what he has to say."

Accordingly the two started off, and in due time reached a big building in which the menagerie had its home. Phil was introduced to Timms, as fine an old soldier as the sergeant-major, and was greatly relieved to hear that his services would be accepted at fifteen shillings a week.

"Come in a week, when your notice is up," Timms said pleasantly, "and your job will be waiting for you. You'll look after the horses at first, and perhaps we'll give you one of the cages later on. You'll want rough clothes and strong boots, and, for sleeping, a couple of thick rugs. Get a bag to hold your kit, and that will do for your pillow as well. Set your mind easy, Williams. I'll look after the lad and see that he comes to no harm."

That day week Phil left the office on the expiration of his notice, having meanwhile written to Mr Western and to Joe. Then he returned to his room, packed the few valuables he possessed, and a couple of changes of clothing in a waterproof bag, and with this under one arm, and a roll of coarse blankets under the other, set out for the menagerie.

"That you, youngster?" Timms asked cheerily. "'Pon my word I hardly expected you. Some fellows back out of a job like this at the last moment. But come along and I'll show you where you will sleep, and who will be your mate. He's a good fellow, and will show you the ropes."

Passing outside the building, Timms led the way to a large yard at the back in which was an assortment of the caravans which usually accompany a circus.

"Jim!" he shouted. "Here, Jim, your new mate's arrived. Show him round."

A jovial and dirty face, with a two-days' growth of beard upon it, was thrust out of a wagon, and a voice called out: "Come right in here, mate. Glad to see yer. Bring your togs along."

Phil scrambled up the steep steps and into the wagon, where, having grasped the hand extended to him, he looked round with some curiosity, noticing with much interest the two neat little bunks, one above the other, at the farther end, the diminutive table close to one red-curtained window, and the stove on the other side, filled with paper shavings of all colours, and gold tinsel, with its chimney of brightly-polished brass.

"Queer little house, mate, ain't it?" sang out the man who went by the name of Jim, busying himself with a pot of hot water and a shaving-brush and soap.

"Yes, I've never been in a van of this sort before," said Phil. "It looks comfortable, and at any rate must be a good shelter on wet nights."

"That it is, mate, and you'll find it so precious soon. We start at daylight to-morrow on a long trip to the south, and I tell yer it's mighty pleasant to know as there's a warm fire, and a dry bed to get into, when the water's coming down in buckets, and the wind's that cold it freezes yer to the marrer."

Phil noted every little article in the van, and listened to the scrape, scrape of the razor as Jim removed his bristles. When this operation was completed, Jim took him round the horses, and having initiated him into the mysterious duties of a stableman, invited him back to the wagon to tea.

"Timms and I sleep here," he remarked, with his pipe firmly clenched between his teeth, "and you'll put your rugs down on the floor. We'll mess together, and you'll find that five bob a week joined to our two fives will feed us well and leave the rest in our pockets. The other chaps has their own messes. I'll take yer round to see them soon. They're a queer lot; some has been sailors and soldiers, and some anything at all. Others has been at this game all their lives. You'll learn to know them all in a few days, and I'll give yer a hint—keep clear of the rowdy ones. They soon gets the sack, for the boss is very particular, and won't have no drinking and such like goings-on.

"Now about your job. What do you know of animals, and what class are yer on top of a horse what ain't 'xactly a camel?"

"I am sorry to say I am hopelessly ignorant of the first," Phil answered. "I've ridden horses often, and can manage to keep in my saddle as a rule, but cannot boast that I am a good horseman."

"Oh, you'll do! besides, I can see you're willing to learn and has got the grit to stick to things that might bother others of your sort. You're to be my mate, and for a time, at any rate, we shall be on the move. The gent who runs this business keeps five and six such vans as this moving most of the year, besides the cages, of course, which follow.

"You see, agents in furrin parts collects lions and every sort of animal down to snakes, and sends them to England. No sooner does the ship come alongside the river dock than some of us are there with cages, mounted on wheels and drawn by horses. We unload the animals, slip 'em into the cage, and bring them here. A day or two later, perhaps a week, or even as long after as a month, someone wants one or other of them beasts, and arranges to buy him from the guv'nor. Then in he goes into the travelling-cage again, and off we take him to wherever he's been ordered. Of course there's railroads nowadays; but they are risky things at any time, and the wild beasts we deal in catch cold, and fall sick so easy that it's been found cheaper and safer to take 'em by road. And a very pleasant life it is, to be sure. With two of us on the beat, and drawing our own house, we're as comfortable as chaps could wish for. Every day there's something different to look at and ask questions about, and every evening, when yer pull up on some wayside piece of ground and start to water and feed the animals, there's new scenery and new people around yer, the last always ready to be civil and polite. Yes, it's a free, easy life, with plenty of change and movement to make yer work come pleasant and light. You'll like it, lad. By the way—what's yer name? Ah, Philip Western! Well, Phil, I've told yer pretty nigh all I can think about. Timms and me start early to-morrow, as I told yer, so turn in soon to-night. We'll teach yer all yer want to know while on the road, and if yer only keeps yer eyes open you'll soon get a hold on the work." Jim nodded pleasantly, and having invited Phil to sit down for a short time and rest himself, he ran down the steps of the van and went to complete his daily work.

"Of course all this is very different from office life," mused Phil, looking round, and still finding many little things in the quaint travelling house to interest and amuse him, "I can see that any kind of work is expected of me, and I must not be afraid of dirtying my hands. A few months at this will show me whether or not I shall like the army, for I remember the sergeant-major told me that there too the men have numerous fatigues to do, cleaning barracks and quarters, carrying coal, and a hundred-and-one other things. Yes, I've come to rough it, and I'll do my utmost to prove useful. It seems, too, that this travelling with wild beasts is very much liked by the other men. It will be funny to be constantly on the move, and constantly seeing fresh places. Well, I think I shall like it. It will be what I have hankered after—an open-air life,—and since Jim is to be my companion I feel sure I shall be happy, for he looks an excellent fellow."

Indeed, though outwardly rough, Jim was a sterling good fellow, with a kind heart beating beneath his weather-stained jacket. Already he had taken a liking to Phil, and seeing that he was altogether different from the new hands usually employed, and moreover having heard something of his story from Timms, he determined to look after his charge and make life as pleasant for him as possible.

That evening the three who were to be companions supped at a little coffee-stall standing close outside the menagerie, and, having returned to the van, indulged in a chat before turning-in. Then Jim and the old soldier Timms climbed into their bunks, while Phil spread his blankets on the floor, and with his kit-bag beneath his head soon fell asleep, to be wakened, however, every now and again by the roaring of a big African lion, which had arrived two days before, and was caged close at hand.

Day had scarcely dawned when Jim turned over in his bunk, yawned loudly, and, sitting up with a start, consulted a silver watch, of the proportions of a turnip, which dangled from the arched roof of the van. "Five o'clock, and not a soul stirring!" he cried. "Up, up yer get, all of yer. Look lively now, or else we'll be moving before we've had a morning meal."

"What! Time for breakfast! Hullo, where am I?" cried Phil, sitting up with a start and staring round in bewilderment. Then the truth dawned upon him, and, throwing off his blankets, he rose to his feet.

"What orders, Jim?" he asked.

"Come along with me, Phil. That's the orders. Timms'll see to the breakfast, while you and me looks to the horses."

Hurriedly throwing on their coats—for they had discarded nothing more when they turned in on the previous night—they ran down the steps to the stables, where they found other men at work busily grooming their animals. Instructed by Jim, Phil started with a brush upon the smooth coat of a fine draught horse which was to form one of their team. From that he went to another, while Jim looked to the other two. That done the animals were fed, and while Phil returned to the van Jim went to see that the lion they were to transport was safely caged and fed in preparation for the journey.

Meanwhile Timms had not been idle. As Phil reached the van he emerged from a doorway opposite, bearing a kettle, from the spout of which a cloud of steam was puffing. Already he had placed a rough folding-table on the ground, and now he proceeded to infuse the tea. Then he dived into the van, to reappear immediately with plates and knives and enough cups and saucers. Ten minutes later Jim had returned, and, sitting down, the three hastily swallowed thick slices of bread and butter, washing them down with cups of steaming tea.

"That'll keep us quiet for a few hours, I reckon," exclaimed Jim, jumping to his feet and hastily filling a pipe in preparation for a morning smoke. "Now, young un, you and me'll slip off and harness the horses, while our mate cleans up the breakfast things."

Half an hour later two fine horses had been yoked to the van, while another pair had been harnessed to the large boxed-in cage on wheels, which enclosed the magnificent animal they were to transport. A sack of corn was placed on the van, and a large joint of horse-flesh hung beneath, and then, fully prepared for the journey, the gates were thrown open, and with nodded adieus from the other hands they issued from the yard and took the road for Brighton, Jim driving the horses in the van, with Phil by his side, while Timms went in front in charge of the lion. Trundling over the London cobbles they crossed one of the bridges, and before very long were out of the great city and enjoying to the full the sunshine and sweet breath of the country.

Chapter Four.

A Gallant Deed.

The outdoor life agreed with Phil thoroughly, and he had scarcely been with the menagerie a month before all his paleness had disappeared, and he felt and looked in the best of health.

Constantly accompanying Jim and the old soldier upon some journey, the beginning of one week would find them at some sunny spot on the southern sea-coast, while at the end they would be slowly trudging to the north, having called *en route* at the headquarters in London, there to take possession of some other animal. And while they carried out this work others did the same, for the menagerie was a large and profitable concern. At the London headquarters there were cages and houses innumerable, in which the various animals were kept. But seldom indeed was any particular one a tenant of his cage for more than a fortnight, for, much to Phil's surprise, the demand for lions, tigers, and other wild beasts was extraordinarily large. Now it was a zoological garden that wished to replace the lose of one of its show animals, and now some wealthy nobleman with a fancy for a private menagerie. Then, too, demands came from the Continent, and had to be attended to. The animals were placed in well-built, warm, but properly ventilated cages, capable of being lifted from their wheels if necessary, and in these they journeyed by road to their several destinations. In no case was the railroad used, for it was as yet very far from attaining to its present efficiency, and experience had taught the owner of the menagerie that beasts from foreign parts required to be treated like hot-house flowers, and protected from the chills and biting winds met with in England.

Two months and more passed pleasantly, and by that time Phil was quite accustomed to his work, and moreover, from frequent calls at the menagerie in London, had met all the other hands.

"I like the life immensely, and am sure it agrees with me," he answered with enthusiasm one day when Jim suddenly turned upon him and asked him the question. "I earn more than I did some weeks ago, and in a very pleasant manner compared with the other employment. Besides, I have been amongst a number of working men and find that I can rub shoulders with them and not quarrel. It is just what I wanted to know, and now that I have had the experience I shall not be long in leaving this employment and enlisting in the army."

"You must do just as you like there, lad," replied Jim briskly. "Each chap settles that kind of thing for hisself. For my part, though, I've been too long and too contented at this here work to want to change."

And indeed there was no doubt that Jim enjoyed his life to the full. A contented and merry fellow, he was just the one to make his companions look upon the bright side of things. Not that Phil was ever inclined to do otherwise. Up at daylight, as blithe as a lark, he was off with the horses to the nearest water so soon as the sun had lifted the mist from the ground. Then, tethering them to the wagon shafts again, he would slip off the thick rugs which covered them and groom them thoroughly, all the while giving vent to that peculiar "hiss" which seems necessary for this purpose, in a way that would have aroused the envy of many a stable lad.

That done, the canvas bin that stretched from the tip of the shaft was filled with corn, and while the sleek-coated animals set to work to consume it, Phil produced an iron tripod, gathered a pile of sticks, and set them alight. A box placed in proper position kept the breeze away on a gusty day, and in a twinkling, it seemed, the kettle above was singing, and a jet of white steam blowing into the cool morning air.

Now came the time he enjoyed most of all. Armed with a frying-pan, he sat down to prepare rashers of bacon, and if it were an extraordinary day, possibly eggs too. A shout would rouse Jim and the old soldier, and in five minutes the folding-table was set up, the tea made, and all three heartily devouring their breakfast.

"We might be in Ameriky, or some such place," remarked Jim one morning. "It's a treat being in the country this fine weather, and it does yer good to get up early and prepare yer own grub."

"A precious lot of preparing you do, I notice," laughed Timms. "Why, ever since Phil joined us he's done all that."

"You've got me there, mate, I owns," Jim grinned. "The young un's a beggar to work, and saves us a deal of trouble. Before he come I used to act as cook. Now I lies abed and takes it easy, as I ought to, on account of my age."

Phil joined heartily in the laugh, for he knew well how Jim and Timms could work. As to his own share, he was glad to have plenty to do, and especially when he found he could help his two comrades, who had shown themselves such excellent fellows.

Phil liked the majority of those he met at the menagerie in London, and as for himself the other hands soon took his measure, and readily acknowledged that he was a hard-working and straight lad, willing to be friends with all. A few, however, were of the opposite opinion. There was a small clique of rowdy fellows who took an instant dislike to Phil, probably because, seeing what they were, he held aloof from them, and these, and in particular one of them, set themselves to make things unpleasant for him.

"Ought to ha' been a lord or summat of the sort," this worthy sneered one day as Phil passed the doorway round which they were lounging. "Thinks he owns the show—that's what it is. I'll take the gent down; see if I don't, and right away too. Hi, you, Phil Western, or whatever's yer name," he shouted, "come here! I want to speak to yer. Now look here, Mr Dook, you're a pretty fine bird, but where do you come from? That's what we're arter. Chaps of your sort don't take to being hands in a menagerie every day, and that's the truth, I reckon. I suppose yer wanted to hide away. That's it, ain't it?"

Now Phil had often been annoyed by this same young man, who went by the name of "Tony", and in particular by the jeering way in which he shouted names and various other pleasantries after him every time he happened to pass.

"You want to know where I come from," he replied calmly, standing close to the circle. "Then I'm afraid you will have to want."

"Eh! What! Have to want, shall I?" Tony growled. "Now none of yer cheek. You're too proud, that's what you are, my young peacock, and you've got to get taken down."

"That's possible," Phil rejoined, and was on the point of turning away to avoid a quarrel when the pleasant Tony sprang to his feet and shouting "Possible! Should just about think it is!" grasped him by the arm and swung him round till they faced one another.

"Leave go!" cried Phil, losing his temper.

"Sha'n't till I've took yer down," Tony snapped.

"Then take that!" and Phil dashed his fist into the young man's face.

A scuffle at once ensued, and after a short and fiercely contested round, a ring was formed. But at this moment the owner of the menagerie put in an appearance and stopped the fight, with the natural result that there was bad blood between Phil and Tony from that day, and the latter never ceased to vow that he would have an ample revenge for the black eye he had received.

Now Tony had another disagreeable trait. Besides being a bully, he was also cruel, and took every opportunity of teasing a big brown bear which happened to be his special charge. The more Bruin snarled and showed his teeth, the harder Tony prodded him with his stick, till at times the poor beast was almost mad with rage. It was a dangerous game to play, and could have but one ending, and that was within an ace of being a fatal one for Tony.

It happened upon a day when Phil and his two companions had returned to London and were enjoying a well-earned rest after a few longer tramps than usual. By the merest chance, too, it was a holiday in the menagerie, for some valuable animals had recently arrived, and in consequence, the wives and children and other relatives of the various hands had gathered, by the owner's special request, to have tea with their friends and see the wild beasts in their new home.

Phil was sitting in the van with Jim, sipping a cup of tea, and quite unaware of the fact that Tony was engaged in his usual practice of stirring up the bear for his own amusement and to excite the fear of a few by-standers.

Suddenly there was a snarl, a crash, and the sound of breaking woodwork, and then shrieks of terror and the noise of a wild stampede.

"What's that? Something's up," cried Phil, and springing down the steps he ran towards the spot where the animals were kept.

A fearful sight met his eye, for the end of the flimsy cage in which Bruin was kept a prisoner was splintered, and close beside it. Tony lay motionless, and full length upon the ground, with the bear crouching over him and clutching his head with a paw armed with murderous-looking claws.

Not a soul was near, for all had fled for their lives. As Phil ran forward, the enraged animal crouched lower over its victim, and snarled fiercely, showing a row of teeth and gums.

"Help, Jim! The bear is killing Tony," shouted Phil, turning his head for a moment, but still running towards the scene of the conflict.

As he passed a wagon he snatched up a long pitchfork. Rushing at the bear, which reared itself on end, Phil swung the fork above his head and brought it down with a smash on the animal's nose, shouting at the same time in the hope of frightening it.

But Bruin was thoroughly aroused, and, stung to further anger by the tap upon his head, he darted from the prostrate man and came open-mouthed at Phil.

It was a terrifying sight, and many another might have taken to his heels and not been called a coward. But Phil's mouth hardened till it was a thin, straight line. Standing with his feet planted wide apart, and the fork well in front of him, he kept his ground and lunged at the animal with all his might, driving the prongs well into its chest.

There was a roar of pain and anger, and Bruin drew back for a moment, but only to rise upon his hind-legs and advance with arms ready to crush the life out of Phil's body, and gleaming teeth with which to tear his flesh.

On he came, and, waiting his time, Phil once more plunged the prongs deep into his chest, where they remained fast. A second later the bear had shattered the pole with his paw, and, rushing at his enemy, had beaten him to the ground and fallen upon him—dead.

It was a narrow shave, as Jim remarked.

"You're the biggest, yes, the biggest idiot I ever see, young un," he said severely, as Phil lay in his bunk. "Here you go and attack a bear as is always pretty wild, and only with a thing as is little better than a toothpick. I can't make yer out. If it was me as was laid under that there beast I might see some reason for it, though even then you'd be pretty mad, I reckon; but when it's Tony, who's always a-naggin' at yer, why, it fairly does for me."

"I didn't think of that, though," answered Phil cheerfully, for by a piece of good fortune he had escaped with a severe shaking and a fright. "There was the bear killing someone, and I was the first on the spot and therefore bound to do something."

"Get on with yer! Bound to do something! Yes, it's run away most of us would do—least—I don't know, though; I expects we'd have had a try to drive the brute off. But for you, a kid like you, Phil, to tackle the job all alone, and with only a pitchfork too, why, it just knocks all the stuffin' out of me. Give us yer flipper, mate. You're a true un, and don't you go a-telling me yer didn't know it was Tony as lay there. I heard yer shout it. So no more of them fibs."

Jim got quite indignant, and then shook Phil's hand, squeezing it so hard that he could have shouted with the pain.

"And that chap Tony's goin' to live too," he went on. "If he don't say summat out o' the ord'nary, blest if I won't set to work and give him the biggest hidin' he ever had. That is, when he's strong again. Now, young un, turn over and get to sleep. You've had a roughish time, and a go of grog ain't sufficient to pull yer round."

Phil obediently curled himself up and promptly fell asleep, but only to dream that it was. Joe Sweetman who lay helpless upon the ground, while the figure that was crouching over him, and that rushed at himself when he ran to the rescue, was none other than "old Bumble", rendered furious by the joke played upon his statue. It was an awful moment when Phil plunged the fork into the old gentleman's massive chest, and so upset him that he awoke, to find himself drenched with perspiration, but decidedly better for all that, while through the open door he could see Jim, pipe in mouth and in his shirt sleeves, squatting over the fire and preparing breakfast.

Another month passed, making the third that Phil had spent in his new employment, and ending also his seventeenth year. Short as the time had been it had done much for him. He had filled out a little, and though his face was still that of a boy, his limbs and body were big, so that, if he could only pass inspection, he was quite fitted to take his place in the ranks as a full-grown man. By this time he had completed a long journey into the country, and having returned to London with Jim and the old soldier, he was not long in looking up his friend, Sergeant-major Williams.

"Back again, sir, and filled out and healthier-looking, too! How do you like the life?" the latter exclaimed.

"I never spent a better or more profitable three months, never in my life," said Phil emphatically. "We've had grand weather, and always fresh scenery. The work was not too hard, and my comrades were all that I could wish for. In addition, I have saved close upon five pounds, which was simply impossible when I was living here."

"Ah, glad you like it, lad! But I thought you would; and now I suppose you'll be off again soon?"

"Yes, but not with the van and my old comrades," said Phil. "The best I can do there is to become a foreman in charge of a number of cages. I mean to enlist and try my fortune in the army."

"Bless the lad!" exclaimed the sergeant-major. "He's as long-headed as a lawyer, and always thinking of the future. But you couldn't do better than that. Keep it always in your mind's eye and you'll get on. Now, what regiment will you go for? I'm from the Guards, and of course I say there's none to beat them. It's the truth too, as others can tell you."

"I've been thinking it over," Phil answered, "and I have decided to become a Grenadier—one of the old Grenadiers."

The sergeant-major's features flushed, and he looked not a little flattered, for he too was one of the Grenadier Guards, and he knew it was because of his connection with it that Phil had decided to enlist in that regiment.

"You couldn't do better, sir," he exclaimed, "and what's more, by joining them I'll be able to make your start easier. I am not so old but that some of the non-commissioned officers—N.C.O.'s as we call 'em—remember Owen Williams. I've many a pal there, and as soon as you're ready I'll take you right along to the barracks and see you 'listed myself."

A day was fixed, and having learned a few more details, Phil returned to his friends. The latter were genuinely sorry to hear that he was to go, and of all, Jim was perhaps the saddest.

"No one to cook the breakfast no more, now you're off, young un," he said, with a ring of true regret in his voice. "Never mind; that chap Tony's come back, and I'll turn him on to the job. If he kicks there'll be trouble, and then I'll do as I promised yer."

But Jim was disappointed. For three weeks Tony had lain in bed at a hospital, and for the first six days it was a matter of life and death. The bear's claws had lacerated his scalp so severely that it was a wonder he survived. But by dint of careful nursing he recovered, and on the very day that Phil had been to see the sergeant-major he returned to the menagerie. But he was a changed man. A double escape from death had cured him of his rowdiness, and when he came towards Phil shamefacedly, offering his hand as though he could not expect it to be shaken, he was filled with deep gratitude for the truly gallant deed that had saved his life.

Phil clutched the hand extended and shook it heartily.

"Ah, sir!" Tony blurted out, with tears in his eyes, "I've been a real brute, and no one knows it better nor myself. But yer saved my life, Phil Western, yer did, and I ain't ungrateful. If you'd left me to be torn to pieces it was only what I deserved, for we wasn't the best of friends, and a chap as can torment a dumb animal must expect something back in the end. And now, sir, I hear you're going, and if you'll let me I'll come too."

"Nonsense, Tony!" Phil exclaimed. "You've got a good job, and had better stick to it."

"I had one, but I ain't now, Phil," Tony replied dolefully. "The boss give me the sack, saying I'd cost him a good fifty pounds by causing the death of the bear. So I'm out of work now, and if you're for a soldier, as they tell me, why, so am I too; and I tell yer I'll stick to yer like a true 'un if you'll let me come, and one day when you're an officer I'll be yer servant."

Phil laughed good-naturedly, and flushed red when he saw that here was one who thought it was within the bounds of possibility that he would attain to the status of officer.

"It will be a long time before I shall be that, Tony," he said, with a smile; "but if you really have made up your mind to be a soldier, come with me. There's been bad blood between us up to this, but now we'll be good friends and help one another along."

"Ah, we'll be friends, sir, good friends too! I've had my lesson, and I sha'n't need another. I've acted like a brute up to this, but now I mean to be steady, and I mean to show yer too that I ain't bad altogether."

Phil was astonished at the turn matters had taken; but he recognised that Tony had really made up his mind to reform, and at once determined to help him to adhere to that resolution.

"Very well, Tony," he said, "we'll enlist together. My month is up to-morrow, and on the following day we'll take the shilling. I'm going to join the Grenadier Guards."

"Grenadier Guards or any Guards for me, Phil. It don't make a ha'poth of difference so far as I'm concerned. Just fix what it's to be, and I'll be there with yer."

"Then it's settled, Tony. We're for the Guards. Come to the house where Sergeant-major Williams lives, at nine o'clock the day after to-morrow."

They shook hands, as though to seal the compact, and separated, Phil returning to the van, where he spent part of the day in writing to Mr Western and to Joe, informing them of the step he was taking. To his previous letter Mr Western had deigned no answer, for he was thoroughly upset by its contents, and from that day firmly resolved never again to have any dealings with his adopted son. He was an utter failure and a scamp, and it only needed Joe Sweetman's efforts to defend him to settle the matter.

M 845

"HE KEPT HIS GROUND AND LUNGED AT THE ANIMAL"

"It is just what I told you would happen," Joe had said defiantly. "The lad has spirit, and far from being the rogue you think him, is filled with the desire to see life and make his way in the world. I am not a great judge of character, but if ever there was a youth unfitted for office life, that one is Phil. You have only yourself to thank after all. You have endeavoured to force a profession on him, whereas you should have given the lad an opportunity of selecting one for himself. Mark my words, Edward: Phil will live to do well and be a credit to you, and one of these days you will acknowledge that the step he is taking now was a good one and for the best. Now I'll write to him, and give him a few words of advice."

And this Joe did, sending a characteristic letter, written not to damp Phil's hopes, but to encourage him, and let him see that there was one old friend at least who still thought well of him.

Find your own place in the world, Phil, he wrote; *and if it is a good one, as I feel sure it will be, there is one who will be proud of you. You start in the ranks, and so fall into discredit among your friends. You are on the lowest rung; stick to it, and we will see where you come out. Meanwhile, my lad, I will send you ten shillings a week, paid every month in advance. You will find it a help, for soldiers want spare cash as well as other people.*

At last the morning arrived for Phil and Tony to enlist, and, attended by the sergeant-major, they made their way to Wellington Barracks. Both felt somewhat nervous and bashful, especially when they passed the sentries at the gate.

"My eye!" exclaimed Tony in a whisper, "what swells them coves look! Shall we wear them hats, do yer think?"

"Of course you will," the sergeant-major, who had overheard the remark, replied. "That is the Guards' bearskin, and you'll learn to be proud of it yet. It's a grand head-dress, and there isn't another half as good; at least that's what I think, though chaps in other regiments would stick up for theirs in just the same way. And you'll find, too, that the forage-cap with the red band round it, that's worn well over the right ear—well over, mind you, youngsters—is as taking a thing as was ever invented."

Phil and Tony both agreed, for the men walking about in uniform with forage-caps on did look smart and well dressed.

"Now here we are at the orderly-room," said the old soldier, a moment later. "Wait a moment and I'll speak to the sergeant-major."

Phil and Tony stood looking with interest across the parade-ground. Then they suddenly heard a voice say in a room at the door of which they were waiting:

"Two recruits, and likely-looking fellows, I think you said, sergeant-major? March them in."

A moment later a big man with bristling moustache, and dressed in a tight-fitting red tunic, came to the door, and in a voice that made Phil and Tony start, and which could easily have been heard across the square, exclaimed: "Now, you two, get together; yes, just like that. Right turn! Quick march!"

It was a new experience, but Phil, who stood nearest the door, carried out the order smartly, and, snatching his hat from his head, followed the sergeant-major. A moment later they were standing in front of a table covered with green baize, and with a number of books and blue papers all neatly arranged upon it. Behind it sat an officer, dressed in a dark-blue uniform, with braided front, and a peaked cap encircled with a dark band and bearing a miniature grenade in front. It was the adjutant, and he at once cross-questioned the new recruits.

"Both of you have been in a menagerie," he remarked with some astonishment, "but surely you—and he pointed towards, Phil—have had some education?"

"Yes, sir, I have been to a good school," Phil answered, "and before I joined the menagerie I was a clerk in an office for a short time."

"Ah, just the kind of man we want!" exclaimed the officer. "And both of you wish to enlist in the Grenadier Guards? Very well; send them across to the doctor's."

"Right turn! Quick march!" The words almost made Tony jump out of his skin, but he and Phil obeyed them promptly, and next moment were breathing a trifle more freely in the open air. A corporal was now sent for, and he conducted them across to another room. Here they were told to strip, and a few minutes later were ushered into an inner room, in which were the regimental doctor and a sergeant who sat with a book before him. Phil and Tony were sounded and thumped all over, and then told to hop up and down the floor. They swung their arms round their heads till they were red in the face, and swung their legs to and fro to show that they had free movement of their joints. Then their eyes were tested, and these and their hearing having proved satisfactory, they were declared fit for the army, and were told to dress themselves.

"What's coming next, Phil?" whispered Tony, with a chuckle. "We've been interviewed—or whatever they calls it—by the officer, and now we've been punched all over, like folks used to do with that prize mare the boss in the old show was so fond of."

"Wait and see," Phil answered, for he too was wondering what their next experience would be.

They had not long to wait. The same corporal who had conducted them before took them round to the back of the building, up a steep flight of stairs, and showed them into the quarter-master's stores. And here they spent almost an hour, during which time a complete set of uniform, with the exception of a bearskin, was served out to each of them. Their civilian clothing was then taken from them and safely packed away, and feeling remarkably queer, and uncertain how to carry the smart little cane which had been given them, they were marched away to the barrack-room, heads in air and chests well to the front, as every new recruit does when in uniform for the first time, and trying to look as though they were well used to their new circumstances, whereas every man they passed grinned, and, nudging his comrade, chuckled: "New uns! Look at the chest that redheaded cove's got on 'im, and don't the other hold his nose up?" or something equally flattering.

But Phil and Tony were blissfully ignorant of these facetious remarks, and in a few minutes had reached the room in which they were to sleep, and had taken possession of their cots.

The following day they were once more inspected by the adjutant, and under his eye the regimental tailor chalk-marked their clothing where alterations were to be made.

In due time both settled down to their new duties and began to learn their drill on the parade-ground. A few days, and they lost all the slovenliness of recruits and held themselves erect. Soon they were as smart as any, and an old friend of Phil's, looking at him now, with his forage-cap jauntily set over his ear, his tight-fitting tunic and belt, and the swagger-cane beneath his arm, would scarcely have recognised him, so much had he altered. But had he only asked Tony, he would quickly have learnt the truth.

"Yus, that's Phil Western, you bet!" the latter would exclaim; "and I tell yer what it is, that young chap is downright the smartest lad in this lot of recruits, and that's saying a deal, as you'll agree if you'll only take a look at 'em."

So thought Joe Sweetman too, when he visited London on one occasion and looked his young friend up. "He's every inch a soldier," he exclaimed admiringly to Mr Western, on his return to Riddington. "As smart and good-looking a fellow as ever I saw; and that lad means to get on and do well. Mark my words! That's what he means, and he'll do it too, or I'm a donkey."

Chapter Five.

A Step in Rank.

Whether or not honest kind-hearted old Joe Sweetman was a donkey was yet to be proved, as the reader will ascertain for himself if he will only have patience to bear with the narrative till the end; but certain it was that Joe and Tony were not alone in thinking well of Phil.

"He's a likely youngster," the adjutant had more than once remarked to the colonel, "and he'll make an excellent N.C.O. once he has sufficient service. He's well educated, and always well-behaved, and with your permission, Colonel, I will give him a trial in the orderly-room."

"Do just as you like," the latter had answered. "I leave these matters in your hands; only, if you make him a clerk, do not take him altogether from his other duties. He might lose his smartness in the ranks, and what I want is not alone N.C.O.'s who can write well, but men who can be an example to the others, and, above all, have authority over them. Keep your eye on the lad, and let me know how he gets on."

"Certainly, sir. I'll see how he performs his duties, and mention the subject to you another day."

Phil had thus already attracted attention, and a hint to that effect, passed from the sergeant-major through the colour-sergeant to himself, encouraged him to persevere in his drill. Not long afterwards the battalion received orders to proceed to Windsor, and there relieve another of the Guards regiments. By that time Phil and Tony had completed their recruits' course, and had taken their places in a company of the regiment.

"We couldn't ha' been luckier, Phil, could we?" remarked Tony, with a grunt of satisfaction, as the two stood on the parade-ground waiting for the bugle to sound the "Fall in". "I said weeks back as I'd stick to yer through thick and thin, and here we are, yer see, both in the same company, and always falling-in alongside of one another. But it won't last long, mate, and don't you go for to try and make believe it will. I ain't so blind as I can't see that before long you'll wear a corporal's stripes. All the fellers says the same, and it's bound to be true."

"I must say I hope it will," Phil replied cheerfully. "It is my aim and object to become an N.C.O. But we needn't think of parting, Tony. We'll still be in the same company, and if we don't stand side by side, we shall be close together in the barrack-room. Besides, you may get the stripes sooner than I."

"Me, mate? That's a good un! There ain't a chance."

"You never know, Tony; and although it seems far away now, it will come, especially if you always keep out of trouble, as you have done up to this."

"Yus, it might," Tony agreed, after a long pause. "Every chap gets a chance, they say, and I'll see if I can't win them stripes just to show yer, Phil, that I've stuck to me oath. And it won't be getting into trouble as will lose 'em for me. I used to be a regular wild un, but I've given that up months ago; besides, I heerd Sergeant Irving a-saying only a few days ago that the chap as was quiet was bound to get on. 'What's the good of larking about as some of these idjuts do?' he says. 'Them as drinks is certain to get into trouble, and come before the colonel, and what good does it do 'em? They loses their chance of promotion, and they ruins their health. Besides that, they goes down the quickest when the troops is on active service.'"

"Yes, that is very true, I believe," Phil answered. "But to return to the stripes. You must win them, Tony, and if only you stick to your work I am sure you will succeed. Then in the course of time you'll be made sergeant, and later perhaps become sergeant-major. What a fine thing it would be! You would have a good pension to look forward to, and one of these days could end your service while still a young man, but with the comfortable feeling that you were provided for for life."

"Hum! that's flying away to the skies, mate," Tony chuckled, "but there's plenty of time to see, and—look up! there goes the bugle."

Both lads fell in with their company, now dressed in all the pride of bearskins and whitened belts and pouches, and having been duly inspected, marched stiffly erect out through the barrack-gate, up Sheet Street, and into the famous old castle.

Many a time did Phil stand motionless by his sentry-box, looking over the terrace-wall at a scene not to be surpassed in any other quarter of Her Majesty's wide dominions—the green fields of Berkshire, with old Father Thames winding hither and thither amongst them, now flowing placidly along between banks of shimmering corn and grass, and anon swirling past with a splash and a gurgle which broke up the reflections of boats and houses brightly mirrored on its surface. Then, sloping his gun, he would march across in front of the terrace gardens and the windows of the royal apartments, and, turning his eyes in the opposite direction, admire the three miles of absolutely straight and undulating road, lined on either side by its double row of grand old oaks and beeches, and ending in a green knoll, surmounted by a pile of masonry, on which is set a large equestrian statue familiarly known as "the Copper Horse". Away on either side the wide stretches of the park would attract his attention, while far beyond the town, appeared the faint blue and reddish band which marks the position of Windsor Forest.

Many times, too, whilst on sentry-go, did he stand as rigid as his own ramrod, heels close together, and gun at the "present", as the Queen and the Prince Consort with their children sauntered by. He had even exchanged words with them, for, attracted by his height, and possibly persuaded by the pleading of the infant princes, the Prince had stopped in front of our hero and questioned him as to his age and his parentage. The remarkable manner in which he had been adopted appealed to their curiosity, and before long they had learned Phil's story.

When not for guard, Phil and Tony generally managed to find plenty of occupation in their spare hours. In the winter there were long walks to be taken, and in the summer there was the river, a never-failing source of enjoyment, and in those days far less crowded than in this twentieth century, when excursion trains, bicycles, and tooting steam-launches have done not a little to mar its pleasant peacefulness. Hard by the Brocas boats could be obtained, and here a number of soldiers were to be found every afternoon, idling by the river-side and gazing at the youth of Eton disporting on the water, or themselves seated in boats sculling up and down the stream.

Phil and Tony were occupied in this way one hot summer afternoon, and having sculled up to the Clewer reach, rowed in to the bank, and made fast there for a while.

"It's mighty hot, young un, ain't it?" remarked Tony, wiping the perspiration from his forehead. "Phew! it is hot! Why, if we was bound to row these boats, we'd hate the sight of the river. What do yer say to a snooze?"

"Just the thing, Tony. It's too hot for any kind of exercise, so let's tie up and wait an hour; then we can pull up to the lock and down again. It'll be time for tea then."

Accordingly the two laid in their paddles, and stretching themselves on the bottom of the boat beneath the shade of an overhanging tree, soon fell asleep, lulled by the gentle ripple of the water. An hour passed, and still they slumbered placidly, the wash of a big boat as it slipped by them failed to rouse them. They heard nothing, and even the hoarse chuckles of a few comrades on the bank above them did not disturb them.

"What say, Jim? Shall we let 'em go?" grinned one.

"Yes, send 'em along, Tom. It'll be a proper joke to watch 'em when they wakes up and looks about 'em," was the answer. "Now, shake off that rope, and pitch it into the boat. So—oh! Gently, man! Shove 'em off as quiet as if they was babies in a cradle."

It was a huge joke to those upon the bank, but upon the unconscious occupants of the craft it was wasted. They stirred neither hand nor eyelid, but, locked firmly in the arms of Morpheus, glided down the river, totally unmindful of the shouts which followed them and of the angry "Boat ahead! Where are you coming to? Steer to the left!" which was hurled at them on more than one occasion. Suddenly a louder shout awoke Phil, and, sitting up with a start, he stared around, his eyes wide-open with astonishment, to find that he and Tony were drifting in midstream past the Brocas, and were already within 50 feet of the bridge.

"Why, we're adrift!" he exclaimed in a bewildered tone. "Here, Tony, wake up or we shall be on the bridge!"

"Eh, what!" grunted Tony, rubbing his eyes. "Adrift! What's that row about?"

The shout which had aroused Phil was repeated at that moment and, taken up immediately, assumed a perfect roar, in the intervals of which a loud clattering as of wheels rapidly passing over cobble stones, and the stamp of horses' hoofs were heard.

"Sounds like a cart or something coming down the street," said Phil. "Look out, Tony, something's wrong!"

As Phil spoke the clatter of hoofs and wheels became deafening, and before either could realise what was happening, two maddened horses dashed on to the bridge, dragging a carriage after them in which a gentleman was seated. On the back of one of the beasts was a postilion, and before Phil had time to exclaim, "It's a royal carriage!" the vehicle had collided with a cart coming in the opposite direction, there was a crash and a sound of breaking woodwork, and next second rider and passenger were shot as if from a catapult over the low rail of the bridge into the water.

"Quick! get your paddle out!" cried Phil, snatching one up and plunging it into the water.

Tony, now fully awake, sprang up and hastily obeyed, but with such vigour that he swung the boat round till it lay across the stream. Next moment, driven by the swirl of the water, it was hurled against a support of the bridge and capsized immediately.

When Phil rose to the surface a few seconds later, and had shaken the water from his eyes, he saw the boat shooting bottom-uppermost through the archway of the bridge, with Tony clinging to it. The stream had already swept him through, and just in front of him, splashing helplessly, was the unfortunate postilion, his eyes glaring round in search of help, and his mouth wide-open as he shouted to the people on the bank.

"All right! I'll be with you in a moment," cried Phil, striking out in his direction. A minute later he was by his side, and, grasping him by the shoulder, supported him till the overturned boat floated past them.

Both clutched it, and hung on for their lives.

"There he is, there's the other!" shouted a crowd of people on the bridge, and, hearing them, Phil hoisted himself as high as possible and searched the water carefully. There was a swirl some fifteen feet away, and two clutching hands suddenly appeared, to be swallowed up an instant later.

Leaving the boat Phil struck out with all his might, to find nothing when he reached the spot; but, plunging beneath the surface, he let the stream sweep him on, and groped with outstretched hands on either side. Something touched his fingers, and, grasping it he pulled it to him; holding tightly with both hands he kicked frantically till his head appeared above the water. Another second and the head of the unconscious passenger was reclining on his shoulder, and a burst of hearty cheering was ringing in his ears. Breathless and exhausted after the struggle, Phil looked round and caught sight of the boat drifting down to him. Treading water for a few minutes he supported the figure in his arms, and at last reached out for and obtained a firm hold of the keel, to which he clung, unable to make another effort, so much was he fatigued.

But help was at hand. A boat had been hastily pushed off from the river-bank, and before long all four had been lifted from the water and carried up the steps on to terra firma. A doctor was hastily summoned, and meanwhile the gentleman and the postilion were removed to a cottage.

As for Phil, five minutes' rest upon the ground made him feel himself again. Then, shaking the water from him, and bashfully exchanging handshakes with the enthusiastic crowd who surrounded him, and would not be denied, he slipped away with Tony, and, aided by a waterman, righted the capsized boat and proceeded to bail the water out.

"Come along, let's get out of this, Tony!" he exclaimed fretfully. "I never came across such a bother, and I hate a fuss like this."

"But you'll stop and give yer name, Phil? They're certain to want it, 'specially as the cove has summat to do with the castle."

"Oh, they can find out later on! Come along and let's get away," repeated Phil, in far more terror now than he had been when the boat upset.

"Wait a minute, my men," suddenly sang out a voice from the bank. "I want to find out who you are."

Phil reluctantly helped to push the boat alongside, while a gentleman who he knew had some connection with the castle pushed his way to the front of the crowd and, coming down the steps, held his hand out towards him.

"Shake hands, my brave young fellow," he said earnestly. "I never saw a more gallant deed, and you can have every cause for satisfaction, for you have saved the life of one of our Queen's most honoured guests. What is your name?"

"Private Western, sir," answered Phil with flushed cheeks. "Private Phil Western, Number 1760."

"Then, Western, you can expect to hear from me again. You are a credit to your regiment, and your officers and all your comrades shall know what a fine lad you are. Now, I will not detain you. You had better get off and change your clothes."

"Three cheers for the sodger boy!" a voice in the crowd shouted; and these were given with a gusto which made Phil's heart flutter, while Tony stood upright in the boat, looking more pleased and proud than he had ever done before.

"Shove off!" cried Phil almost angrily. "Shove off, or we shall never get away." A minute later they were pulling up-stream once more.

"I don't mind guessing them stripes is yours," chuckled Tony over his shoulder. "Young un, I knewed you'd have 'em soon, but you've won 'em now, and no one ought to feel prouder of them than you. Mate, Tony Jenkins is more pleased than if he'd got 'em hisself, and he feels just like a blessed peacock."

Phil made no reply, for he was still confused after his adventure, but for all that the thought that now there was some possibility of promotion elated him. If from this day he was to be known as Corporal Western he determined that he would do credit to that rank, and make use of it as a stepping-stone to a higher one. He wondered what the colonel would say, and was in the middle of imagining himself being thanked by that officer in the orderly-room when the boat banged against the bank.

"Come along, mate," cried Tony. "We'll get along to barracks and change these wet togs."

Squeezing the water from their garments they left the boat in charge of its owner, and made the best of their way to the barracks, where they were not long in getting into dry clothing.

Already a rumour had reached the soldiers, and soon both were surrounded by an eager crush.

"What's happened? What have you two chaps been up to?" they asked.

"Oh, an upset in the river, that's all!" said Phil nervously. "Here, ask Tony, he knows all about it;" and having transferred their attentions from himself he slipped away, while Tony, seated comfortably on the end of a bed, calmly filled and lighted his pipe, and, puffing big clouds into the air, dilated upon the gallant deed performed by his chum.

"He's a good plucked un, you chaps, as I has good cause to know," he concluded. "Once he saved me from a bear as was near tearing me to pieces, and now he's fished a gent out of the river that's staying along with the Queen. He's made, is Phil Western, and'll get his stripes. What's more, I'll tell yer now, so as there won't be no mistakes. When the young un's corporal, we'll all treat him as such. Any chap as doesn't 'll have to square it up with me. So now yer know what to expect."

With this final shot Tony pulled hard at his pipe and went off to find his friend.

Phil had won his stripes without a doubt, but he had yet to go through the ordeal of receiving them.

The very next day his name was down for commanding officer's orders, and when he marched into the orderly-room, and stood to attention in front of the green baize table, there was the colonel looking kindly at him, while a row of officers, no less interested in the young soldier who had behaved so gallantly, stood on either side.

"Western, my lad, it is reported to me that you saved two lives from drowning yesterday," said the colonel. "I have made enquiries about it and find that you behaved nobly, and have been a credit to this regiment. I may tell you that your name has already been mentioned as deserving of promotion, and there is no doubt but that you would have received your stripes ere long. But now you may feel doubly proud of them, for you have gained them by an act of bravery, which is seldom the case unless on active service. From this date you are a full corporal. Now, my lad, get your stripes put on, for we shall want to see them on parade."

Motionless, looking straight to his front, Phil listened as if in a dream. Then he blurted out, "Thank you, sir!" and a second later was obeying the order, "Right turn! Quick march!"

Outside, by order of the colonel, the tailor was waiting for him, and within a quarter of an hour Phil was the proud possessor of two stripes on his right arm, the badge of a full corporal.

"There you are, corporal," said the tailor. "They're fixed on strong, and I hope they'll never want to be taken off. Stick to 'em, and when the time comes I'll sew on another with all me heart. Now you'd better look lively. The 'fall in' goes in a few minutes, and I hear there's something else for you to listen to."

"Something else? Why, what?" asked Phil.

"Well, some message came down from the castle, that's all I know of, but they're rigging up the platform on the square, so it looks like some show or other."

Phil groaned dismally, and went to his barrack-room to smarten himself up, hoping that this new "show" could have nothing to do with himself.

But he was disappointed. The whole battalion fell in, carrying the colours, and having been duly formed up in review order and inspected, they stood at ease, wondering what was coming, and looking with curious eyes at the group of privileged sightseers who had already assembled, and at the red-carpeted platform which had been placed on the opposite side of the square.

Suddenly a movement was noticed amidst the crowd outside the gates; they opened up, and a minute later two royal carriages swept in past the guard-room. All eyes were turned towards them, till a hoarse "Battalion, attention. Royal salute. Present arms!" was given by the colonel, and as one man the regiment went through the movement, colours and officers' swords dropped simultaneously, and a royal personage, dressed in full uniform, was driven up to the centre, where, the carriage having stopped, he descended, and returned the salute.

Then followed a minute inspection, during which Phil's heart beat tumultuously against his ribs. Afterwards, with colours in air and the band playing, the regiment marched past in column—a sight worth going many miles to see—and finally drew up in quarter column and faced inwards towards the platform.

"Corporal Western!" the colonel cried.

Phil started and flushed crimson. Then, recovering his composure, he stepped from the ranks, and, marching forward, halted a few paces in front of the platform.

"Officers, non-commissioned officers, and men," commenced the royal personage who had reviewed them, stepping forward, "it has given me great pleasure to come here to-day and witness the fine way in which you have marched, and the smart, soldierly appearance you present. You have fully upheld the traditions of the regiment to which you belong. I have now another pleasant duty. One of your number performed a gallant act yesterday. He was then a private, and is now a corporal. He has won his promotion by bravery, as every soldier desires to do, and as a mark of the Queen's gratitude for saving the life of a distinguished guest, and in order that he may never forget this day, I now present Corporal Western with this watch and chain, and I feel sure he will always prize it. It comes from his Queen. May it one day be carried in the fob of an officer!"

Bewildered, and scarcely knowing whether he stood on his head or his heels, Phil took the watch handed to him and returned to the ranks. In a dream he heard the regiment answer the colonel's call for cheers as the royal officer stepped into his carriage, and in the same condition he stood, whilst his comrades tore off their bearskins, and, hoisting them on their bayonets, shouted cheers at him for his gallantry.

It was a bad half-hour for Phil, but, like all things, it came to an end. Soon he was back in the barrack-room, with friends crushing round and eagerly gazing at the gold watch and chain presented to him.

What Phil valued most was the crown set with brilliants on the back, and the inscription beneath, which ran:

"Presented to Corporal Philip Western, of the Grenadier Guards,
In recognition of his gallantry,
By Victoria R."

Many and many a time did Phil pull out the watch and gaze at that inscription, and often too did he determine that one day it should lie in the waistcoat pocket of an officer.

"It's my first step in the regiment," he said quietly to Tony, when talking over his promotion, "and I hope it will not be the last."

"Never fear, young un! You'll get higher yet, I know," Tony replied earnestly. "In these days of peace it will take a time, no doubt; but if there's war, as seems likely, then you'll go up, and I don't mind telling yer it's my opinion you'll be an officer yet afore I gets my stripes."

"Humbug, Tony! It takes years and years to get a commission, even when on active service. But I mean to have a good try for it, and should troubles come with some foreign power, then, as you say, there is all the more chance of my being successful. Now I am off to the quarter-master to ask him to put this in his safe and keep it for me. I wouldn't lose it for worlds."

Chapter Six.

War with Russia.

The summer months flew by in the pleasant surroundings of beautiful Windsor. Guard duties alternating with drills, and odd hours spent in the office of the regimental orderly-room, kept Phil pleasantly occupied, and when off duty he and Tony had always plenty of ways of amusing themselves, so that the latter days of September found them loth to leave the garrison and march to London. But orders had come for the battalion to go to Wellington Barracks, and in due course they found themselves once more installed in their old quarters, facing the park across the celebrated Bird-cage Walk.

"We've had a real good time down there," remarked Tony, some two months after their arrival, jerking his thumb in the direction of Windsor, "and it'll be long before we strike against such another.

"What's to be done here? Nothing—simply nothing! It's drill and go on guard nigh every day, and when you're free, kick yer heels in the square, or go out walking. I'm getting tired of it already."

"Oh, come, Tony, it isn't quite so bad as that!" laughed Phil. "We're no harder worked here than we were during the summer, and in our free time we can find heaps to do if we only set about it. They say that thousands of Londoners know far less about their own surroundings than do occasional visitors. Now I propose we get some sort of a guide, and every day we are able, go off to see some gallery or museum. It will cost us little or nothing, and will be good fun. In any case it would take weeks to exhaust all the sights, and before that, if all one hears is true, we are likely to be setting our faces south for some other country."

"PHIL STRUCK OUT WITH ALL HIS MIGHT"

"Oh, you mean we'll be off fighting, do you, Phil? Well, I ain't so jolly certain. Seems to me that England ain't keen on a row just now. It takes a scholar to know anything about it, but I hears that the Queen and her government want peace, and I suppose what England wants she's bound to have. Leastways that's how I reckon it, for we'd whop the heads off any nation what tried to interfere."

"Ha, ha! You've rather a big idea of England's power," laughed Phil; "but there's a good deal of truth in it, I expect. I must get to know about this row, and meanwhile we'll do as I said, if you're agreeable."

"Yes, it'll suit me well, young un," answered Tony, who was fond of addressing his friend in that way. "I don't drink, and I ain't never in trouble nowadays, thanks to you, but there's no saying what might happen if I hadn't anything to do. What's that kind of saying about idleness?"

"Idleness is the root of all evil."

"Yes, that's it, Phil. Give me plenty to do, and I'll be better able to keep that promise I made yer."

Accordingly Phil and Tony laid out a couple of shillings in a guide, and commenced systematically to investigate the sights of London, commencing with the Tower, where a regiment of Guards was quartered, and turning their attention next to the British Museum, which itself occupied several days.

"We must do the thing thoroughly," said Phil, as, book in hand, he and Tony strolled through one of the larger rooms. "I'll tell you what will be a good plan. We'll pay a visit to the map room, look up a certain country, and then investigate whatever curios there happen to be from that part."

"I'm with yer, Phil," Tony answered cheerfully, wishing to please his companion, and secretly imbued with a firm determination to make up as much as possible for his ignorance. "But you'll have to show me everything. I don't suppose I'd be able to tell the difference between a map of France and one of England. You'd better start with the lot, and point 'em out one by one."

Anxious to improve his humble friend, Phil took up his education in this way with zest, and spent hours in scanning a map of the world. So deeply interested did they become that on the second day they did not observe that a little man, dressed in respectable black, and wearing a large white stock, had stolen up behind them, and with smiling face, and eyes which peered through a pair of glasses, was peeping over their shoulders and listening with interest to the harangue which Phil was delivering for the benefit of Tony.

"There's the Black Sea, communicating with the Mediterranean by means of this narrow channel," Phil was remarking, as he placed his finger on the Dardanelles, and ran it up and down to show the communication between the two seas. "There's Turkey, and there's Russia; and it's between those two countries that war is imminent."

"Then Russia and the Czar, or whatever he's called, ought to be ashamed of theirselves, that's all I've got to say," answered Tony with disgust. "See what a size the first one is. Why, the other's only a baby."

"She'll fight for all that, Tony, so people say, but why or for what I don't know. Russia wants something, and Turkey says 'No'. Russia has answered that she will have it or war, and now I believe the Sultan is on the point of replying."

"Yus, that's clear enough, young un, but what about Old England? Where does she come in? Why should she fight Russia when the row's between the Czar and the Sultan? It beats me altogether."

"And me too, Tony. I'm in a regular fog."

"Then allow me to help you," came in suave tones from the dapper little stranger, with such suddenness, that both Tony and Phil started back in surprise.

"Ah! did not know that I was there, I suppose," remarked the stranger, with a smile. "But I've been listening—listening with interest for some time. You have had some education, I observe, young sir," he continued, addressing Phil, "and if you and your companion would really care, I will clear up this mystery for you."

"Thank you! It would be very kind, sir," exclaimed Phil. "We have bothered about the matter many days."

"And there is no one who ought to be informed more than you, my friends," the stranger remarked earnestly. "As sure as my name is Shelton, you of the Guards, and many another soldier boy, will be off towards the Black Sea before many weeks have passed. For war is practically certain."

"Horroo! You don't say so, sir!" cried Tony, snapping his fingers with delight and drawing himself up stiffly as though to show Mr Shelton what a fight he would make of it.

"But I do, my young friend," the latter replied, with a grave smile. "War is undoubtedly imminent, and the Powers are about to grapple with an enemy as subtle and as courageous as exists in any part of the world. But come, glance at the map and I will try to tell you all about the trouble, and when I have finished I feel sure that you two will go out with all the more determination to do your duty for the sake of the oppressed and for England's honour, for if ever there was an act of bullying the Czar is guilty of it.

"You must know that Russia's teeming thousands are, as a mass, densely, hopelessly ignorant. Peasants for the most part, they live a life of abject misery. They are little better than slaves, and, ruled over by various lords, they one and

61

all look to the Czar as all-powerful, unconquerable, and as a tyrant whose word is law, and whose hand, lifted in anger, is worse than death itself. He is, in other words, an autocratic ruler, and he, like those who held the throne before him, has diligently followed out a policy of keeping his poor subjects in a state of ignorance. What a work it would be to lift those poor people from their lifelong condition of serfdom! A work fit for the best of rulers; but educate them, teach them to think for themselves, and at once your autocratic government ceases, for the masses will unite and rise against a galling system of tyranny and oppression. They will no longer bow to the will of one man—to thousands in the far-off districts a ruler only in name,—but, goaded to rebellion, they will fight for that liberty sweet to every man.

"Thus, you will follow me, education is opposed to autocratic rule. But such a rule, bringing in its train misery and poverty, breeds discontent, and even the most pitiable of wretches, if sufficiently ill-treated, will brood over their wrongs till the fury of hate seizes them, and once more the reign of the absolute ruler is threatened. So well is the Czar Nicholas aware of this, that to distract the attention of his subjects from their grievances he has filled their minds with the alluring spectacle of foreign conquests. Look at the map. See how big the Russian empire is, and remember how a great part is almost uninhabitable owing to excessive cold. Then look at her capital, Saint Petersburg, and see how far from European ports it is. How much better for her if she possessed a town in the position of Constantinople. Then, with the narrow Dardanelles to guard, she could post a fleet of war-ships in the Black Sea, and at any moment swoop down into the Mediterranean. She would become at once mistress of that sea, and as such could intimidate her neighbours. And in peace times what an outlet the Turkish capital would prove for all Russia's surplus manufactures, and how easily a vast quantity of stores could be imported through it! It would be the making of Russia, my young friends, and she knows it, has known it, and has steadily worked for that end."

Mr Shelton paused, and, drawing the map closer, pointed out the various points of interest in Russia and Turkey, while Phil and Tony followed him.

"Ah, now I begin to see!" said the former; "Russia wants Turkey, or rather that part of it on the Dardanelles, and that I suppose is the reason for this trouble. But surely she would not deliberately attempt to deprive the Sultan of his capital?"

"By no means, young sir; the Czar is far too clever for that. He wanted a pretext for war, and one which would appeal to his people; and what more powerful one could he have found than a religious one, that is, one in which those of the

Greek Church were shown to be the martyrs, for Russia belongs to that persuasion.

"There was one at hand. The Holy Land, which of course is under the Sultan's sway, is the home of large numbers of priests and others belonging to the Latin and the Greek Churches, and the Czar promptly demanded that the latter should have more religious privileges than the former, while France, whose interests are with the Latin Church, demanded the very opposite. What was the unhappy Sultan to do? Himself a Mahometan, he could not be expected to favour either of the two infidel sects practising their religion at Jerusalem.

"It was an exceedingly difficult problem, and it is not to be wondered at that he failed to please both parties. The Latins were moderately content, while the Greek Church was roused into a fit of the warmest indignation, and with it the Czar, who at once despatched two army corps over the Turkish frontier and occupied the country between it and the Danube, in the opinion of all right-thinking people an act of monstrous injustice."

"I should think so indeed!" Phil blurted out. "How could the poor Sultan be expected to satisfy both parties? It was a regular trap."

"Undoubtedly, undoubtedly, my friend! It was an example of high-handedness never before surpassed," remarked Mr Shelton gravely. "But still war might have been averted, for the Sultan now agreed to the Czar's demands, and in the eyes of Europe Russia could not but withdraw.

"Such a course, however, was far from her intentions. With this point gained, she now demanded a protectorate over all subjects of the Greek Church, a suggestion which, if complied with, would have at once led 14,000,000 people resident in Turkey to own the Czar as their ruler, and thus leave the unfortunate Sultan with merely a sprinkling of subjects.

"Turkey might have declared war promptly, but now the Western powers, much to the Czar's chagrin and anger, intervened. Look at Austria. If Turkey were occupied by Russia, the emperor's territory would be partially enclosed, and a feeling of insecurity would naturally arise. Therefore he is opposed to the scheme. France has perhaps no very definite reason for opposition, save the upholding of the rights of the Latin Church. But we must remember that she has ever been a belligerent power, and that success in arms would place Louis Napoleon more firmly on a throne at present in a decidedly shaky condition. Also, if she took Russia's part, she would have England and her fleet to cope with, an item that I can assure you, my young friends, is not to be lightly thought of.

"And now for England. Ever the mainstay of justice and right, and the protector of the oppressed, she has, considerably to the astonishment of everyone, and particularly of Russia, awakened from that long peace enjoyed since Waterloo, and, shaking herself free for the moment from her absorbing interest in trade, has thrown herself heart and soul into the cause of Turkey. With the French, some of our ships sailed to the Bosphorus; and as Russia refused to withdraw her troops from the Danube, the combined fleets entered the Dardanelles and anchored before Constantinople.

"And now comes the crux of the whole thing," said Mr Shelton, with emphasis. "We are not at war, but our interests are aroused, and our sympathy with Turkey is deep. It wanted only a match to set us flaring, and cause us to engage in a war of what magnitude no one can say, and that match has been applied. On the last day of November a small fleet of Turkish ships, which had anchored at Sinope, close above Constantinople, was destroyed, together with 4000 men, by a fleet of Russian war-vessels. It was a cruel and unnecessary act. Capture would have sufficed. But the fatal deed is done, and now I fancy both England and France are launched into the struggle, for their peoples are clamouring for the punishment of the Czar and his subjects. In any case a few days will determine the matter, and then, my lads, your country will have need of you, and thousands more like you."

"Then I for one, sir, shall fight all the better and all the harder now that I know exactly what the trouble is!" exclaimed Phil; while Tony gave a grunt of marked approval, showing that if he had failed to grasp exactly the real reason for war, he had at any rate a decided grudge against the Czar and his people, which he would endeavour to satisfy at the earliest opportunity.

"And where do you think the fighting will take place?" continued Phil. "Shall we invade Russia, or will our fleets go in chase of the Russian ships? In that case we soldiers would have precious little to do, and the sailors would come in for all the honour and glory."

"Rest easy, my young friend," replied Mr Shelton, with a smile. "Both services will have their hands full, or I shall be much surprised. At present matters point to a campaign on the Danube, while our fleet holds the Dardanelles and the Black Sea; but for all I know Russia may be invaded. In that case Sebastopol is likely to be the port fixed upon for attack. Situated in the Crimea, it is an immense naval and military arsenal, which in itself is a constant menace to Turkey. Look at the map once more and note the position of the Danube and of Sebastopol, you will then more readily see the truth of my words."

"Don't matter to me where it is, sir!" exclaimed Tony bluntly; "if it's war we'll fight and lick the beggars, see if we don't; and if it comes to invasion, or whatever yer calls it, well, all the better, I say. 'Tain't nearly such good fun sticking behind stone walls and keeping fellers out as it is rushing forts and such like things, and turning the garrison out with the end of a bay'net. That's the boy for 'em. Give me and all my mates a good half-yard of steel at the end of our guns, and see if we don't make it warm for the Russians. We'll do as well as the Froggies at any rate."

"That you will, I am sure," laughed Mr Shelton, patting him on the back. "Fancy how strange it is that we who have always been fighting with France, who is, as I might say, our natural enemy, should now be side by side with her, and in all probability will soon be fighting for the same object. It will lead to tremendous scenes of emulation, for no British soldier will care to allow a Frenchman to beat him at anything."

"I should think not, indeed," Phil snorted. "There was a chap at the school I first went to who was a regular Froggy. His people had come to England to save him from conscription; it would have been the making of him, for he was a regular donkey, conceited and all that; curled his hair and put scent on his handkerchief. Pah! How we disliked that fellow!"

"It sounds as though you had had something to do with him," said Mr Shelton, with a quizzical smile, "for we were saying that no Englishman would suffer a Frenchman to beat him."

"Oh—er, yes, there was something like that!" Phil replied, with reddened cheeks. "You see the beggar got so uppish and disagreeable there was no doing anything with him; then, when I called him Froggy, in pure jest, he threw a stump at me, and caught me a crack on the head. I didn't like that, and—er—"

"Yes, you did what?" asked Mr Shelton, with the same quizzical smile.

"I licked him till he blubbered," Phil blurted out shamefacedly, conscious that he had been dragged into saying more than he had at first intended.

"Ha, ha, ha! you licked him till he blubbered," roared the old gentleman, losing in a moment his appearance of gravity, and beaming all over his face. "You licked him, and a very proper thing too, my friend! But you must not be trying such games now. It would mean a court-martial, or even something more serious. But I must be going now. Bear in mind what I have told you, and be sure of this—war—red war—is at hand. Now good-bye and good luck!—you are just the class of lads that England will want."

"Thank you, sir! Good-bye!" cried Phil and Tony, saluting the old gentleman. Then, tucking their canes under their arms, they strode out of the building and away to the barracks, discussing as they went the possibility of war, and the share they were likely to take in it.

"I'm going to get a book on Russian!" exclaimed Phil, the day following their visit to the British Museum. "People tell me it is the most difficult of all languages to learn, but I may be able to pick up a few useful words. I remember now that the firm I acted as clerk to did business with another trading with Russian ports, and they had a Russian clerk. I met him once or twice, and I'll just go along and see what he says about the matter."

"It's a good thing, right enough, Phil," Tony replied, with a shrug, "but it's far beyond me, as far as the clouds; but you have a try at it, old man, and I'll be bound you'll succeed. I never knew yer beat yet."

Accordingly Phil went off at the first opportunity to see the clerk he had mentioned, and after a chat with him bought a book, and was shown the characters as a first lesson.

"Take my advice," said the clerk, who was the son of a Russian mother and an English father, and almost entirely English in his ways and thoughts, "and buy a really good map of the country, and a reliable compass. Supposing you get cut off from the troops, it might prove of the greatest service to you. As regards the language, come along to my rooms as often as you like. I am always in about six o'clock, and will be glad to give you a lesson."

Phil was not slow to take advantage of the offer. Every day he was free from guards and other duties, and had no engagement with Tony to see the sights of London, he repaired to the rooms of his Russian friend, and there worked hard at the language.

If Mr Western could have seen him and his earnestness, he would have been agape with amazement. This his idle adopted son? This the wilful lad who would never settle down to work, and never take a leading place in his class at school? Could this young soldier—this fine, stalwart young fellow (even he would have been obliged to admit it)—who slaved so many hours day and night at the dryest of dry and uninteresting subjects, be really the lad who had always gone contrary to his wishes, the unmanageable boy full of daring and mischief, who had occasioned the vicar of Riddington so many anxious and bitter thoughts? To him it would have been almost beyond belief. His dull and rigidly narrow mind could not have grasped the change. But Joe Sweetman, what would he have said? How he would have chuckled, with just a suspicion of pride and elation, and blurted out: "Didn't I tell you so. Leave the lad alone. Wild and unmanageable? Pshaw! Look at him now. His heart's in the right place. He's got hold of a subject he's interested in, and he's got the backbone to stick to it, though it means a lot of hard work."

And Phil had indeed the backbone and perseverance to continue to work at the language. A month passed, and he had apparently made no progress, and the alphabet was still almost a troublesome maze to him. But when some weeks more had flown by he could join a few words together in the semblance of sense, though he was still far from being able to carry on a conversation. By the middle of February, 1854, the year in which the eventful Crimean war began, he could even acknowledge to himself that he was getting on, and that a little more practice would find him fairly proficient. Never for a moment did he forget this ambition of his, this self-imposed task, to master the most difficult of languages. Who is there who cannot imagine the labour it meant, the constant grinding, the late hours when, beneath a flickering gas-jet or a smoking oil lantern, he opened his book and devoured its contents till his eyes were almost falling from his head? Few, indeed, would saddle themselves willingly with such a labour, but to Phil to take up a subject, however trivial, was to succeed, and that very success was the reward he received. The alphabet and more difficult words having now been mastered, the work was far more pleasant, and invited him to persevere.

"There's no doubt about it, it is a grind, an awful grind," he one day admitted in muttered tones to himself. "But I'll stick to it. It comes easier to me every day, and who knows what the knowledge may do for me? Interpreters will certainly be required, though to imagine myself one is flying rather high."

On parade, at musketry practice, everywhere he would repeat sentences in low tones, and would attempt to put the orders for the soldiers into Russian. Then, at the first opportunity, he and the clerk who had so befriended him would retire to the latter's room and there carry on a long conversation, in which no English was admitted on pain of a small fine. Thus, as the days passed, his proficiency increased, till he was almost competent to find his way through the heart of Russia without much difficulty, so far as the language was concerned.

But a far from unexpected interruption occurred. France and England were on the eve of despatching an ultimatum to Russia, and the usually placid life of the Guards was disturbed by orders to embark for active service.

Chapter Seven.

Good-Bye to Old England.

What excitement there was! What bustle and hard work! Though the brigade of Guards had for long expected, and indeed anxiously awaited, orders to prepare for embarkation, when at last the time did actually arrive, they found still hosts of matters to be dealt with.

Men had to be examined as to their physical fitness for rough work in the field; kits had to be looked to, new boots issued, and a hundred-and-one points attended to. Then there were good-byes to be said, for many of those fine, brave lads, the last they would ever have an opportunity of saying, for the Crimea was to claim them, and the deep-trodden mire and mud of the heights round Sebastopol was destined to form a covering for thousands—thousands, alas! of England's bravest soldiers. And the Queen—God bless her!—she too must take leave of her Guards, and wish them a safe return.

Ah! it was a grand time, and books on Russian were forgotten in the whirl Phil had too many other things to think about. True, he had few friends to part with, and in that he was to be congratulated, for partings are ever painful; but he had hosts of duties to carry out, and his services in the office of the orderly-room were daily in requisition.

"I never see such a time," grumbled Tony disgustedly. "I never get a word with yer now, young un. You're stuck in that office or on some other job all day and every day. I for one shall be jolly glad when we're off, and then I expect every one of us will be precious sorry for a time. The Guards makes a fine show on parade, but aboard a ship, about the size of one of these here barrack-rooms, they'll have to be squeezed like herrings, and then if it blows won't there be a scene! I remember I went for a week in a fishing-boat once, and spent about as miserable a time as I ever did. Lor', how jolly ill and wretched I was!"

"Yes, I expect it will take a little time to get our sea-legs, Tony," Phil replied cheerily; "but once the Bay of Biscay is passed we ought to have fine weather, I'm told, and then we shall enjoy it. As to never seeing me, the job is now practically finished. To-morrow the Queen reviews us, and on the twenty-eighth we sail from Southampton. That's only a few days away. Then hurrah for Russia and a campaign!"

How loyal every one of those stalwart Guardsmen felt as he stood paraded before Queen Victoria on that eventful day. How he fixed his eyes on that figure standing on the balcony of Buckingham Palace, and swore silently that he would fight and die if need be for her and for the country she ruled. Gone, in the excitement and fervour of the moment, was all thought of coming misery and privation. Gone all fear of death or injury by cannon-shot or bullet. Before them was the Queen, and beyond them, far across the sea, the Russian enemy. Ere they returned they would humble the Czar's pride, or perish in the attempt.

And the good and beloved Queen Victoria, as she scanned the long lines before her, did she forget what her soldiers might meet with? Did she know of the horrors ever associated with war that must inevitably fall upon some of the devoted fellows standing proudly erect before her? Yes, she knew, and she did not forget. She knew, too, the need for England to assert herself in support of the oppressed, and though it filled her heart with grief to think that many of those she looked at, many of those stalwart officers from amongst the highest in the land, and lads from amongst the bravest, must fall in the fight, yet she sent them forth with smiling face and words of God-speed and encouragement, for such is the duty of a queen.

But at length it was all over. With colours flying and bands clashing before them, the Grenadier Guards marched through a seething crowd which filled the streets of London, and entrained for Southampton. It was a day to be remembered. The masses were full of excitement, and cheered till they were hoarse. Those on foot pressed forward, and, defying all regulations, marched beside their heroes. Sweethearts struggled to clutch the arms of lovers, and wives, poor things! held up their babes and gazed fondly and with tearful eyes at departing husbands. Ay, and it was a time full of trials for the higher as well as the humbler in the land. How many of those fair damsels, dressed in all the finery that money could buy, waved a handkerchief to some devoted lover, and how many women sent all they cared for away to war and duty with dry eyes and an encouraging smile, while surrounded by their sisters, only to retire later and weep in private as if their hearts would break? God knows! Only such things are, and ever will be, when men go out to fight. But at last it was all done with. The train was off, and the din and shouts, the cheers and strains of the National Anthem left far behind.

"Thank goodness, we're off!" exclaimed one big fellow who happened to be in the same carriage with Phil and Tony, and who had just waved a last adieu to quite a number of girls. "I wouldn't go through it again for the wealth of the Queen. It makes yer almost wish there wasn't such things as sweethearts."

"Get along, George, old man!" another man replied, with a poor attempt at a laugh, as he hastily drew his sleeve across his eyes. "Yer know yer wouldn't be without 'em, bless their little hearts! It's fine to think as there'll be someone at home a-thinking of yer; and just yer wait till we're back again. My eye, what a time we'll have! What do yer say, Corporal Western?"

"I fancy I haven't an opinion to give, Billy," Phil said, with a smile. "I haven't a sweetheart yet, you see."

"Then yer ought'er, Corporal. You're smart. Why, blow me if you aren't one of the smartest in the regiment, and if yer liked yer could have ten of 'em, and all thinking they was the only one. You've been wasting opportunities." Billy looked quite reproachfully at Phil.

"Then I'll have to wait, Billy, I expect. Sweethearts are not to be found in Russia," was the laughing answer.

"No, I d'say not. You ought to know, Corporal, for I hear yer can speak the Russian lingo; and knows lots about the country. What's all this row about? None of us chaps knows, and you'd be doing all of us a good turn if you'd tell us."

Nothing loth, Phil promptly commenced, and a heated argument following as to the real intentions of Russia, and as to the merits of the French soldiery compared, with the British, the time slipped by, and Southampton was reached before anyone expected it.

The men at once tumbled out, and lined up on the platform, kit-bag and rifle in hand. Then in perfect order, and as if performing an every-day movement, they filed up the gangway on to the decks of the *Orinoco*, which lay alongside the wharf, with the *Ripon* and *Manilla* astern of her. Weapons were passed from hand to hand along the decks, down the gangways, and into the hold, where they were secured in racks. Then bearskin helmets were collected and stored in an out-of-the-way room, and in less than half an hour every man had disappeared into the hold, and had taken possession of his hammock.

"It's a pretty close fit," remarked Tony, looking round; "but I expect we shall be comfortable."

"We ought to be, Tony. I hear the Guards have been given extra room owing to their size, and as far as I can see, we shall have just sufficient room to sling our hammocks and lie in them without touching one another."

This was the case. From beams screwed to the deck, and supported by pillars, rows of big iron hooks depended in such a manner that, when slung, the hammocks were only a few inches apart, while the foot end of each of the next row just protruded between them as far as the head of the occupant.

"Now, we'll stow our kits here," said Phil, "and go on deck. I heard the captain telling the colonel that he should cast off at once, so we may as well see as much of the old country as possible. Who knows when we shall set eyes on it again? Perhaps it will be a year or more before the war is over and we are at liberty to return."

"Then we'll say good-bye to it, though I tell yer, Phil, I'm fair tired of this yelling. It makes yer feel curious just here," and he pointed to his throat. "I ain't got no friends to bother about, but I feels for the poor chaps as has, and I hates to see the girls a-blubbering. Poor things! They was just a-crying their pretty eyes out back there in Lunnon."

"Yes, it's a trying time for sweethearts, husbands, and wives, Tony, but let's hope all will meet again, though I suppose that isn't possible, unless we find that the troubles have been settled before we reach the Black Sea. It would be a merciful thing, though bad luck for us."

"Bad luck! I should think it would be, Phil. Why, remember what we're after, you and me. Promotion—quick promotion. You've got to get that commission and become a toff of an orfficer, and I've got to win me stripes; and how's it all to be done unless we smell powder? No, there's going to be a jolly war, and we Guards are going to be in the thick of it;" and having settled the matter, as it were, Tony gave a grunt, expressive of the disgust he might feel if the troubles really were to disappear in smoke, and, turning on his heel, climbed up the gangway ladder to the deck.

There were numbers of soldiers already lining the rails, and a crowd of people on the quay, all chattering, calling to one another, and attempting to look cheerful and gay under obviously depressing circumstances.

Then a man with a grey beard, upright carriage, and a general appearance which did not need the row of medals displayed on his waistcoat to proclaim him an old soldier, stepped forward, and, producing a cornet, played "The British Grenadiers."

Already the hawsers had been cast off. Two panting little tugs were slowly towing the paddle-ship into the open water, and hoarse voices sounded from the bridge. The tune changed to the National Anthem, and hats were doffed by the crowd, while every lad on board stood at attention. Then the strains of "Auld Lang Syne" came across the water, at first loud and distinct, but gradually getting fainter, cheers passed from deck to quay, handkerchiefs and sticks were waved, the railway-engine screeched a last farewell with its whistle, and the *Orinoco* trembled from stem to stern at the beat of her paddles, like some powerful animal making a terrific struggle to escape its bonds.

The parting was over. Men gazed at the rapidly receding shore, and then turning, dived below decks and busied themselves in arranging their hammocks. What was the good of being downcast? Who could look into the future? As well make the best of matters and take things cheerfully. Soon all were laughing and joking, perhaps a little more soberly than before, but still far more happily than an hour ago.

"Now, my lads," cried the sergeant-major, "each man to his hammock, and we'll serve out to-day's allowance of rum. It'll cheer you up and keep the cold out."

One by one the men were served with the spirit, and soon after, having been joined by the sailors off duty, Jack Tar and Thomas Atkins sat themselves down to a convivial evening. Pipes were produced, and some thoughtful fellow extracting a concertina from the depths of a kit-bag, an impromptu concert was commenced and kept up till "lights out."

"This kind of thing won't be allowed every night, I expect," said Phil, as he sat by Tony's side, for many of the sailors, liberally helped to a portion of the soldiers' rum, were reeling away to their quarters.

"Ah! well, it's only the first night out, mate, mind that. The officers, I expect, knows about it as well as we do, but they knows the boys want cheering. But I expects there'll be a change."

And as a matter of fact there was, for on the following day, when the hour for the serving out of grog came round, the men were drawn up in their several messes. Then under the eye of the sergeant-major one mess was served, and at the order, "Men served one pace forward and swallow," the spirit disappeared.

It was a strange feeling to lie for the first time in a hammock, but the men took to it like ducks to water.

"It's jolly comfortable, and ever so much softer than a barrack-bed, ain't it, Phil?" remarked Tony, as he lay full length close beside his friend, with only his face showing, and a pipe projecting from his lips.

"I've slept in a harder bed many a time," laughed Phil. "But I'm tired; so good-night, Tony!"

At 6:30 a.m. the next morning *reveillé* sounded through the ship, and the men tumbled out, to find a fresh, cold breeze blowing and a nasty sea on. Faces fell, for soldiers, like other mortals, fall victims to *mal de mer*. Breakfasts were looked at askance, and scarcely touched, and soon the rails were almost as thickly crowded as on the previous day.

"Lummy! How jolly bad I feel!" groaned Tony. "I'm off to me bunk as fast as me feet will take me."

Phil nodded curtly, and very soon followed his example, for he too was not exactly enjoying himself.

On the following day the ship was on an even keel once more, and bright faces and merry jokes were everywhere. In seven days Gibraltar was reached, but no one was allowed to land, and no sooner had the ship coaled than she paddled on to Malta. Arrived there, the troops disembarked, to hear the welcome news that France and England had declared war on Russia on the day after their sailing.

"That's all right, then!" exclaimed Tony with a grunt of satisfaction. "We shall soon have a taste of fighting, and the sooner it comes the better. See them coves over there, Phil? Ain't they smart, just. Wonder how they'll tackle the Russians!"

He alluded to a ship-load of French artillery which had arrived only a few hours before in the harbour. Smart, athletic men they looked, as they crowded the decks and shouted back greetings to the British.

"They are said to be amongst the finest gunners trained by any nation," answered Phil, "and I've no doubt they will do well. But look out, Tony; there goes the bugle. I expect we shall have to disembark."

The bugle notes rang out clear, waking the harbour of Valetta with the echo; and the hoarse voice of the sergeant-major penetrated to every hole and corner of the *Orinoco*.

"Fall in, lads," he shouted. "Smartly now; by companies."

Phil and Tony soon found their places, and then for half an hour were busily engaged in passing rifles and bearskin helmets and in securing their kit. When all were ready, the disembarkation proceeded apace, and in an hour the Grenadier Guards were ashore and comfortably housed in casemates of the forts.

"I wonder how long we shall stay here," remarked Phil about a week later, as he and Tony stood on the ramparts and gazed at the town. "The sooner we leave the better. Our men are having a splendid time, and have struck up a great friendship with the Frenchies, but at this rate it won't do. Look at those fellows over there."

"They are pretty bad; you're right, Phil," Tony grunted, as he watched a tiny French artillerist staggering down towards him, with two burly British linesmen on either side, with arms firmly linked in his, and all three roaring a refrain to be heard in any *café* in the town.

"Pretty bad! I should think so, Tony. But it won't last. Our officers know what is going on, and we shall sail very shortly. The new life and excitement here and the low price of spirit make it easy for our men to get intoxicated and behave in a riotous manner. After all, one cannot exactly blame them. They are going to a rough country probably, and are making the most of the present time. But much of this sort of thing will play havoc with them in the end. Only yesterday I heard our doctor say that disease was far more dangerous to armies than bullets, and that men who entered upon a campaign in indifferent health were certain to go under if hardships had to be faced. I mean to take plenty of exercise, and beware of eating too much fruit."

"Then I'm with yer, mate. Yer know drink ain't nothing to me now, and I can see as the feller what keeps himself fit, takes walks and plenty of fresh air, and don't eat nor drink too much, finds himself better able to enjoy his life. Why, ever since that ugly old bear gave me a mauling I've been a different man. I have, Phil. A different and a better man. But come along, mate, let's take a stroll about and see what's happening. Some of those French blokes is going to do a gun drill, I hear, and we may as well look at 'em."

It was a wise resolution on Phil's part to keep himself in good trim, for no one possessed of common sense can doubt that nothing is more prejudicial to a young man than riotous living. For a time an excellent constitution may stand the unusual strain, but sooner or later health is shattered, and with additional strain, when met by cold and exposure, and perhaps insufficient food, disease finds a ready victim, and another patient falls into the hands of doctors already heavily pressed by work.

Fortunately for all, orders were not long in coming, and soon the Grenadiers were on the sea again. A short and most interesting voyage followed till they reached the entrance to the Dardanelles and dropped anchor.

It was pitchy dark, and the outlines of the forts which guard the narrow entrance could not be made out; but excited shouts and an occasional blue flare which lit up a limited area, showing gesticulating figures clad in Turkish costume, proved that the coming of the *Orinoco* had not passed unnoticed.

On the following morning the ship weighed anchor, and, steaming into the Bosphorus, drew up opposite Scutari, fated to prove the scene of awful misery to the British. That evening Phil and his comrades were ashore, and were safely housed under canvas. Two days later they obtained permission to visit Gallipoli, where the bulk of our army had landed, with numbers of the French, and, hiring a native craft, were rowed across.

"Looks like a fairy place, don't it, Phil?" remarked Tony as, seated in the boat, he gazed at the shore of Gallipoli. "Look at them things like white fingers a-sticking up into the sky, and those white houses amongst the green trees."

And, indeed, seen from a distance, and, above all, from the sea, Gallipoli with its immediate surroundings is a paradise. It consists of a collection of all sorts of houses scattered here and there hap-hazard on the foreground, other houses built on the hill behind, and the whole swathed in green patches of luxuriant tree-growth, and backed by the distant hills. It was an enchanting spot, and its charm was greatly increased by the fact that it was situated in a strange land, where large domed mosques and white-washed minarets reared high in the air, and reflected the rays of a glorious sun from their glistening surfaces.

Phil and Tony were delighted with it, but as the boat drew nearer, and dirt and squalor became visible, their faces fell.

"Pah! It's worse than a farmyard," exclaimed Tony, with disgust, as he sniffed the air. "And look at that mud!"

"Wait a minute, and let us see what the streets are like. Perhaps they will be interesting," answered Phil, with a laugh. "Certainly this part of Gallipoli is rather unsavoury, and the sooner we are away from it the better."

The boat touched the shore, and, having paid the small sum demanded, the two set off, and were soon in the centre of the town. Every moment some new sight arrested their attention, and in the excitement of the moment they quickly forgot the dirt and foul gutters to be seen everywhere. Grave Turks accosted them, politely stepping on one side to allow room for them to pass; Greeks weighed down with huge baskets of merchandise staggered past; and ever and anon a swarthy, unclean-looking Armenian Jew flitted down some by-street as if fearing to be seen. Soldiers in every variety of uniform, Highlanders, lithe, plucky-looking little riflemen, and daintily-dressed Zouaves came by singly and sometimes arm-in-arm, a burly Englishman fraternising with some dapper little Frenchman, and endeavouring vainly to carry on a conversation with him.

Phil and Tony were greatly interested, but to their astonishment, though the sight of foreign soldiers must have been a rare one indeed to the Turks, not a single inhabitant of this oriental spot showed any curiosity or looked up when they passed. In every little shop or doorway a Turk was seated cross-legged on a low divan, puffing moodily at his chibouk, each and every one, whether grey-bearded or otherwise, motionless, immovable, and absolutely uninterested.

"Well, I never!" exclaimed Phil. "Did you ever see such a sleepy lot, Tony? They look as though an earthquake would not move them; and the children, too, seem just as little upset by the arrival of the troops."

"They are about the sleepiest lot I ever see," growled Tony in reply. "That old cove over there might be made of wax; and what's this a-coming down the street? I suppose it's a woman, but she might just as well be a sack. Ugh! Give me England and English girls! Let's get on, old man, and see what these here Frenchmen are up to."

Everywhere the streets were labelled with French names, and indeed the French seemed to be far more *en evidence* than the British. They had inaugurated a

75

café, the best building in the town was utilised as their hospital, and their general had his quarters in a prominent position. One might have thought that the British were not there at all, save that Highlanders stepping briskly along the pavements, and an occasional infantry-man or a mounted orderly passing through the streets showed that our forces too were represented.

"It is curious to see so much that is French and so little that is English," remarked Phil in a disappointed voice. "Everywhere it's Rue this or Rue that; never an English name, from the landing-stage to the edge of the town. What can our people be doing?"

"They're awake. You trust 'em for that," Tony answered with conviction, "Just because they haven't christened all the streets and painted their names everywhere, don't you think they're not every bit as good as these here Froggies."

It was almost nightfall when Phil and Tony reached Scutari again and rejoined their comrades, and there they remained until early in June, passing the greater part of their days in drills and musketry practice, and in exploring the surrounding country.

Chapter Eight.

Lost in the Crimea.

"Bustle up, you boys! Put your kit together, Tony, as quickly as you can, for we are off at last!" cried Phil excitedly, on his return one morning from the tent which had been set apart for the orderly-room clerks. "I have great news for you."

"What is it? Out with it, Phil!" came in a chorus from the nine men who shared the tent with him. "A move at last! Hurrah! We're all precious tired of this place. Is it Russia we're off to?"

"No, not that, but Varna," answered Phil. "We sail to-morrow, I have been told, and with the French march against the Russians. It will be the opening scene of a grand campaign, for I hear they are besieging Silistria, in the province of the Danube."

"Then all them yarns about the Crimea, or whatever they calls it, and taking Sebastopol, is all wrong 'uns," exclaimed Tony, with disgust. "Never mind, boys. I expects Silistria's better than that. It'll be warm at any rate; at least that's what people say; and I shall be precious glad, for if there's anything that upsets me, it's freezing cold weather, and that's what we'll have in the Crimea."

"Anything's better, I reckon, than sticking in this here place," chimed in another. "What have we been doing? Simply drilling day and night, it seems, and eating our rations. Wasting time, I calls it. Then every chap has been sick. See how many of our poor fellows has died. Let's get out of this, I says. Anything's better than sitting still."

There was a grunt of assent from all, for disease had already picked out many victims from amongst the men of the combined armies, and inaction amongst a number of troops living in more or less confined quarters had already had disastrous results. Accordingly the move to Varna was hailed with delight, and the men of the Guards embarked with feelings of unmixed pleasure.

Arrived at Varna, a picturesque spot on the sea-coast, they found the French already there, and other troops arriving daily. Not long afterwards a French force set out to march towards Silistria, but with terrible results. Cholera had dogged their footsteps from Marseilles, and seven days after leaving the coast this dread disease attacked the two divisions under General Canrobert with malignant fury, bringing no less than 7000 of the unfortunate men to an untimely end. It was an awful example of sudden death, for in three days the divisions crawled back into Varna more disorganised and downhearted than if they had sustained a terrible defeat.

"It is terrible!" exclaimed Phil when the news reached him; "and worse still to think that the epidemic may come into our camps. If it does, God help us! for thousands will die. Remember our rule, Tony, no fruit. It is the most dangerous article of food at present, and has already killed many by causing dysentery. So beware of it, as you value your life."

Indeed, so certain was this, that the men were warned against over-indulgence in fruit and vegetables, and the regimental doctor earnestly advised all to boil any water before drinking it. In spite of the warning, however, many were too thoughtless or too careless to heed it, and scarcely had the shattered ranks of the French crawled into Varna when cholera broke out amongst the British. Of these there were some 22,000, whilst the bulk of the garrison was composed of 50,000 French and 8000 Turks. As if by the hand of the Destroying Angel the dread scourge spread through the camp, striking down men on every side, irrespective of race, creed, or age. Hundreds died, and the hospitals were filled to overflowing. As for the still hale and hearty, they went about silently, and as if fearing to laugh or sing, for on all sides their comrades were dying. Instead they stared moodily at one another with wide-open eyes which seemed to ask: "How much longer will this misery last? When will our turn come to fall victims to this dreadful scourge—this terrifying sickness which strikes silently and unawares, and yet so surely and so fatally that he upon whom its grip is fastened can scarcely hope to see the light of another day?" Phil often asked himself these questions.

"The doctor has called for volunteers to nurse the sick," he said one morning as he sat in the tent and looked at his comrades, whose numbers were already sadly diminished.

"What? Volunteers to nurse them with cholera!" exclaimed one in awe-struck tones.

"Yes, to nurse the cholera patients."

"He'll never get any—never!" said the man moodily. "It's bad enough to know it's here amongst us. But who's going to run against it if he's able to keep away? It's like shooting yourself."

"There's risk certainly," remarked Phil calmly, "but the doctors take it, and so do their orderlies; and after all, one must die some day. Won't any of you fellows volunteer?"

No answer was returned, though Tony looked up at his friend with a frightened, half-guilty face, and then, like his comrades, stared moodily at the ground.

"Well, good-bye, in case!" said Phil shortly, and stepped out of the tent.

"Here, what's this you're doing, Phil?" gasped Tony hurriedly, following him, and looking searchingly at him as if to read his inmost thoughts.

"I'm going to help, Tony. The men are dying like flies, poor fellows! and the hospital staff is simply overwhelmed. Volunteers are asked for, and I'm one. At any other time I wouldn't dream of it, but now it's different. Besides, this inaction is too trying, and I feel that I must have something to occupy my thoughts."

"Don't say no more, mate, I'm with yer," Tony blurted out, flushing red with shame and grasping his friend's hand. "It's just what a chap like you would do, and I'm blowed if I don't come along too."

It was a desperate undertaking for Tony, for, like all uneducated people, he had a far greater dread of cholera than others better informed. But his friend's decision was enough for him, and, swallowing his fears with a gulp, he wiped the perspiration from his forehead and followed Phil to the hospital.

"There, it's not half so bad as you imagined, and, for the matter of that, not nearly so serious an undertaking as I thought," said Phil, some two weeks later, as he and Tony sat on the door-step of the hospital, taking a little fresh air after their unpleasant work.

"No, 'tain't as bad, but it's trying," remarked Tony thoughtfully.

And he was right. It had been trying work. Gifted with considerable common sense and a fair education, Phil had rapidly picked up the duties of a nurse sufficiently well to be able to render real help to his comrades who were suffering from cholera, and was now in charge of a large ward, with Tony to help him. And together they had worked day and night, relieving one another, and earning the praise of doctors and patients alike.

"You shall never regret this sacrifice," said the doctor gratefully. "I have already mentioned you to the colonel; and be sure, when honours are given at the end of the campaign, you will not be overlooked. I know what it means to you, and that you would far rather face the guns of the Russians than this disease."

"It's not so bad, now we're used to it, sir," said Phil; "but I own I'd far rather be in the fighting-line; not so much because I fear the disease, as because it is so distressing to see all these poor fellows die in agony."

"Right, lad, right! I know what it means," the doctor answered, with a sigh. "But, thank Heavens! the epidemic is abating."

By the middle of August there was a considerable decrease, though the fleet was suffering severely in spite of having severed its connection with the shore. A week later the number of cases was infinitesimal compared with what it had been, and in consequence arrangements were pushed forward for another move. "We shall go to the Crimea this time," said the doctor, who seemed to have taken quite a fancy to Phil, and often indulged in a chat with him. "Austria has moved 50,000 or more of her troops down Silistria way, and the Russians have raised the siege and retired. Now we are going to show them that war cannot be commenced with impunity on such trivial grounds. It is supposed to be a secret, but Sebastopol will undoubtedly be our object, and we shall endeavour to destroy it."

It was evident to all, in fact, that something was in the wind. A huge fleet of East Indiamen and other craft assembled off Varna to act as transports, and immense barges were prepared for the reception of artillery. Stores, too, stood in enormous stacks down by the shore, and everything pointed to a change of quarters.

The news of a possible move spread like fire through the camp, and at once the spirits of the soldiers rose. Despair gave way to cheerfulness, and whistling and singing were again to be heard. At last came the orders to embark, and on September 4th the British fleet, which stretched away to the horizon, set sail for an unknown port, and with an agreement to meet the French and Turkish vessels *en route*. It is unnecessary to detail the vexatious dallying and delay that occurred. Had fixed plans been drawn out before the departure from Varna, the allied armies could have reached the Crimea and landed upon its shores in three days, but nothing had been arranged. The fleets sailed hither and thither aimlessly, it seemed, and finally anchored, while a party was sent forward to reconnoitre. The natural result was that the Russians suspected that a descent was contemplated upon Sebastopol and at once prepared for emergencies, entrenching the landward face of the town and fortress, which till then was almost devoid of batteries and fortifications.

But at last something was decided, and at daybreak on September 14th the huge fleet of transports, now joined by French and Turks, dropped anchor off Lake Saki, near Eupatoria, some 34 miles from Sebastopol.

The boom of a gun at once echoed along the shore, followed by a puff of smoke from a port-hole of the French flagship. At once a boat shot away from her stern and made for the beach.

"Ah! the beggars!" exclaimed Phil. "They will be the first ashore. Why does not our general send a boat to race them?"

"Plenty of time, mate," growled Tony, no more pleased than his friend to see their dapper allies to the front. "We'll show 'em yet; see if we don't."

All eyes were fixed on the boat. It ran gently on to the beach, its crew sprang out, and within a few minutes a flagstaff was erected, and the tricolour run up to the accompaniment of a shrill "Vive l'Empereur!" faintly heard across the water.

"Yes, shout if yer like," cried Tony in disgust. "See how we'll show yer. It don't take much to put up a flag there on the shore, but wait till it comes to planting it in a fort; we'll be there with yer, and p'r'aps show yer the way."

"Come, come," laughed Phil. "It's all your jealousy. The French are a brave nation and can fight; though I'm glad to think that we have always beaten them. Ah! there goes another gun, and see, they are disembarking."

"Yes, so they are; but look away over there," exclaimed Tony, pointing to the shore, where on an upland plateau, above the lake, some two hundred yards from the sea, stood five shaggy-looking ponies with figures seated on their backs holding long lances in their hands.

"Cossacks!" remarked Phil. "They are watching us. It seems strange that the Russians have made no preparations to oppose our landing, but I suppose they were quite uncertain as to the exact spot we should hit upon."

Transferring their attention from the figures on the shore to the French fleet, they watched, not without some amount of envy, the rapid disembarkation of the soldiers. But very soon another gun boomed out, and boats dashed from the British men-of-war towards the transports.

"Now our turn has come," remarked Phil. "Come along, Tony. We'll get our kit strapped on, and then we shall be ready at any moment."

"Pass the word along there for Corporal Western," sounded across the deck at this moment; and, hastily making his canteen fast, Phil shouldered his Minié rifle and stepped up to the adjutant.

"Take two men," the latter ordered, "and mount guard over the boxes of ammunition. You will land with them and see them safely stacked out of reach of the water, and remain in charge of them till you are relieved."

"I understand, sir," said Phil, saluting smartly by bringing his disengaged hand across to his rifle and striding away.

"Tony, I want you," he said, "and we'll take Sam Wilson as well. We're to mount guard over the ammunition."

It was the first really responsible charge that Phil had had entrusted to him, and he felt proud of it. Taking Tony and Sam with him, they stacked the boxes which had just been hoisted from the hold, and while one strode up and down in front, the other two sat down and waited for the order to disembark. Soon it came, and the men, who had fallen in, two deep, slowly filed to the gangways.

It was a difficult undertaking to disembark so many, but with the help of the sailors the greater part of the work was completed by nightfall.

"By Jove, it's really grand to see how those Jack Tars work," remarked Phil. "They have made no end of trips to the shore already, and here they are preparing to tow us."

Honest Jack indeed worked like a slave. As if to show his comrade-in-arms what he could do, and that he was master on the sea, he handed each soldier down into the boats as tenderly as if he were a child, remarking: "Now sit down there, matey. It'll soon be over, and this here swell's simply nothing;" or, "Hang on to that there ladder with yer eyebrows. Yer ain't used to these monkey tricks, and I've seen a better man than you let go and get a sousing."

Thomas Atkins listened to it all good-humouredly, and took his place obediently, while the sailors pulled the heavy boats and flats ashore.

Phil and his charge were taken in a special boat, and on landing the boxes were carried up and stacked in the centre of the camp selected for the Grenadier Guards. By this time the wind had risen, and rain had commenced to fall.

"It looks like raining all night, Phil," said Tony ruefully, staring up at the heavy clouds. "It's a fine look-out for us, for there ain't a single tent amongst us."

"Then we're no worse off than our officers, Tony. I see, though, that those Frenchies are housed under tiny tents they call '*tentes d'abri*'. Why shouldn't we make a kind of hutch with these boxes. One of us must do sentry-go outside, of course, but the other two may as well keep dry, and for the matter of that there are sufficient boxes to make a regular hut big enough to lie down in, and high enough to cover the sentry."

"Lummy, that's a cute dodge!" cried Tony. "We'll fix it up at once. Come along, Sam; lend a hand before this rain goes through us."

The boxes were heavy, but within a quarter of an hour quite a respectable house had been formed, with a blanket for a roof, and the opening turned away from the wind. Into this two of them crept, while the third stood on guard under the covering. By this means, while everyone else in the British lines spent a miserable night, and was drenched to the skin, Phil and his comrades escaped the rain, and awoke in the morning refreshed by a good sleep.

Phil was not relieved from his charge, but, with the two men helping him, remained on guard all the following day, when a native cart, called an "araba", was provided for the carriage of the ammunition, and he was informed that he would be in charge of it, and must see to having it loaded before the troops marched.

"A precious nice game," snorted Tony, when he heard the order. "Here we are, stuck right in rear of the troops, in charge of a few boxes of ammunition. Why couldn't someone else have been chosen?"

"Don't you grumble," replied Phil severely. "We have a responsible charge, and for all we know we may have even more fun and adventure than the others. Now it's your turn for sentry-go, so out you get. You can grumble there to your heart's content."

Tony departed abashed, and Phil and Sam looked on at the debarkation, which still continued. By the 17th all were ashore, save the sick, of whom there were still a large number. Even to a veteran soldier it was indeed a most interesting sight to see the huge allied army assembled on the upland slopes above the lake. In the distance the Turks, sitting contentedly and composedly in their tents; the French, like so many ants, bustling hither and thither and busily superintending the mid-day meal; and the lines of the British, now provided with tents for the few days before they marched from the shore.

It was a large force, and as many regiments were to make themselves for ever famous in the course of the campaign, it will perhaps be advisable to explain how our army was divided.

In chief command was Lord Raglan, an officer who for many years had lived a peaceful life, and had therefore little, if any, experience of warfare. His army consisted of six divisions, each made up of several regiments and commanded by a brigadier, or in some cases divided into two portions under different leaders.

The Light Division consisted of the 2nd Battalion Rifle Brigade, 7th Fusiliers, 19th Regiment and 23rd Fusiliers, under Major-general Codrington, and the 33rd, 77th, and 88th Regiments, under Brigadier-general Buller.

The First Division, under the Duke of Cambridge, included the Grenadier Guards, the Coldstream and Scots Fusilier Guards, now the Scots Guards, with Major-general Bentinck in command, and the 42nd, 79th, and 93rd Highlanders, fine brawny sons of the heather, under Brigadier Sir C. Campbell.

The Second Division comprised the 30th, 55th, and 95th Regiments, under Brigadier-general Pennefather, and the 41st, 47th, and 49th, under Brigadier-general Adams.

The Third Division, under Sir R. England, was composed of the 1st Royals, 28th, 38th, 44th, 50th, and 68th Regiments, commanded by Brigadiers Sir John Campbell and Eyre.

The Fourth Division, under Sir George Cathcart, consisted of the 20th, 21st, and 63rd Regiments and of the 2nd Battalion Rifle Brigade. The 46th and 57th

Regiments, which were to form part of it, had not yet arrived, but were *en route* from England.

The Cavalry Division, under Lord Lucan, was divided into a light brigade, under Lord Cardigan, which was made up of the 4th light Dragoons, the 8th and 11th Hussars, the 13th Dragoons, and the 17th Lancers; and the Heavy Cavalry Brigade, in command of Brigadier-general Scarlett, which comprised the Scots Greys, 14th Dragoon Guards, 5th Dragoon Guards, and 6th Dragoons, the first regiment not having yet put in an appearance.

It was indeed an immense force, and of course needed a huge commissariat train to feed it.

On the 18th the allied armies moved out of camp towards the Alma, the French being on the right, next the coast-line, and supported there by the guns of the fleets, while the brigade of Guards marched in rear. Phil took his place behind his regiment, and, slinging his rifle, acted as driver of the araba, while Tony and Sam trudged along on either side.

"It won't be long now before we hear guns," he remarked cheerfully from his elevated perch on top of the ammunition-boxes. "The Cossack fires were only a couple of miles in front of us last night, and it is scarcely likely that we shall be allowed to advance far without opposition. So look out for squalls, you fellows."

"It's what we've come for, mate," Tony replied with a shrug of his broad shoulders, "but it strikes me as we'll have to be looking out for trouble with this here old cart afore long. This wheel won't stand much of this kind of jolting."

The roads were indeed in places extremely rough, and a foot or more deep in mud after the recent rains and the trample of the troops in advance.

"Didn't I tell yer so," cried Tony a moment later, as the araba sank almost axle-deep and stopped abruptly. "Whip up them horses, Phil, or we'll get left behind."

Phil promptly applied the whip, but to no effect, and before the cart was again set in motion by the united efforts of his comrades and the horses, they had lost a considerable amount of ground. Then, to their intense vexation, one of the animals stumbled, and, falling upon the shaft, snapped it in two.

"What a misfortune!" exclaimed Phil, surveying the wreck. "But we are in charge of this ammunition, you fellows, and must bring it through. It is getting dark already, so I expect the troops will soon be halting. Lend a hand, both of you, and we'll splice this break, and catch the regiment up later on."

"You'll have to unload first, mate," Tony answered. "This weight is too much for one horse to keep up while we're mending, and besides, we'll get the job done in half the time if we take 'em both out and empty the cart."

Accordingly all three set to work and lifted the heavy boxes out. Then the horses were unharnessed, and with a length of rope and a batten of wood a shift was made to mend the break.

"That will do, I think," said Phil at last, surveying the work with satisfaction. "Now in with the animals, and let us get along as quickly as possible. We must be a couple of miles behind the troops, but fortunately the road is clear, and though it is a dark night we ought to reach them without trouble."

Once more they set out on the road, and were congratulating themselves on the fact that they were close to the camp, when Tony called a halt.

"What are them coves over there?" he asked, pointing ahead to a collection of camp-fires, in front of which mounted figures were flitting. "If them ain't Russians, I'm a Frenchie."

"They look remarkably like Cossacks, I must say, Tony," replied Phil anxiously. "Stop here a few moments while I go forward and make certain."

In another minute he had disappeared in the darkness. Walking boldly forward for three hundred yards he then judged it wise to observe some caution, and, stooping low, crept forward on the turf at the roadside, which completely muffled his footsteps. Suddenly a figure loomed up in front of him, followed by another, and, flinging himself on the ground, Phil crawled behind a growth of low bush and hastily hid himself from view.

"There, Petroff," he heard a harsh voice say in Russian, "that is your post. Remain there till you are relieved. If these pigs of Englishmen advance this way gallop back and warn us. See that you do not sleep, my man, or as the Czar, our master, lives, I will hang you to the nearest tree."

"Excellency, your orders shall be obeyed," the Cossack trooper answered humbly, and then, as his officer rode off, swore in a low but audible voice.

"Hang me to the nearest tree!" he muttered angrily. "Ah! Will he! Wait, your most noble excellency. Who knows how soon a bullet shall put an end to your threats, and should it come from behind instead of from these foreign pigs, then—ah, well! the fortune of war."

The man gave a stamp, as if to show his hatred, and, turning his horse, led it back a few paces. Phil at once rose to his feet and took to his heels in the direction of the cart.

"We have lost our way," he said, on rejoining his friends. "I cannot imagine how it has happened, but perhaps the British camp lies in a hollow, and we have mistaken the Russian fires for theirs. We evidently went off to the left, and now we must keep to the right."

Whipping up the horses, they pushed on once more, but two hours passed and still there was no sign of the camp.

"We're lost, that's what it comes to," said Tony calmly. "What shall we do, Phil? Seems to me 'tain't no use going ahead like this, for we shall be into the middle of the Russian army before long."

"That's what I'm afraid of, Tony. I think we had better stop here for to-night, and start again at daylight. We'll take the horses out and tie them on behind. No smoking, you fellows, and keep as quiet as you can. A match might lead to our capture, and we don't want to see the inside of a Russian prison so early in the campaign."

"Then, if we're stopping here, I vote we prepare for the worst," said Tony. "Supposing daylight shows us Cossacks all round, we sha'n't stand a chance. It won't take no more than an hour to build a wall with these boxes, and it may come in useful, for it's better to lie behind cover and fire than stand out in the open."

"That's a good idea, Tony, and we'll see to it," agreed Phil readily. "Now all together and get these horses out. Tie them with a long rope. In that way they will get a feed of grass, and as for water, there is plenty of dew falling to quench their thirst."

An hour later a wall some six feet long had been built close alongside the cart, leaving room for Phil and his friends to lie between it and the wheel. Then, having done all that was possible, they ate a portion of the three days' rations which each carried in his haversack, and, wrapping themselves in their blankets, lay down to sleep, one of their number, however, being left seated upon the boxes to keep guard.

Three hours later, when Phil's turn came for duty, the sky was already brightening in the east, and he waited anxiously for daylight. Gradually the dawn lit up the sky, chasing the dark clouds away, and finally banishing the grey mist which hung like a pall over the ground. Phil looked round in search of the British, but there was not a sign of them. A moment later a shout from behind attracted his attention, and turning, his heart leapt into his mouth at the sight of five wild-looking Cossack horsemen spurring their wiry ponies towards the cart, with their long lances already lowered and ready for the charge.

Chapter Nine.

An Exciting Adventure.

"Cossacks, by George! Wake up, you fellows!" shouted Phil, frantically kicking his comrades and caring little for the pain he caused, while at the same moment he saw to the loading of his Minié rifle.

"What's up? Why are you kicking us like that?" grunted Tony, lazily sitting up on his elbow. Then, as he saw Phil's anxious face and his preparations for defence, he sprang to his feet, and, grasping his rifle, cried, "Cossacks, is it? All round us, too, Phil. I guess we're trapped. But we'll make a fight of it."

"Fight! Of course we will. Do you think them fluffy-looking beggars is going to collar us without a little shooting?" growled Sam, grimly ramming down a charge, while he gazed over the top of the ammunition-boxes at the advancing enemy.

"Are you all loaded?" asked Phil shortly. "Then creep under the cart, Sam, and fire between the spokes of the wheel. Whatever you do, though, wait till I give the word. Our rifles carry a good long way, and we'll be able to get in a couple of volleys before they reach us."

In a twinkling Sam had dived beneath the cart, and a "Ready, boys!" shouted in a cheery voice, which scarcely showed a trace of the excitement he felt, told Phil and Tony he was prepared for any emergency.

Seeing three heads appear above the boxes, the Cossacks at once spread out, and completely surrounded the cart. Then, without pausing in their headlong gallop, they came full tilt at it, lance heads well in advance, each with his face close to his pony's neck, and his spurs buried in its flanks.

Phil and his friends singled out their men, and waited a few moments to get them well in range; then at the command "Fire!" from the former, three jets of smoke and flame spurted out from their rifles. Almost instantly the man at whom Phil had aimed tossed his arms into the air, and, falling heavily from his saddle, with one foot jammed in the stirrup, was dragged across the grass right up to the wall of ammunition-boxes, where the frightened animal came to a sudden halt, and having sniffed at it suspiciously, and snorted as if in disdain, lowered its head and commenced to crop the grass as if nothing out of the usual had occurred.

Sandy's bullet also found a mark, for another of the shaggy ponies fell as if struck by a pole-axe, and the rider shot out over its head and remained stunned and senseless upon the ground.

A grunt of disgust from Tony showed that his shot had missed.

"Well, I'm bothered! Missed!" he cried. "But here goes for another."

Reloading as rapidly as possible, they fired again, with the result that one of the horsemen was hit in the chest, and, doubling up, with arms hanging limply on either side of his pony's neck, was carried past the little fort like a whirlwind.

"Load up, boys!" cried Phil excitedly. "They'll be here in a minute; we must stop them, or those lances will be into us."

But to fire at a rapidly-moving object, even when coming directly at one, is no easy matter, particularly when a long, cruel-looking shaft, armed with a glittering spear-point, is held directed at one's chest. It takes nerve and coolness to make a careful shot, and it takes real courage to ride on towards that shot, knowing that it must reach its mark sooner than the lance can find its home in the enemy's breast. All honour therefore to the two gallant Cossacks who still were left. Without a pull at their reins, and without so much as a shadow of hesitation, they charged the harrier. All three rifles spoke out, and next moment with a crash one of the lances met the piled-up boxes, and, unable to throw them on one side owing to their weight, or pierce the thick woodwork, shivered into a thousand splinters, while the brave Russian who held it glared savagely at Phil, and making an ineffectual effort to draw a pistol, groaned and fell lifeless from his saddle with an ugly wound gaping in his neck.

The other Cossack was more successful. Dropping the point of his lance, he charged full at Sam, and escaping his bullet by a miracle, pinned him to the ground by a thrust through the shoulder.

"Bayonets! Come along, Tony!" shouted Phil, and without waiting to see if he were followed, he dashed over the wall, and flung himself upon the Russian, with his drawn bayonet in his hand. It was a narrow shave for him, for a pistol exploded almost in his face, and carried his bearskin away. Next second he had thrust his weapon through his opponent's body, and dragged him from his pony.

"Give a hand here, corporal," sang out Sam at this moment. "This beast of a spear holds me so tight I can't move. I feel just like a butterfly pinned to a board."

"Half a minute, Sam. Now, hold on," cried Tony, grasping the spear. Then, with, a sudden tug he wrenched it from the ground.

"My eye, don't it hurt!" groaned poor Sam, suddenly becoming pale. "Go easy with it, mate. Let the corporal have a turn."

Phil crept under the wagon, and finding the spear protruding almost a foot on the other side of the shoulder, pulled out his clasp-knife, and opening a small saw, which was a special feature of it, proceeded to cut the point off. That done, he grasped the shaft and gently pulled it from the wound.

"Come and help here, Tony," he cried. "But—wait a minute. Have a good look round first of all, and tell me if you can see any more of those fellows."

Tony climbed on top of the cart, and gazed all round.

"Not a single one of 'em in sight," he cried; "but they'll be here soon, you may be sure."

"Then come and give a hand here with Sam," answered Phil, pulling out his handkerchief. "I want a pad of linen or something."

"Here's the very thing, Phil;" and, pulling his bearskin off, Tony produced a large woollen muffler.

Ripping the seams of the coat with his knife, Phil quickly exposed the wound, and at once bound the muffler round it. Then with Tony's help he propped Sam with his back against the wheel, and placed the arm in a sling.

"Stay there, old boy," he said gently, "and as soon as the pain goes off, crawl in behind the boxes. The Russians will not be able to reach you there."

"Here yer are, mate," said Tony, handing Phil his bearskin. "It's about as near a go as you'll ever want. See, there's a hole bang through it, and the fur's all singed off the front."

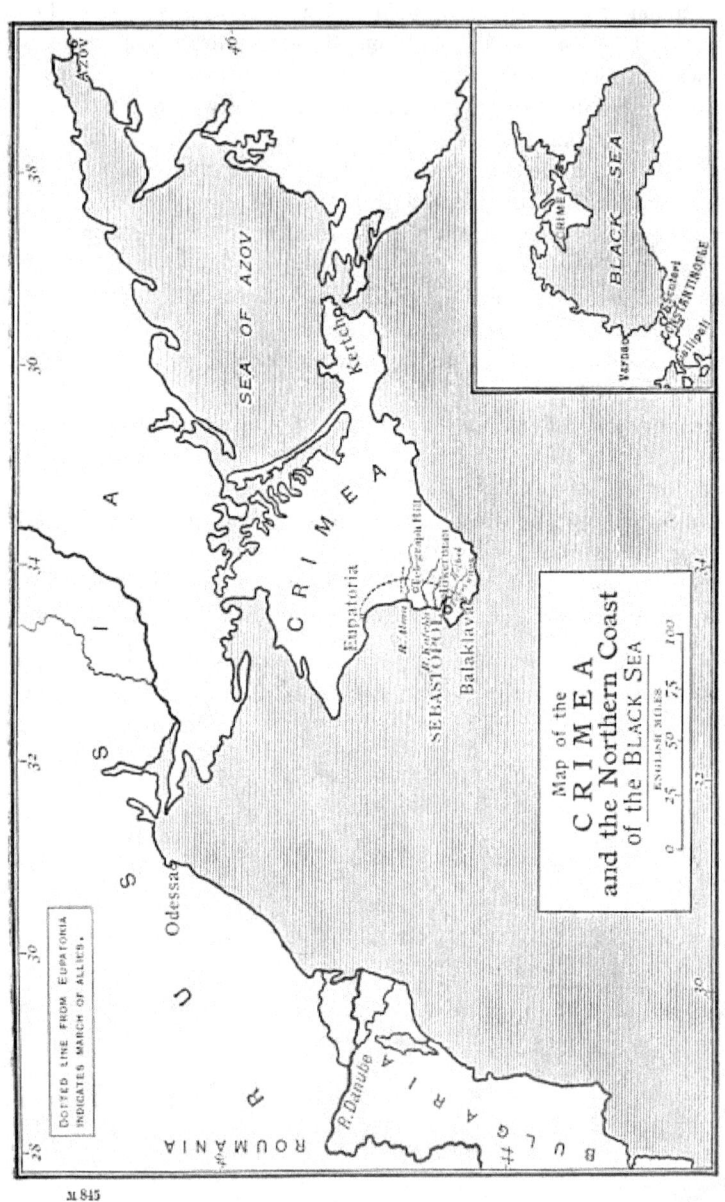

Map of the
CRIMEA
and the Northern Coast
of the BLACK SEA

ENGLISH MILES

0   25   50   75   100

DOTTED LINE FROM EUPATORIA
INDICATES MARCH OF ALLIES.

M 845

Phil inspected it with an outward show of coolness, but as he jammed it on his head he muttered beneath his breath a fervent thanksgiving to the Almighty for his preservation, for had he not ducked at the critical moment, that hole would not have been blown through the helmet, but through his head.

"Get up on top, and keep a look-out, Tony," he exclaimed. "We're in a tight hole, and it will only be by keeping our eyes well open that we shall get safely out of it. First of all, though, break open one of those boxes, and load the rifles. We shall want plenty of ammunition, and had best have it ready and close at hand, in case of a sudden attack. I will have a look at these poor fellows."

Crawling from beneath the cart, he knelt beside the Cossack into whose body he had thrust the bayonet. The poor fellow was evidently at his last gasp, but hearing Phil's voice he opened his eyes, and gazed wonderingly at him. Then, as he recognised him, he feebly raised his hand.

A feeling of terrible grief and dismay surged through Phil's heart, for he was a lad who would sooner have lost his own life than taken that of another in cold blood. And yet, though this had been done in war-time, and whilst battling for life and liberty, a pang of regret oppressed him, and he felt only as a young man can feel who, for the first time in his existence, has been the cause of suffering and death to another.

He took the hand of the dying man, and gently pressed it.

"Are you in great pain, my poor fellow?" he whispered.

The wounded Russian shook his head, and answered something. Phil placed his ear close to his mouth and listened.

"We were enemies," the Cossack gasped, "bitter enemies, for you have invaded our country. But now we are friends, friends until death. Hold my hand, brother, and the Virgin will bless you. Feel round my neck when I am gone, and you will find a cross. Take—take it for yourself, and when you glance at it think sometimes of him who died for his beloved Czar and country."

"I will, I will!" whispered Phil, with a groan of anguish.

"I see my old peasant home," went on the dying Cossack in a voice that was scarcely audible. "Ah, I see it better than ever—ever before. My poor mother!—thank God she has long gone to her rest!—and my brother. The stream in front, and the trees all round. Hold me, Englishman! Everything is dancing and blurred before my eyes. I—I am dying. Good-bye! Think some— sometimes of the man who died for his country."

The poor fellow, who had struggled into a sitting position, fell back, and Phil thought that he was dead. But he opened his eyes again, smiled, and with a sigh his spirit fled.

Deeply impressed, Phil knelt by his side and offered up a short prayer. Then he rose to his feet, and, climbing on to the cart, looked round.

Phit! A bullet struck the corner of one of the ammunition-boxes, and, glancing off, buried itself in the heel of his boot.

"That's a close one again, Phil, old boy," laughed Tony, who seemed to enjoy the risk of being shot. "It's that fellow over there. He's just below the hill, and you can only see him by standing up on top here."

This was the case. Another Cossack had ridden up, and, choosing a convenient position within range, sat upon his pony, with only his head showing above a ridge, and fired at Phil and his friends.

"This won't do," muttered Phil. "If he were in sight we could make it warm for him, for our rifles carry farther. But as it is, he hits us at every shot, while we might pour volleys in his direction, and only bag him by the merest chance. There, didn't I say so?" he exclaimed, as a second bullet whirred past between himself and Tony. "Look here, Tony," he continued, "climb down behind the boxes, and fire as often as you can at the beggar. That will distract his attention."

"Yes, and what game are you up to, mate?" asked Tony wonderingly.

"I'm going to creep round and drive him off," Phil answered with decision.

"Take my tip then and ride round, Phil. Soon as he sees you move he'll change his position, but if you're riding you'll be able to stop his game. But anyways I think the job belongs to me," he added, as if the thought that his friend would be running into greater danger had suddenly occurred to him. "You ain't the only chap as can ride, and as you're boss here, should stay in command of our fort."

Phil looked at Tony sternly, and for the moment was on the point of ordering him to do as he was told. But, changing his mind, he picked up a rifle, and without a word dropped over the wall of boxes. The pony was still standing, quietly cropping the grass, and did not move when he disengaged the foot of the dead man from the stirrup. A second later he had mounted, and, picking up the reins and holding his rifle across the pommel of the saddle, nodded to Tony and cantered off.

Striking away to the left he galloped to the top of the rise, only to find the Cossack spurring away from him, evidently with the intention of gaining another post from which to fire.

"By George, I'll bag that chap!" muttered Phil. "It would be great to rejoin the regiment with a captive."

Kicking his pony with his heels he was soon flying across the turf, the nimble and sure-footed little animal leaping the few holes that came in his path with an ease that showed how accustomed he was to it. Soon the flying Cossack had disappeared over another ridge, and Phil was not surprised to hear the report of a rifle a moment later and an angry hiss above his head.

"He'll certainly knock me over with one of his shots if I ride on like this," he thought. "I'll dismount and stalk him."

Acting on the thought he pulled up sharply and leapt from the saddle, the pony immediately dropping his head to graze. Then, flinging himself on to hands and knees, he scrambled forward until he reached a patch of long grass, where he lay full length, and, bringing his rifle to his shoulder, pointed it in the direction of the Cossack and waited breathlessly.

An instant later the Russian appeared in sight, and Phil pressed the trigger; then, jumping to his feet, he rushed forward to secure his prisoner, for the Cossack had dropped like a stone. He topped the ridge, and was on the point of running down, when a bullet struck the butt of his rifle and shattered it, while the Russian, who had been merely acting, rose on one knee not fifty yards away, and commenced to rapidly reload. What was Phil to do? He hesitated, but the sight of some eight or nine more Cossacks galloping up to help their comrade decided him.

"I'm off," he muttered hurriedly, and, dropping his useless rifle, he took to his heels. It seemed as though he would never reach the pony, but at last he did and, flinging himself astride it, galloped madly back to the fort, glancing anxiously over his shoulder at the Cossacks. They had closed together, and, topping the rise at this moment, came thundering down, shouting encouragement to one another.

Phil reached the cart, and was off the pony's back and in the fort in a trice.

"Shake hands, old man!" exclaimed Tony grimly. "This here will be our last. There's a hundred or more of these fellows charging."

"Nonsense! Pick up the rifles," gasped Phil. "Now get ready to give them a volley. Sam, where are you?"

"Here, and ready to lend a hand, mate," the wounded man answered, crawling from beneath the cart at that moment. "I've got hold of these barkers," he said, with a grin, producing two pistols which he had taken from the Cossacks lying dead close at hand, "and I bet yer if those Russian coves gets close enough, I'll give 'em some of their own lead to swallow."

But though the three put the best face on the matter, there was no doubt that they were in desperate straits. The first volley failed miserably, and already the fiery horsemen were within a hundred yards of the cart, when there was a shout from behind, and to the joy of Phil and his comrades a patrol of dragoons came cantering across the grass.

"Pals, hooray!" shouted Tony. "Phil, we'll join 'em. Get hold of your nag and I'll take this other here. Now, up we get; and when the boys come along, we goes at them beggars with them."

Caught by the excitement of the moment Phil vaulted over the wall, and just as the dragoons came spurring by with drawn swords poised ready for the encounter, he and Tony dashed out and joined them.

"What ho, mates!" sang out the troopers. "Coming for a picnic with us, are yer? Good, boys!"

There was no time for more. Setting spurs to their horses, the troop, which was only ten strong counting Phil and Tony, went headlong at the Cossacks. The latter pulled up immediately, hesitated for a moment, and were on the point of flying, when the impossibility of getting away from dragoons mounted on fresh English horses occurred to them. They threw down their arms and sullenly waited to be made prisoners.

"Each of you catch hold of one of their reins and come along, quick," sang out the non-commissioned officer who was in charge of the dragoons. "That's it. Now off we go, back to the cart."

"How far is the camp away?" asked Phil.

"Five miles, I should think, corporal. We'll have to look precious smart. As soon as we get the horses in, and the boxes loaded up, we'll scatter. I've enough men to spare—two in front, and two well out on the flanks. Then if we're attacked we'll make a running fight of it."

"We've a wounded friend under the cart," replied Phil, "but I expect if we perch him up on top of the ammunition-boxes he'll be able to drive. Then Tony and I will give a hand by looking after the prisoners. It'll be grand getting back to camp safely with our charge, and with a few of the Cossacks in addition, though, mind you, we would have been prisoners if you fellows hadn't ridden up in the nick of time."

"You're right there, corporal. You chaps made a fine stand of it, we can all see, and we'll not forget to say something about it when we get into camp. But you were fair goners if we hadn't been out and heard the firing. Now let's get smartly ahead. Some more Cossacks will be riding down before long, and though we're all game for a brush with them, we don't want to lose this chance of bringing in prisoners."

By this time the cart had been reached, and while half the patrol guarded the prisoners, the remainder set to work and rapidly loaded it with the ammunition. Then the horses were yoked, Sam was placed upon a folded-up blanket on top of the boxes, and the cavalcade started, Tony and Phil forming the flank guard, and proudly riding their newly-acquired steeds.

94

"I should have liked to give those poor fellows a decent burial," said Phil with a sigh of regret as they rode away, "but it is impossible. We haven't any spades or picks, and, above all, it would not do to wait."

"Don't worry about that, mate," one of the troopers answered. "Their chums is certain to come over and see to that, for these Russians ain't bad chaps when you take 'em all round, and I hear they're as kind as possible to one another."

An hour later the party rode into camp and caused quite a sensation.

"Why, Corporal Western, we gave you up for lost!" said the adjutant of the Grenadiers, coming out to meet them. "We made sure you had been killed or captured, and now you turn up with prisoners. How has it happened?"

"Quite simply, sir," Phil answered, with a smile. "We were left behind when the shaft of our cart broke, and then we took the wrong road. This morning we were attacked, and beat off five Cossacks. Then others appeared, and just as we were thinking of giving in, a patrol of dragoons rode up."

"Giving in!" exclaimed Sam in high disdain from his elevated seat. "Tell you what it is, sir. That Corporal Western don't know when the time to hoist the white flag arrives. He meant sticking to it, so we just backed him up."

"Whoever was the cause of your holding on, my lads, it's much the same in the end," exclaimed the officer heartily. "You have done well, and your names shall be mentioned to the colonel. Now you had better see what the cooks have left, while the doctors take your wounded comrade in charge."

Handing the cart over to the quarter-master, Tony followed Phil to the cook's fire, and both were soon devouring a meal of bully beef and bread, for they were almost famished, having been too much engaged and too highly excited to eat while threatened by the Cossacks.

They found the Allies encamped a few miles from the River Alma, and almost in sight of the Russian position.

"It'll be hot work to-morrow," said one of the sergeants that evening, as they sat wrapped in their blankets round the fire. "The enemy has chosen a splendid position along the heights the other side of the river, and I expect our job will be to turn him out. It will be a big fight, or I'm mistaken, and as we shall all have plenty to do I'm for turning-in at once and getting as long a sleep as I can. Good-night, you chaps! Corporal Western, you'll have them three stripes this time to-morrow if you do only half as well as you and your two mates did to-day."

The stalwart sergeant laid his blanket on the ground, rolled himself in it, and, placing his head on his haversack, was very soon in a deep sleep, untroubled by the fact that to-morrow might be his last day on earth.

As for Phil and Tony, they sat up an hour or more longer, chatting over past events and the probabilities of the next day's fight, never dreaming that it was destined to be on historical one, and one in which the mettle of British troops was to be tested and found of the staunchest, by as fierce a storm of shot and shell as ever assailed an army.

Chapter Ten.

The Glorious Alma.

The misty grey of early dawn lay over the smooth grassy slopes of the Crimea when Phil and Tony turned over on the following morning and looked about them. Here and there men were moving about like big ghostly shadows as they trudged down to the banks of the River Bulganak to fill their water-bottles and mess-tins in preparation for the morning meal. Some were crouching over smoking fires, encouraging them to burn up brightly and give out sufficient heat to cook the food. Close at hand others were grooming officers' chargers, and on every side there was the clatter of an awaking camp, the stamp of restive hoofs, cheery calls from man to man, and the startling notes of reveillé ringing out clearly in the morning air, and warning all that another day had arrived, and that it was time to throw off sleep and be ready to try conclusions with the enemy.

"Lummy, ain't I sleepy just!" yawned Tony, throwing off his blanket and sitting up to rub his eyes with his knuckles.

"I too could have done with a couple of hours more," answered Phil peevishly. Then, springing to his feet, he shook the heavy dew from his blanket and looked towards the river, the smooth and sluggish surface of which had just caught the first rays of the rising sun.

"Who's for a dip?" he cried briskly. "Come along, Tony, boy; we shall never wake up till we have douched ourselves with water."

"'Tain't a bad idea, Phil, and I'm with yer," exclaimed his friend, shaking himself like a dog. "There ain't no towels, as I can see, so I suppose it's a case of dry as best you can."

"Yes, of course. The sun will be up in another ten minutes, and will serve our purpose well. Come along; we've a clear half-hour before breakfast."

Another five minutes and Phil, accompanied by many comrades, was hastily pulling off his boots and clothing close to the bank of the stream. Then someone waded in and tried the depth, and having found a deep pool the others dived in, splashing the water in every direction. The pastime caught on like fire, and very soon a hundred or more were enjoying a bathe. Officers, too, came down to the river, some to look on, and others to join the men in the water.

By eight o'clock the whole of the Allies were under arms and waiting anxiously for orders, the French on the right, while the British took care of the left flank, where danger was to be expected. In rear of all were the arabas and cavalry, besides herds of cattle and sheep. Phil and Tony had been relieved of their charge, and were in the ranks with their comrades.

"I ain't sorry to say good-bye to that old cart, araba, or whatever they call it," exclaimed Tony. "Yer see, we shall get a chance of seeing most of the fun if there's a fight, whilst if we was in charge of the ammunition where should we be? Right away behind, there ain't a doubt, kicking our heels and waiting till some chance cannon-shot come bowling along our way and chopped our heads off. Halloo! who's that?"

This exclamation was caused by the sudden appearance of a smartly-dressed officer, with glittering epaulettes and waving plume, cantering down before the British lines.

"It's Marshal St Arnaud, him as commands the Froggies," shouted someone. The news spread through the ranks, and at once, lifting their rifles, the troops greeted the Marshal with three hearty British cheers, a compliment which evidently caused him much gratification.

M 845

"A PISTOL EXPLODED ALMOST IN HIS FACE"

"We shall move now, Tony," remarked Phil gravely, "so we'll just shake hands, old man. One never knows what may happen. Perhaps it will be unnecessary, but we've a big fight before us, and who can say that we shall both come safely through it?"

"No one, Phil. No one but Him as sits above," Tony answered earnestly; "but I tell yer we're coming through it, you and me, and you're going to do something for them stripes. I feel it somehow. But here's my hand, old pal. You've been a good 'un to me, and if I go this day, I'll have a better chance than a year or more ago. I shall, and yer know it."

Tony grasped Phil's hand and wrung it, while tears stood in his eyes. Phil returned the pressure earnestly, and then they leant on their rifles and waited for the word to advance.

Between nine and ten it came, and the Allies trudged forward over a wide sweeping plain leading to a ridge, beyond which lay the valley of the Alma, the valley—fair though it looked on that grand morning—of the shadow of death. And now guns in front boomed out, answering the shots of the Russian batteries, and each man grasped his rifle more firmly at the sound, while a keen, strained look came over his face, as though he had braced himself for the trial which was coming.

Trudge, trudge, trudge! On moved the mass of men, looking grand in their varied uniforms, and all seeming anxious to get more quickly to that ridge in front and look upon the enemy.

"Ah! there they are," exclaimed Phil with a sigh of relief as his company topped the rise and came in full view of the Russian position. "See, they are right in front of us if we only march in the direction we are taking now, so there will be plenty of work for us, you fellows! Hurrah for the fight!" and in the excitement of the moment, he snatched his bearskin from his head, and, tossing it into the air, caught it on his bayonet with the skill of a juggler. Instantly a wave of cheering spread along the British lines, and a forest of bearskins and head-gear of every description was thrust aloft on the gleaming bayonets, soon—very soon—to be used in deadly and desperate earnest for another purpose. A minute later the answering cheers of the French came echoing along the lines, their "Vive l'Empereur!" piercing the morning air with a shrill note, showing that they too were roused to the highest pitch of enthusiasm.

"Look, Tony!" exclaimed Phil a few minutes later, having calmed down sufficiently to be able to make a good examination of the Russian position, "those beggars have chosen a splendid spot on which to manoeuvre. You can see them massed on the slope of the hill close upon the other side of the river, and to reach them we must cross the open and plunge through the water. That makes it pretty well impossible for our cavalry to help us by a flank attack. But we'll go for them tooth and nail, in the regular old bull-dog way, and if we don't rout them out of their position, well, I'll—I'll never speak to you again."

"Yer won't, won't yer?" answered Tony, with a curious grin, staring at his friend with no small amount of astonishment. "Young 'un, I never see yer so wound up afore. I never thought yer was that bloodthirsty. Me and all yer mates took yer for one of them quiet kind of coves what takes a lot of rousing. But now—blow me—I can see yer monkey's up, and I'll have to keep an eye on yer, else yer'll be trying to fight the whole of them Russian coves alone." Then, having smiled once more at Phil, the honest fellow's face suddenly assumed a sterner look, his eyes glistened and his cheeks flushed, while he hurriedly fumbled at the fastening of his ammunition-pouch. "Beat 'em, Phil, old boy! in course we will. If the Grenadier Guards don't find their way to the top of that there hill, and take every one of them big guns yer see, it'll be because there ain't none of 'em left to do it. We'll manage it or die on the way."

And indeed, to look at the disposition of the Russian troops and guns made by General Menschikoff, there was every possibility that before they were forced to retire many a gallant British and French soldier would be laid low upon the grass. In front of the Allies stretched the river Alma, forming a sharp bend, the apex of which was opposite the division between French and English troops, and pointed towards the Russians. In the bend was the village of Bourliouk, soon to be the scene of sharp skirmishing, and on the right a road crossed the river and ascended the opposite bank, which at that point sloped easily towards a conical hill known as Telegraph Hill. To the right of this road, and exactly facing the French and Turkish troops, there was a steep cliff on the other side of the river. Up this, however, two roads ran, one of which was available for guns.

In front of the British, grassy slopes descended to gardens and vineyards which stretched to the river-bank, and through them passed a broad post-road from Sebastopol to Eupatoria, crossing the Alma by a bridge, and ascending between Telegraph Hill and another height known as Kourgani Hill. On either side of this road the banks of the river ascended in easy slopes, and here it was that Menschikoff had disposed his forces, planting a formidable battery of fourteen guns, of large calibre, behind an earthwork thrown up on a terrace one hundred yards from the water, while farther to the left was another battery, the two supported by nine field-batteries of eight guns each—a truly formidable armament.

"Heavens! what guns!" Phil heard one of the officers mutter. Then, gripping the colours he bore, the young fellow tossed his head proudly and added: "By Jove, we'll have the lot before the day is out!"—a resolution which every soldier had also made.

What it was to cost them only the future could disclose, but those who had seen war before, who had trained themselves to conduct the movements of armies, could not but expect a heavy list of casualties; for even an amateur might have seen that the Russian position was one of extraordinary strength, while the expert able to grasp its salient points could tell at a glance that it presented an extremely difficult and anxious problem to the attacker. Even Phil, boy though he was and inexperienced in warfare, could not but be struck by the formidable works towards which the Allies were advancing.

"They seem impregnable," he muttered. "Look at the batteries. They must have 100 guns at least, and all trained for the slope upon which we are advancing. Then there is the river to cross. It may or may not be fordable, but in any case it means a disadvantage to us and an advantage to the Russians. When that is crossed there is the rush uphill in the teeth of those guns, and opposed by the enemy's bayonets. It will be hot work, Tony, very hot work, for I suppose we shall be compelled to make a frontal attack."

"If that means marching straight to our front, without turning so much as an inch, then I says yes, I hope we shall," Tony answered with a growl, assumed only to cover his excitement. "How else should Englishmen attack? Go straight for them is our way of doing business, and I reckon it's the best."

And this in fact seemed the only way of attacking the Russians successfully. Perhaps a flanking movement to the left might have proved successful, but even then the river must first be forded, no doubt in the teeth of a murderous fire. But this had not struck the British leader as possible, and the whole force marched on steadily, shoulder to shoulder, and with a martial tramp which seemed to shake the ground.

And upon them as they advanced was fixed the anxious gaze of some 50,000 Russians, horse, foot, and gunners, who marvelled at their boldness and seeming unconcern, and waited only for the long red lines of the British and the brisk-moving masses of French blue to come a little nearer, when they promised themselves that they would sweep them out of existence with a tempest of shot and shell the like of which had never been experienced. Yes, all was ready. Their guns were trained for the ground over which British and French must pass; but not for an instant did it occur to them that French and Turks might think of attacking the cliffs on their left. The narrow road, its steepness, and the proximity of their guns seemed to make such an attempt impossible, and, safe in the thought, they brought every piece they possessed to bear upon those slopes and vineyards across which the British were soon to march.

"Halt!" The command came hoarsely through the air and was emphasised by the shrill notes of a bugle.

"Now, what is going to happen?" asked Phil. "Ah! I see; we are to get into our proper formation, ready to march down to the river. Then I suppose we shall deploy till we have ample elbow-room, and afterwards make a dash for the Russian position."

Ten minutes later the British divisions were swinging along over the green turf, their centre marching almost directly on the village of Bourliouk, and the whole face to face with Menschikoff's huge army, and destined to bear the brunt of the fighting.

The French and Turkish troops took but a small part in the battle. Seeing the difficulty of the two cliff roads ascending the river-bank to the left of his force, Menschikoff had failed to occupy them, as has been mentioned, and had placed but few troops in the neighbourhood, for the guns of the allied fleets commanded the cliffs. Taking advantage of this, the lithe and active little Frenchmen were soon crowding the narrow road in their front, and in an incredibly short space of time their guns had been hauled to the top of the cliff, and from there boomed out at the Russian batteries and long lines of massed infantry, doing much execution and threatening them from their flank. Farther to the right the Turks swarmed up the other road, and having gained the cliffs, took up their position there.

Meanwhile the red lines of the British, who, it had been arranged, should not be launched at the main army till the French had commenced their flank attack, moved down the grassy slope, solemn and grand, and as steadily as a mass of moving rock, the front line composed of the Second and Light Divisions, the next of the Third and First Divisions, in column formation, while behind them the Fourth Division marched in echelon, with five regiments in rear as reserves. Stretching for nearly two miles, with its right close to the village of Bourliouk and its left near that of Tarkhaular, the mass of men advanced slowly and evenly, with a cloud of skirmishers from the rifle battalions thrown out in front. Soon these became engaged with the Russian skirmishers posted in the vineyards and in Bourliouk, and the sharp rat-a-tat of musketry and an occasional hiss above the heads of the gallant men in red showed that the battle of the Alma had commenced. A grunt, almost a shout, of satisfaction and pent-up excitement, instantly went down the lines, and the regiments at a sharp order commenced to open out and deploy, the foremost line, composed of the Second and Light Divisions, stepping forward at a smart pace, which soon became almost a double, as the men eagerly advanced against the Russians.

Boom! The big battery had opened fire, and, as if this had been a signal, every gun on the Russian side blazed out and covered the slopes with smoke, while their shot searched the whole British front, tearing remorselessly through the ranks and crashing into the village houses.

"This is hot!" shouted Phil in Tony's ear, as they squatted with their comrades upon the grass, awaiting the order to advance. "I'd rather march straight against that battery than sit here and be pounded into a jelly before having a chance of a smack at those beggars."

"'Tain't nothing," grunted Tony reassuringly, tilting his bearskin back to dash the perspiration from his forehead. "Ah, that was a bad 'un!" he muttered hoarsely as, with an awful screech, a cannon-shot plunged into the men close at hand, laying five of the poor fellows dead and maiming two others in its flight.

But now the first line had reached the river, and, holding their pouches and rifles above their heads, they plunged in boldly, and were soon massed on the other side, where they waited, standing waist-deep in the water, and sheltered by the steep bank from the fire of the batteries above. But it was only a momentary halt. Dashing through the river, Sir George Brown put his horse at the bank, and, surmounting it, turned in his saddle and called upon the brave fellows to follow him, waving his sword in a manner that showed all who were out of hearing what his wishes were. And he had not to call a second time, for, hastily gulping down a mouthful of water, the thin red line climbed the bank with a shout, and, falling into their places with as much coolness as though on a parade-ground, advanced shoulder to shoulder up the slopes.

A glance at them, however, displayed the curious fact that the advancing troops were in no regular formation. Compelled to deploy and often make wide détours in passing through the vineyards on the other bank and in marching round the village, regiments had been split up into smaller portions, and in many cases men had lost sight of their comrades altogether. But still discipline and coolness were second nature to them. Without orders but of their own initiative they fell in, and forming a double line—the favoured formation for British attack,—they pressed up the hill; dark-coated riflemen and red linesmen intermingled, and were swallowed up in the clouds of eddying smoke.

Up, up they climbed, steadily and with heroic bravery, and, passing through a storm of hurtling iron and lead, at length flung themselves upon the deep columns of the Russians.

One moment visible, they were seen surging from side to side, desperately using their bayonets; and next moment, with an appalling roar, the batteries would open once more, and clouds of white smoke would swallow them up, only their excited cries, and the hoarse, encouraging voices of the officers nobly leading them, showing that they still survived.

"It's grand to see them," cried Phil, carried away by the excitement of the moment. "When will our turn come? They will be swept away by those crowds of Russian soldiers. Look at them, Tony! Now they are at close quarters, and the enemy is giving back. Hurrah, now we have them!" and, springing to his feet, he would have broken from the ranks and rushed to join the fighting-line had not Tony clutched him by the arm and dragged him to the ground, while a hoarse and well-timed "Steady, youngster, you're tiring yourself; keep all your gristle till we come up against them," from a veteran sergeant who sat close at hand, smoking calmly, served to quieten him again. But Phil was not the only man there who longed to be up and doing. Not one but was restless and chafing at the delay, especially at Phil's last shout, for a turn had taken place in the tide of the battle which indeed gave the British a far better chance of victory. Awed by the mass of advancing men, the big Russian battery, which had done such damage in our ranks, suddenly limbered up and retired over the hill—a disgraceful retreat which proved disastrous to the enemy.

But though the attacking force had thus gained an important advantage, the masses of the Russians now poured down the slope and threw themselves upon the gallant British line. Bravely did the latter resist, and with desperate courage strive to continue their advance; but the enemy opposing them were equally brave and equally stubborn, and moreover had the advantage of position and numbers. For a few moments there was a seething mixture of red and grey coats, glittering bayonets, and darts of flame; and then, broken by sheer weight, the British retired upon the ranks of the now advancing second line.

Side by side Phil and Tony stepped forward with their comrades, and almost in a dream plunged through the river and climbed the opposite bank. But now the voices of their officers recalled their wandering senses, and, falling into their places, the brigade of Guards pushed on in perfect formation, with the Highlanders abreast of them.

What a scene it was! What excitement and what movement! A double line of stalwart Guardsmen as well-ordered and as rigidly erect as if drilling in the green parks at home; and in line with them brawny Highlanders, all dripping with water, deafened by the crashing artillery, and yet determined to a man to get to close quarters with the enemy. And retiring upon them, war-worn, bedraggled, and bareheaded, with faces and hands black with the smoke of powder, some limping heavily, and others even crawling, came the gallant first line, loth to turn their backs upon the foe, and yet compelled to do so by overwhelming numbers. Had the second line advanced earlier it would have supported them at the critical moment, but owing to the fact that Lord Raglan and his staff had already crossed the river and ridden close to Telegraph Hill, it received no direct order from him; and when it did advance, it was on the responsibility of the division commander. But now, opening its ranks for the moment to pass through the broken first line, it marched at a rapid pace, and immediately plunged into the tempest of bullets. Men fell to right and left, biting the dust and struggling in their agony, while others lay motionless, sometimes with contorted limbs and faces, and sometimes in peaceful repose as if asleep, stirring not from the position in which death had found them. Ah! it was war, red, cruel war, and well might that second line have wavered and turned back. But theirs was not that sort of courage. Determined to be beaten by nothing, they kept steadily marching up the hill, and soon disappeared, for volumes of smoke were pouring from the village of Bourliouk, which was now in flames, and, mingling with that from the guns, enveloped the combatants in a dense cloud.

And as the line advanced into the thick of the fight, and while rifle fire brought havoc to the ranks, the Russian skirmishers, still clinging to their positions amongst the trees of the river-bank, picked off all the stragglers, and even turned their volleys and the fire of a few light field-guns upon the main body.

"Keep together, mate. We'll fight 'em side by side," shouted Tony, closing up to Phil. "Got yer rifle loaded? Then keep yer charge till we gets to close quarters. It'll come in handy then."

"Right! I thought of that," Phil shouted back. Then, closing up to their comrades, they advanced at a rapid pace and flung themselves upon the lines of grey-coated Russians.

To this day Phil cannot quite recall what happened. If you press him he will perhaps tell you that he recollects a young officer falling at his feet, while a huge Russian prepared to bayonet him. Next moment the man was down and Phil was standing over him, while Tony's rifle laid low another who was in the act of dashing his friend's head to pieces with the butt of his weapon.

On pressed the red line resistlessly and with never a pause, leaving behind them friend and foe strewn upon the grass, and on, ever in front, went the officers and the colours into the heart of the struggling mass of grey. There was no need to call to their men and beg them to follow. The British lion was aroused in desperate earnestness, and with grim and awe-inspiring silence the men rushed on headlong and regardless of bullet or bayonet. There was a crash, the bang, bang of an occasional shot, and the clash of steel upon steel, and then the trample of thousands of feet as the enemy gave way and fled.

Side by side Phil and Tony had fought their way into the middle of the famous Vladimir regiment, and as the Russians turned, found themselves mixed up with brawny Highlanders, who, with the light of battle in their eyes, were pressing resistlessly forward. Suddenly Phil caught sight of a figure in advance bearing a British colour. It swayed this way and that, now endeavouring to get closer to the Highlanders, and next moment swept forward as the retreating Russians slowly gave way and drove the bearer before them.

"The colour! the colour!" he shouted frantically, dashing forward with Tony at his heels. Scattering those who barred their path, they made their way to the flag, and falling-in on either side, fought grimly to help its bearer back to the ranks of the Highlanders.

"Thanks, my men!" shouted the young officer who supported the flag. "Now, help me, and we'll get out of this hole. All together! Rush!"

With their weapons held well in advance, the three dashed at the enemy, while the Highlanders, seeing the predicament into which the colour had fallen, with a shout of wrath flung themselves in their direction. But though beaten, the Russians had in no way lost courage, and, turning fiercely, they bore the gallant Scotsmen back, while others opposed Phil and his comrades.

"Rally, rally! The colour!" shouted Phil, thrusting right and left with his bayonet, and turning just in time to discharge his rifle at a man who was attacking them in rear.

So fiercely did the little band of three fight that the Russians in their immediate neighbourhood gave way, and, standing in a circle round them, glared at the gallant red-coats who had thus far been too much for them.

A glorious picture they presented. At bay, with a host of the enemy surrounding them and glowering at them with fierce hatred, the officer and his two supporters indeed were men of whom Britain might well feel proud. With flushed faces and flashing eyes, which looked into those of the enemy with no signs of fear, but with keen glances of stern determination, they stood there a mere drop in an ocean of struggling men. Smoke-begrimed, dishevelled, and with bearskins tumbled in the mud, Phil and Tony clutched their rifles and looked ready and willing to fall upon the hundreds around them. Thoughts of home, danger of capture, or death by bayonet or bullet were lost in the delirious excitement of the moment. They thought only of the flag for which they fought, and, hemmed in and panting with exhaustion, they listened to the deafening din of the battle still raging a few feet from them, and nobly determined to die sooner than permit the Russians to capture it.

"We're done, lads," groaned the officer, sinking on his knee. "Corporal, take the colour. I'm hit, and can't hold it any longer. Fight on for it!"

Phil grasped the staff, and, hoisting the flag still higher, looked round with proud defiance, while Tony, with a grim smile of exultation on his face, stepped nearer to him.

"Ay, well fight on for it, sir, never fear," he muttered. "We'll fight till we're dead."

Phil nodded.

"I'll borrow your sword, sir," he said, grasping the weapon as he spoke. "A rifle and bayonet are too heavy to use one-handed."

"Look out, lads! Here come the cavalry!" the officer exclaimed at this moment; and almost instantly Cossack horses dashed through the Russian infantry, scattering them and surrounding the colour. There was one last desperate fight. Phil's sword smashed in two at the first vicious cut, and for a minute he continued the defence by belabouring the horsemen with the colour-staff. Then that was dashed to the ground, and before he was aware of it a lasso-noose had been slipped over his shoulders, securing his arms to his side, and he was being dragged away.

The last backward glance as he was hurried away showed him a grand rush by the Highlanders. The grey-coats retreated precipitately, and amid hoarse shouts of exultation the rescued colour was borne back to the British lines.

Chapter Eleven.

A Russian Villain.

The celebrated, the historical battle of the Alma was over almost as soon as Phil had been dragged away, for there was no stopping the British troops, and once the Russians had turned to retreat, our brave fellows pressed forward till the summit of the slopes was gained. They had fought magnificently against desperate odds, and without ever having need to call upon their reserves. And while the infantry had been busy, other arms of the service had been by no means idle. The cavalry protected the left, and the guns, after firing for some time across the river, had limbered up, and while some crossed by the bridge which carried the post-road, others plunged through the water to its right, and ascending close to Telegraph Hill, raked the Russian batteries and struggling infantry with their fire.

It was a sight to see—an example of the dogged pluck which characterises our nation; and an example which the French, perched upon the cliff on the right, did not fail to watch with admiration, and with a secret determination to emulate it on the first occasion.

And now that the enemy had retreated, the British guns still plied them with shot. Lord Raglan longed to convert their retirement into a rout, but the French had discarded their knapsacks before fording the river, and on the plea, that without their kits it was impossible to pursue, the marshal refused to agree to the plan. Consequently a hard-won victory, which might easily, by energetic action, have been changed into one of the greatest importance, proved of little use, and hardly affected the latter part of the campaign at all. It was a lamentable mistake, for had the Russian forces been driven pell-mell from the field, Sebastopol might have surrendered, and thousands of brave and valuable lives on both sides might have been saved. As it was, a glorious victory had been achieved at great cost to British and Russians alike, and all that could be said was that the Crimean campaign had opened favourably for the Allies.

The victorious army that defeats one portion of the enemy's troops, and thereby causes the whole force to retire, achieves a success which, brilliant though it may be, is as nothing compared with that obtained when the whole of the opposing force is hopelessly crushed and afterwards captured or driven, a mere herd of terror-stricken beings, from the field. For the Allies the Alma was a glorious victory, but no more. The fact that the general and his staff were isolated from the attacking army at the critical moment, and that in consequence the troops advanced at wide intervals, while the reserves were never called into action, ruined all hopes of a really great and telling success. Had it been otherwise, had the British divisions been poured unceasingly upon the Russians, they would have engaged the whole of Menschikoffs great army, and so severely handled it as to hopelessly mar its future effectiveness.

It was a sad, sad army that bivouacked that night near the river Alma. Comrades and dear friends were missing; while the flickering lights hovering over hill and valley showed that the search-parties were at work, the doctors busy at their merciful and pain-relieving duties, and the burial-parties delving to prepare huge trenches for the reception of the dead. It was a terrible ending indeed to a glorious day, but one that ever follows the crash and turmoil of a battle. It is impossible to realise its sadness, its awful horror, till you stand beside one of these trenches, and, with helmet in hand and the bright sun overhead, read the last rites over your comrades of a few hours ago, who have been called suddenly, and by the aid of your fellow-men, from beside you.

For two days the Allies remained here, and then, loading arabas, they advanced by easy stages on Sebastopol. To attack the town and fortress from the northern side was impossible, for the harbour intervened, and in consequence the march was resumed till finally the British left approached the harbour of Balaclava; the rest of the allied forces extended along the slopes of the Chersonese heights surrounding the town, and prepared to throw up earthworks in readiness for a gigantic bombardment.

Meanwhile the Russians in Sebastopol were by no means idle. All civilians left the town and forts, and, under the great Todleben, their engineer, thousands set to work with pick and spade to improve their defences on the south and mount extra guns, relying on their huge army in the field to keep the allied enemy busy. Unlimited supplies poured into the town, and thus, though the Allies were besieging it on the southern side, and the harbour-mouth was blockaded by the opposing fleet, it was in a position to hold out for an indefinite period.

Meanwhile what had become of our hero?

A burly, grey-clad Cossack had charge of Phil, and noticing that he was exhausted after the struggle in which he had been engaged, he turned and spoke kindly to him.

"We will go along easily till you have got your wind," he said. "You must be tired after such a fight. My word, what gluttons you English are for hard knocks and desperate battles! I watched from the summit of the hill and saw you and your comrade rush to the rescue of the flag. It was a mad act, Englishman, but bravely done. But come, I am forgetting. You are a comrade in distress. Take a sip from this bottle. It is vodka with a little water added, and will put new life into you."

Phil thanked him heartily, and as soon as they were out of range of the British batteries, sat down on a boulder and took a pull at the Cossack's flask.

"Thank you, my friend!" he exclaimed earnestly. "A short rest here will do me a world of good. Have we far to go to-night?"

"What! You speak our language, Englishman! Good!" and the Russian's broad and rugged face lit up with a kindly smile. "Yes," he continued, "we have a long way to go. But you are tired. Give me your word that you will not attempt to throw me, or get the better of me, and I will let you mount behind on the crupper. Come, there is no one about, and before we join the squadron again you can dismount."

Phil readily gave the required promise, and, vaulting up behind the friendly Cossack, they pushed on amongst the retreating infantry.

"What has become of my comrades?" asked Phil after a pause, for he was terribly afraid that Tony and the officer were killed.

"Comfort yourself, Englishman, they too are prisoners, and you will meet them at the camp; but I doubt whether they will reach there so easily as you, for Alexoff has charge of your soldier friend, while the brave wounded officer walks by the side of our commander, who is not too kind to us, and hates all Englishmen bitterly. Yes, I fear it will go hard with him, for we have lost heavily, and Stackanoff will not easily forget it."

"And is Stackanoff your commander?" asked Phil.

"Yes, that is his name. His excellency rules us with a rod of iron. Ah! my English comrade, there is a little girl waiting for me about half a verst from Moscow town, and I long to break from this life and return to her. I have served my time, and should have been free long ago, but Stackanoff keeps me. Ah, how I hate him! Some day, perhaps, I shall repay him, and meanwhile I will fight for my country, for she has need of us all."

"Yes, it will be a big struggle," agreed Phil, "and if your comrades fight as pluckily as they did to-day, Russia will need many brave men to fill the gaps."

The Cossack gave a hearty grunt of satisfaction, for, though longing to reach Moscow, he was at heart a patriot, and liked to hear his brothers-in-arms well spoken of.

"We are friends from this day," he said, grasping Phil's hand. "But prepare to get down. We are nearing our bivouac, and it would not do to let Stackanoff see you mounted behind me. Wait, though, I will tell you when to jump off."

Putting his horse into a gentle trot the Cossack jogged towards a collection of tents and horsemen. Suddenly there was a shout from behind them, and just as Phil and his captor joined a squadron of Cossacks, a small, fierce-looking man, with a bristling moustache and a face deeply pitted by smallpox, cantered up, dragging beside him an unhappy captive, who was scarcely able to retain his feet.

Phil's blood boiled, for he recognised in an instant that the prisoner was the officer who had so bravely carried the colour.

Pulling his horse in with an angry jerk close alongside Phil's captor, Stackanoff—for it was none other than he—glared at him, and in a harsh voice, and with many an oath, snarled: "How is this, Vilnoff! What do you mean? Are these cursed prisoners then to ride upon his majesty's horses? Come off, you Englishman!" and, dropping his reins, he stretched out his hand, and, clutching Phil by the shoulder, hurled him to the ground.

It was not very far to fall, but Phil came an undoubted cropper, and the sudden and unlooked-for jar, and a yell of derision which rose from the Cossack ranks at the sight, set his blood aflame still more, for he had not yet shaken off the excitement of the recent battle. His eyes flashed angrily, and, picking himself up, he was within an ace of throwing himself upon the brutal Stackanoff when better counsels prevailed.

The Cossack commander eyed him suspiciously, and then, with a malicious glance at Vilnoff and the remark, "You, beast that you are, I will deal with you to-morrow," dug his spurs into his horse with such force that the animal sprang forward so suddenly as to upset the unhappy English officer and drag him along the ground.

"Come, get up, you weak-kneed fool," cried Stackanoff, striking at the poor fellow with his riding-whip.

It was a brutal act, and even the Cossack horsemen were ashamed of it. As for Phil, a blind and unreasoning rage seized him, and, dragging the lasso-noose over his head, he sprang at the Russian, and, lifting him like a child from the saddle, threw him heavily on the ground and stood over him, ready to knock him down if he should try to rise, or treat any other in a similar manner who dared to interfere with him.

"Hurrah, well done, Phil, old boy!" came an excited bellow from the Cossack ranks; and next moment Tony, who was there, a prisoner, had torn the rope which held him from the hands of the man who was in charge of him, and, aiming blows right and left with his fists, rushed forward and joined Phil.

To say that there was a clamour in the camp is to describe the scene mildly. For a moment the horsemen were too astonished to move; then, recovering from their surprise, they lowered their murderous-looking lances, and would undoubtedly have run all three prisoners through, had not another officer ridden into the circle at that moment.

He was a tall, dark man, with heavy features and a settled look of depression on his face. Mounted on a magnificent horse, and bearing the badges of a staff-officer, there was no doubt that he was a person of no little importance and authority.

"What is the meaning of this?" he demanded, quietly looking round with a cold and gleaming eye, which showed that though outwardly calm he was more than angry at the incident. "These are prisoners, by their uniform, and one an officer too. Do we then murder captives taken in battle? Does our august master, the Czar, will it that we should take the lives of gallant Englishmen in cold blood? Answer me, dogs! Whose doing is this?" And, slowly glancing round the circle, he fixed the men with his eyes, each one trembling in his turn and feeling relieved when his scrutiny was finished.

Then Vilnoff, who had remained close beside Phil all the time, turned in his saddle and humbly told the officer what had happened.

"Ah, is it so, man?" the latter replied thoughtfully. "Stackanoff captures prisoners, and leads them away in nooses, as he would drag an ox. And one is wounded, too. Get down, man, and shake this commander of yours."

Vilnoff obeyed, doing as his officer ordered him, and at the same time administering a sly kick. Stackanoff at length opened his eyes, and, struggling to his feet, stared at the new-comer. Meanwhile Phil and Tony had relieved their wounded officer of his noose, and were holding him erect between them.

"Tell me," began the staff-officer, fixing the Cossack commander with a piercing look, "tell me, my good friend, why you would kill our prisoners. Have not the enemy many of our brave comrades in their hands? Do they drag them with ropes and fling the wounded ones to the ground? Dog!—worse than dog!—your command is taken from you. This night our sappers return to the fortress and you with them. Go now before I do worse for you!"

Like a beaten cur the Cossack commander saluted, humbly bowed, calling the staff-officer "Prince", and then retired.

Now was Phil's chance of asking for good treatment for the wounded officer, and, leaving Tony to support the poor fellow, he advanced to the Russian prince, and, standing politely at attention, begged that a doctor might be sent for.

"So it seems that besides doing your best to kill one of my officers, you are acquainted with our language," said the prince with a smile, "Yes, my man, your officer shall have good treatment, and so shall you. Here, you! your name?

Ah—Vilnoff—then you will take charge of these men for to-night. Send this wounded gentleman into the fortress with any of our own that may be leaving. A column has been ordered to start soon after daybreak."

Turning his horse, he nodded to Phil and cantered away.

"My word, but there will be trouble!" said Vilnoff after a few moments' silence. "That demon Stackanoff is disgraced, and he will never forget. He will learn that it was I—Vilnoff—who told the prince the whole truth, and he will repay me. Ah, he will not forget! And you, too, you Englishmen; he will take his revenge on you also. A Cossack never forgives. But there will be time to talk of this. Come with me. You can be free and lie with me beneath my blankets if you will only promise to stay and not give me the slip."

Phil held a few moments' hurried conversation with Tony before giving the desired promise.

"We must remember that we are prisoners, Tony," he said, "and though this good fellow, Vilnoff, is evidently inclined to be most friendly, and act differently from the majority of his comrades, thereby making our lot easier, yet we have a duty to perform. We must escape at the earliest opportunity and try to rejoin our comrades."

"Should think so," Tony grunted. "If it hadn't been for this here chap there's no saying what would have happened. Most like we should have been run through with their pig-stickers same as poor old Sam. Those Cossacks gave me a taste of their gentle treatment on the way here. They trotted pretty nearly all the way, and if I dragged a bit on the rope, the brute who was in charge of me just picked up the slack of his lasso and whopped me over the shoulders. I can feel the sting yet. He was a big black-bearded chap, and I shall know him and be able to talk to him in the proper way next time we meets, see if I sha'n't. Yes, Phil, we've got to get out of this as quick as we can. As for the promise to Vilnoff, you do as you like."

"Very well," said Phil, turning to the Cossack. "How long are we likely to be in your charge?" he asked.

"Only till to-morrow, Englishman. Then we Cossacks will leave the camp and act as outposts and scouts, while you and your friend may be sent into the fortress. In any case, you will be handed over to the infantry. Do not fear. I will speak a word for you."

"Then we promise not to attempt to escape while in your charge, Vilnoff."

"Good!" exclaimed the Cossack. "You will promise, and that is enough, for we have heard that an Englishman prides himself upon his honour. After I have left you can do as you wish," he added, smiling in their faces. "And perhaps it were better that you should risk anything rather than Stackanoff's vengeance. Ah, that man is a brute! Now, follow me, and I will see what can be done in the way of food."

Following the friendly Russian, Phil and Tony at length entered the Cossack lines, and, passing between the horses, reached the farther end, where Vilnoff rapidly removed his saddle and bridle, and, picketing his shaggy animal, went in search of some grain.

"The sooner we are out of this the better," muttered Phil. "Just look round without attracting attention, Tony. These Cossacks are scowling at us as if they would like to cut our throats."

Tony drew an extremely black pipe from his pocket, and, holding a cake of plug tobacco above the bowl, dexterously cut shavings with his knife, ramming them down with his finger till the pipe was filled. Then he placed it in his mouth, and, calmly stepping over to a fire, which was burning close at hand, he lifted a blazing stick and applied it to the weed, turning as he did so, and swiftly gazing round the Cossack lines. A crowd of the horsemen were standing a few yards away, scowling heavily at their prisoners and muttering amongst themselves.

"Ugh! a bigger set of blackguards I never see," Tony remarked calmly. "'Git', as the Yankees say, is the word for us, Phil. It'll be safe to-night with Vilnoff, but to-morrow, when he's gone, they'll pass on their tale to the other coves who've got to look after us, and a precious poor time of it well have."

At this moment Vilnoff returned, and, beckoning to his prisoners, led them to where his blankets and saddle lay. The former were spread upon the ground, and Phil and Tony sat down on them.

"The horse is fed and watered, and now we will look to ourselves," said Vilnoff, with a friendly smile. "I have managed to get an extra allowance of meat, and here is plenty of bread. Now we will have a fire to ourselves;" and stepping across he quickly returned with a blazing stake. Round this sticks from a bundle tied to his saddle were piled, and soon a cheerful fire was burning. Over the blaze was placed an iron tripod, from which a small kettle full of water was suspended, and into this the meat was thrown, after having been cut into small pieces.

For an hour the three sat gazing at the blazing embers, while Phil and Vilnoff discussed the prospects of the campaign. At last the stew was ready. The Russian produced three tin plates and as many mugs, and soon they were enjoying their meal. A small tot of vodka, diluted with water, followed, and then, having smoked a last pipe, and being thoroughly tired out, Phil and Tony lay full length on the rugs, while Vilnoff, producing an enormous kaross of sheep-skin, spread it over them, crawled beneath it himself, and with a guttural

"Good-night, Englishman!" placed his head on his saddle, and was quickly in the land of dreams. As for Phil and Tony, they were worn out, and scarcely had they turned over when they too were asleep, in blissful forgetfulness of the stirring events of the day, and of the dead and dying, who lay not ten miles away on the blood-stained slopes of the Alma.

The next morning the Cossack lines were early astir, and horses and men were fully ready to set out when two officers came towards them, one dressed as a Cossack, and leading his horse. The men were quickly drawn up, and having explained that he was their new commander, the Cossack officer turned to his companion and formally handed over the two prisoners.

"There, comrade," he said, "take them and look well after them. I heat they have already done harm enough, though, indeed, I cannot say much against them, for Stackanoff was too harsh with the wounded prisoner, and, besides, his dismissal has given me this command and a chance of distinguishing myself, and having my name brought before our master the Czar."

The infantry officer answered that he hoped the long-looked-for opportunity would not take long in coming, and beckoning to four men who had followed him, ordered them to march the prisoners off.

Phil and Tony shook hands heartily with Vilnoff, and the former thanked him for his kindness.

"If ever we meet again, Vilnoff," he said, "perhaps we shall be able to do as much for you, and in any case, when we get back to our friends, as we mean to do, we shall tell them how good one of the Cossack horsemen has been to us. Now, good-bye and good luck! I hope Stackanoff will do you no harm, and that before long you will be seeking the girl you spoke of near Moscow."

"Ah!" the Russian grunted, while a broad grin overspread his usually grave features, "you give me hope, Englishman. Good-bye, and may the blessed Virgin see you safely to your friends!"

Phil and Tony were surrounded at this moment by their infantry guard, and marched smartly away to the rear of the camp. Here they were ordered to enter a large shed adjoining a farmhouse, and this they found was filled with other prisoners like themselves.

"Halloo, mates," voices sang out, "when were you taken? What's going to happen to us?"

Phil hastily explained, and then suddenly seeing the wounded officer who had borne the colour on the previous day, and who had been removed from the Cossack lines a few minutes after the brutal Stackanoff's dismissal, he walked over to him and asked him how he felt.

"Much better, thanks to you, Corporal," answered the young fellow. "The doctor dressed my wound, and then got this mattress for me. After all, it was only a flesh wound, and but for severe loss of blood I should have been all right and the colour saved. It is sad to think that it was captured."

"The colour is all right," answered Phil. "As I was dragged away I saw that the Highlanders had rescued it."

"That's good news! Excellent news!" exclaimed the young officer in tones of relief. "Look here, Corporal, my name is McNeil, and I am sending in an account of our little affair. The doctor here has promised to have it taken over to our lines under a flag of truce. What is your name and your friend's? I am going to recommend you both for distinguished gallantry."

Phil gave the required information, and after a few more words returned to Tony flushed with happiness and pride that he and his friend had so early won praise for their deeds.

Half an hour later four Russians entered, and, lifting the wounded officer, carried him outside, and with great gentleness placed him in an araba. The other prisoners were ordered to file out, and in a few minutes they were marching, surrounded by guards, for the grim fortress of Sebastopol. Phil and Tony longed to escape, for once behind the stone walls of Sebastopol there would be little hope. But no opportunity occurred, and by nightfall they, with their comrades, were safely under lock and key, the officer having been taken to separate quarters.

Chapter Twelve.

Close Prisoners.

It was a wearisome time that Phil and his friend spent in prison. Confined in a huge stone building, they passed the greater part of the day in a court-yard open to the sky. Here they discussed with their comrades every possible means of escape, but they could hit on no plan that was likely to be successful. The windows were small and heavily barred, sentries with loaded weapons stood all round the walls of the court-yard, and at night occupied a room commanding the prison, being separated from it by a wall perforated for rifle fire.

"Don't worry, Tony, old chap," said Phil one day, seeing that his friend was becoming despondent. "Our chance will come yet, and we shall get away. If we don't, the Allies may take the place by storm and set us free. After all, we have little to complain of, for our quarters are moderately comfortable, and our food, though plain, is plentiful."

"Right yer are, Phil! I'll cheer up," answered Tony brightly. "When I comes to think of it, we ain't got much to grumble at. Think of them poor chaps as had arms and legs blown off at the Alma—we're far better off than they. But I expects this being caged up ain't for long, and any day the army will be breaking in, as you say, and setting us free."

And indeed, had the prisoners but known it, the Allies were hard at work preparing to take the fortress and town. To do so from the north was, as has already been said, impossible, for the harbour was far too broad to allow of an effective bombardment, and, moreover, its northern shore was commanded by heavy batteries. Therefore, as we have seen, the Allies marched to the Chersonese heights, the British left resting upon Balaclava, while the French lay to our right. Opposite them was the southern face of Sebastopol, up till then undefended by very formidable works, though the plan of defences had long ago been sketched and partially executed. But no sooner was the object of the allied army discovered than hordes of Russians quickly transformed this side of the fortress, throwing up powerful earthworks, and arming them with guns drawn from the inexhaustible arsenals at the dockyard. And while they slaved, the British and French planned their own earthworks, and set fatigue-parties to work. By October 16th they were completed, and after a council of war, in which naval as well as military officers took part, it was decided that the bombardment should commence on the morrow, the batteries on the Chersonese heights doing their utmost to reduce the works in front of them, while the ships engaged the forts on the sea-face to distract attention. The cannonade was to be followed by a general assault.

A moment's reflection will show the reader that nothing could have been wiser than a preliminary battering with cannon-shot, followed by an assault; but how the ships could have aided in one or the other it is difficult to understand. As the forts were placed on elevated plateaux, and in some cases on the cliffs, an assault by means of landing-parties was out of the question. Therefore the Russian commander would not, and did not, trouble to garrison them with infantry, but merely assured their having a sufficiency of gunners to replace possible casualties. Then again, compared with a heavily-armed stone fort, what is a wooden ship? It was a hopeless and a foolish undertaking, and it is not surprising that the allied fleet retired, having done little damage, although they had suffered severely themselves.

On shore things were perhaps a little more satisfactory. Three star shells fired from Mount Rudolph, the French battery, gave the signal for the bombardment at an early hour on October 17th, and from that moment for four awful hours the Allies' combined 126 heavy guns poured a hail of shell into the Russian defences. These consisted of outworks and of various forts of formidable power known as the Flagstaff Bastion, the Malakoff, and the Redan, the whole armed with 118 guns, not to mention a thousand and more of lighter casting to be used in case of assault.

But for an untoward event Sebastopol might have fallen on that very day, and the Crimea as a campaign have sunk into comparative historical insignificance. After four hours' firing a shell unluckily struck the magazine of Mount Rudolph, and with a roar which shook the surrounding camp the battery was destroyed. The French fire at once ceased, and was not renewed for two days. As for the British, they battered the Malakoff, reducing the stone-work to ruin, and silenced its guns. Soon afterwards the magazine of the Redan exploded, and though our fire still continued furiously, it was answered only feebly and at intervals, showing that the enemy too had suffered heavily like the French.

And now let us consider, before returning to Phil and his comrades, why an assault was not delivered either at once, or on the following morning. But for the calamity to the French this would have occurred; owing, however, to the destruction of their chief battery, and the consequent failure to destroy the defences in front of them, assault became almost impracticable, while now that they were to some extent demoralised, it was utterly hopeless. Also it must be borne in mind that the force in Sebastopol was greatly superior in numbers to the Allies, while an attack in rear by the Russian army in the field was always to be dreaded, and, as will be seen, was not long in actually occurring. As to an assault on the following day, dawn showed that it was useless to attempt it, for the brave and energetic enemy had already reconstructed the defences, and made good all the damage that had been done.

Almost a whole month had passed from the date of their incarceration, when one morning the prisoners in Sebastopol were awakened by a roar of exploding artillery.

"What's that?" asked Phil, starting up suddenly and throwing off his blanket. "Listen, you fellows! Yes, there it goes again. That banging is the Russian artillery. Wait a minute and we shall hear our own at work."

A moment later a distant, muttering growl told them that the Allies were answering the fire, while, had there been any doubt, a peculiar shriek overhead, which all had heard before, and the fall of a wall close at hand, told them that a shell from the far-off guns had found a mark.

"Blow me!" exclaimed Tony excitedly. "Supposing one of them shells found its way in here!"

"What, yer ain't afraid!" jeered a big rifleman who was amongst the prisoners. "You 'as helped to save the colours, too!"

"Afraid! Booby! I'll punch yer head if yer don't mind what yer saying," retorted Tony hotly. "It ain't that I was thinking of, but of trying to get out of this. Supposing a hole got knocked in the wall, couldn't we chaps climb through it, and shy bricks at the sentries. Then we'd make a rush for it. You may bet all these Russian soldiers are busy in the forts."

A grunt of assent went round the gathered prisoners, and far from being nervous or anxious lest a shell should knock the house about their ears, they sat there longing to hear the crash and make a dash for liberty.

That such an eventuality might occur had evidently struck the Russians, for that night the doors of the prison were thrown open, and the prisoners ordered out with their blankets. Then they were marched under a strong guard to the harbour and ferried across.

"Where do we go?" Phil asked the soldier who sat in the boat by his side.

"That you will see," was the gruff reply. "But you leave the Crimea at once, and I do not envy you your long march. It is fine weather now, but as you get north you will meet the rains and cold winds, and you will wish yourself back in Sebastopol."

Arrived on the northern bank of the harbour, the prisoners were grouped together, and a meal of hot coffee and bread given them. Then they set out, two ranks of armed guards marching on either side, while some twenty fierce-looking Cossacks hovered here and there, only too ready and willing to transfix any man sufficiently foolhardy to attempt an escape.

"This won't do," muttered Phil, whose wits had been at work. "It won't do," he repeated almost unconsciously.

"What won't?" asked Tony brusquely. "It ain't over nice, I know, but I can't see that anything's extra wrong."

"Where do you think we are marching to, Tony?" asked Phil. "You don't know. Then I'll tell you. We are going due north, out of the Crimea and into some part of the Russian interior. Once there, what chance shall we have of ever getting back?"

"There you puzzle me, Phil," Tony answered, scratching his head. "I suppose it's a long way off."

"Yes, a long way, Tony; but that is not the difficulty. The weather is on the point of changing, and soon we shall have rain and snow. We must get away within the next few days or not at all, so keep your eyes open for the first chance that comes along."

"Trust me, mate," whispered Tony, unconsciously dropping his voice. "I don't want to spend the next year or so in a Russian prison. A month's been enough for me. But it'll be a job to get away from these fellows: and what shall we do for food once we are free?"

"That we must chance, Tony. The main thing is to get safely away, and, of course, we must make the attempt when it is dark. To-night our guards, knowing we are close to the allied camp, will be extra watchful, but a couple of nights later, when we are well on the way, and the Russian field-army is between us and our friends, they are certain to become slack and careless about keeping a watch. That will be our time, and we must make the best of it. There are plenty of small farmhouses scattered about this part of the Crimea, for it is famous for its vineyards, and if the worst comes to the worst, we must break into one and obtain food in that way. In any case there are grapes to be had in abundance."

Having agreed that it was useless to attempt an escape for two days or more, and that it was unnecessary to inform their comrades of their intentions—for where two might chance to slip away, it was hopeless for fifty or more to make the attempt,—Phil and Tony marched on stolidly. Amongst the prisoners were Riflemen, Guards, and Highlanders, some slightly wounded, and all more or less in a tattered and forlorn condition, for head-gear had been for the most part lost, and the bright red of tunics had long ago been dulled by lying on the dirt and mud.

That night they pressed on, and halted only when the field-army was reached. Then they bivouacked and waited till the following day, when the march was resumed in a leisurely manner, the guards, however, still keeping careful watch over their prisoners, while the fierce and restless Cossacks rode their shaggy ponies on either flank and kept a scowling eye on the captives.

Phil and Tony saved some portion of their meal of bread daily, cramming it into their pockets. But it was not till the third night that they dared to attempt an escape.

"Keep an eye on those Cossack fellows as we bivouack, Tony," said Phil in an undertone, as the column came to a halt. "They are the ones we have most to fear. Up to this, I notice that half of them have nightly gone out as pickets, ready to cut off any escape, while the others have camped alongside us. If only we can see the positions the outposts take up, and get away from here without rousing an alarm, we ought to be able to hide up in some vineyard."

Lying down on the ground, as if tired out, the two watched eagerly, and carefully noted the position of the Cossacks. Riding some three hundred yards from their comrades, each of these wiry horsemen leapt from his pony, removed the bit and slipped it under its jaw, and left it there with the reins on the neck, so that in a few moments it could be replaced. Girths were then loosened, and while the animal cropped the grass its watchful master trudged backwards and forwards, lance in hand, and with his face always turned towards the distant camp.

"Sebastopol lies over there," said Phil, nodding in the direction they had come, "and we must make a bolt for it some other way. The outposts are certain to be more vigilant behind us. Look at that fellow over there on our right. I have had my eye on him these last two days; he is evidently lazy and careless of his duties, especially now that no Cossack officer is with the horsemen guarding us."

Tony glanced in the direction indicated, and noted that the man Phil had called his attention to was standing by his pony's side, with one elbow resting on the saddle, and his head on his hand, as if already asleep.

"Yes, that's the beggar for us, Phil," he whispered. "If we crawl over there we ought to be able to slip by him unawares. To-night will be fairly light—just sufficient for us to spot him at twenty yards,—and once we know where he is, it won't be much of a job to slip between him and the next."

At dusk a meal was served, and having eaten their portion, Phil and Tony threw themselves down upon a blanket, and spread the second over them, for the nights were already chilly, and they had discovered that with only one blanket apiece greater warmth and comfort could be obtained in this way.

122

"It won't do to fall asleep now," whispered Phil. "We have had a tiring uphill march, and are both in need of a snooze and inclined to take it. Let us talk about something interesting, so as to keep awake."

Tony yawned loudly and rubbed his eyes.

"I was precious near off then," he answered. "Tell yer what, Phil, teach me a few words of this Russian lingo. That'll wake me up."

Accordingly Phil commenced with the simpler words, and when Tony had heard and repeated as many as he was likely to remember, they commenced to chat about their life in the menagerie, taking care only to whisper, and keeping a vigilant watch upon the sentries close at hand.

"We must clear out of this about an hour before midnight," whispered Phil. "The sentries are changed at twelve o'clock, and the Cossack outposts too. If we wait till then they are all sure to be wide-awake in expectation of relief, and after midnight there will be little chance of slipping past the fresh ones. As it is, I see it will be a far more difficult job than we had imagined."

"That's so," grunted Tony, staring at the nearest sentry. "In course if we could get alongside that feller we could double him up like a rag before he'd got time to shout, and I doubt that the ones on either side can see him. But I fear it would be a failure. We'd never be able to get close enough to smash him before he pulled his trigger."

"I have it, Tony," whispered Phil after a few minutes' silence, during which he cudgelled his brains for a means of escape. "We should never get away together, for where one might slip through two would be certain to be discovered. Fortunately many of our comrades are still moving about or sitting up talking, so that my little scheme has a chance of working. Tony, we must have a row and separate."

"Have a row, Phil? That we don't, while I can help it!" exclaimed Tony hotly.

"Not a real one, Tony," answered Phil, with a smothered laugh. "We must pretend. Listen. It now wants two hours before we must make our attempt, and we must do our best to judge that time pretty nearly. No doubt the sentry has noticed that we have been lying quietly as if asleep, for he has passed close by us several times. Let us peep out, and wait till he is near again, then you must roll over and pull the blanket from me as if in your sleep. The movement is certain to attract his attention. I will then start up and tear the blanket away from you, and after that we can easily come to words and almost to blows. No doubt the sentry will watch us and enjoy our quarrel, and as soon as we have made sufficient noise, I will get up in a regular huff, pull my blanket from you, and go to the other end of the camp. Two hours later I shall do my best to creep between the sentries, and once through I will imitate the whinny of a horse. The men on guard will think it comes from one of the Cossack ponies, and are not likely to stir, while you, knowing it is my signal, will take the first chance of slipping through and joining me."

A suppressed chuckle burst from Tony's lips, and the blanket shook as he attempted to smother his amusement and delight.

"Phil, you're a good 'un," he stuttered. "Yer fairly walk away with it. Blest if yer ain't the smartest chap I ever see! There ain't nothing more to be said. It's bound to work is that there scheme, so the sooner we has that row the better. But—look here, old man, how do we join one another out there in the dark?"

"That I was just going to mention, Tony. Once through, crawl on for a hundred yards, and then sit down. You must take care to go straight to your front. I am going to lie down over there on the right, and I shall know you are on the left. I shall give you a quarter of an hour to get through, and then I shall crawl over in your direction. If after a good search I fail to find you I will give another whinny, and you must crawl up to me. Now is everything clear?"

"Everything, mate," answered Tony, with evident delight. "We just plays this little game, and then I waits for the signal. Once through, there comes that Cossack chap, and if he so much as flickers an eyelid, bust me if I don't smash him like an egg. Now, mate, give us yer flipper, cos, yer know, things might go wrong, and I specks those Russian coves have a nasty way of shooting if they spots a fellow giving them the slip."

Phil stretched out his hand, and meeting Tony's, gave it a cordial grip. Then for some ten minutes the two lay still, Tony snoring heavily, while the sentry passed them twice on his beat, humming a tune as he did so. Close at hand were the other prisoners, some asleep, while others sat up round a fire smoking a last pipe.

"Now, here goes," whispered Tony, and with a loud snort he rolled over on his opposite side, clutching the blanket and dragging it from Phil.

The action was beautifully timed, for the sentry was just opposite them and within a few paces, and halted to see what would happen.

Phil awoke suddenly, sat up, and shivered. Then he felt for the blanket as if expecting to find it over his knees, but failing to hit upon it he looked at his sleeping comrade, and instantly, and with an exclamation of wrath, seized the blanket and dragged it away.

"Here, what are yer up to?" growled Tony hoarsely, sitting up and grabbing at the blanket. "Want it all yerself, yer greedy beggar? Let go, will yer?" They struggled together, while their anger apparently rose till they were on the point of blows.

"Whose blanket is it then?" cried Phil angrily. "It's mine, and I mean to have it. There's yours; you're lying on it. Stick to it, and I'll stick to mine; but not here. I've had enough of you. Every night it's the same. I'm getting worn out for want of sleep."

"Hurrah! here's them two bosom friends a-fighting," laughed a linesman who formed one of the number round the fire. "Have it out, boys. We're getting stale for want of a little fun, and now's just the time for a fight."

Phil and Tony took no notice of this encouragement, but, tearing the blanket angrily from his friend, Phil trudged away with it to the other end of the sleeping line, leaving the sentry, who had watched the whole scene, doubled up with laughter, which was loudly echoed by the men sitting round the fire.

"Stop that noise," came a harsh voice at this moment from the tent occupied by the officer in charge of the party; and instantly the sentry commenced to tramp his beat, while the prisoners rose and went to their hard and uncomfortable couches.

Phil chose a spot between two sleeping figures on the right, and, throwing himself down, apparently fell into a deep sleep. But part of his face was uncovered, and his eyes were fixed in the direction of the sentry, whose figure was now indistinguishable in the darkness. A weary hour and a half dragged by, and then he prepared to make the attempt. Leaving his blanket, he crept on all-fours through the grass, and within five minutes was safely through the sentries, where, having put a sufficient distance between them and himself he sat down and indulged in a whinny—a curious collection of sounds which every school-boy is an adept at, having, no doubt, times out of number, tried the nerves of some irascible master by repeating them from the remote and unobserved depths of his class-room, together with cat-calls and other pleasantries. Half an hour later Phil and Tony had met, and were crawling away towards the Cossack outposts. Stealing through the long grass, and avoiding stones and small patches of corn which were spread thereabouts, they were soon near the post occupied by the horsemen.

"We'll get alongside that wall," whispered Phil, pulling Tony's sleeve in the direction he meant. "It is not a long one, and by crawling to the end and squeezing against it, we ought to be able to see our gentleman without ourselves being observed."

Accordingly they crept to the wall, which surrounded a potato field, and advancing cautiously were soon at the corner, where, lying side by side, they searched the darkness for the Cossack horseman.

"Can't see him anywhere," muttered Phil in an undertone.

"Here, what's that?" asked Tony excitedly, pointing in front of him.

Before Phil had time to answer, there was a hoarse cry of astonishment, and a figure which had been leaning upon the wall just round the corner started out, and, lowering a lance, rushed at them. The weapon struck the ground between them, narrowly missing Phil's arm. Next moment Tony had sprung at the Cossack with a low cry, and had felled him to the ground with a powerful blow from his fist.

"Didn't I say I'd do for yer if yer winked yer blessed eye?" he said breathlessly. "Move again and I'll stick yer through with the lance."

But even if the Russian had been able to understand, he was not in the condition which would allow him to prove offensive, for the fist had crashed like a sledge-hammer into his face, and he now lay motionless and stunned upon the ground. Phil picked up the lance, and while they lay still, in case the slight noise should have aroused the next outpost he produced his knife and commenced to cut it in half. It was soon done, and, keeping the head armed with the spear-point, he handed the other to Tony, and they once more rose to their knees and crept stealthily away into the darkness. Ten minutes later they were walking briskly in the direction of Sebastopol.

Chapter Thirteen.

The Highroad to Liberty.

When they had placed half a mile or more between themselves and the Russian outposts, Phil caught Tony by the sleeve and came to a halt.

"We'll have a breather and a consultation now, old chap," he said with a cheery note in his voice. "We're safely through so far, but there's a lot to be done before we reach our comrades. It was bad luck our hitting up against that fellow, for when the outposts are relieved at midnight he will be found, and our flight discovered. So we may take it that we have barely an hour's start."

"It were bad luck," agreed Tony, "but I don't see as though it weren't worser for him. We hit up against the beggar, but I can tell yer the knock he give us wasn't nothing to the smasher I got in on his face. It fairly knocked the senses out of him, and will teach him to mind his own business in future."

"Now, what's to be done, Tony?" asked Phil. "We have an hour's start, and barely that. I am for making across to the road, and trotting along it at our best pace. They are sure to send horsemen back by that way, and we shall be able to hear them if we keep our ears open. Then we will slip across the grass and hide up in some vineyard, where I expect we shall do well to stay until the search is over."

"Look here, Phil, you're bossing this show," said Tony with some emphasis. "I haven't a doubt but what yer proposes is the best, so let's get off at once."

Having settled the point they promptly swung to the right, and soon were on the post-road. Then, taking to their heels, they ran steadily along it. Every ten minutes they halted for a few moments to listen, but, hearing nothing, set out again. In this way they had covered some five or six miles before shouts and galloping hoofs striking hard upon the road behind them caught their ears. Instantly they turned on to the grass, and, climbing a wall, ran through a large cultivated field and hid themselves in a patch of corn beyond. It was well that they did so, for when opposite the wall the pursuing Cossacks halted, while two of their number dismounted, and, vaulting over it, searched in its shadow for them.

Finding nothing they returned to their companions, and soon the beat of hoofs again resounded along the post-road. Phil and Tony were congratulating themselves on their safety thus far, when the latter, who had pushed his head up through the ears of corn, strained his eyes towards the road, and clutching Phil by the shoulders, whispered, "Hush! I hear something." Both listened intently, but for some minutes could neither see nor hear anything; the moon, however, was rising, and very soon they were able to make out a solitary horseman patrolling the road.

"That settles it," muttered Phil. "Of course by creeping up to the wall we might manage to silence that fellow, but it would do more harm than good. At present they are uncertain of our whereabouts, but his disappearance would tell them at once that we were in the immediate neighbourhood. As it is, I doubt if they will think we have got so far, for the sentries are certain to declare that they noticed our sleeping figures up to the last moment. Tony, we must make a move, and find some better hiding-place than this."

Stealing through the corn-patch they were not long in reaching its margin, and then, to their chagrin, nothing but open fields met their view.

"I fear it means lying where we are," said Phil dejectedly. "We might easily slip across unobserved, but as far as one can see in this light there is not a vineyard or cover of any sort in sight. We must do something, for a couple of horsemen would quickly rout us out of this."

"I seem to remember some kind of house along this way," muttered Tony, trying to recall the spot. "Yes, I'm sure of it, and it's away over there, half a mile or more, I should think;" and he stretched his arm and pointed to the right.

"Then we'll try to find it," said Phil with decision. "There is nothing else for it, and we cannot be in a worse spot than we occupy now. I blame myself for not having kept a better watch on our surroundings as we passed along the road with our escort. That Cossack has ridden away a little, so now is our time; we'll strike straight across, and trust to luck. We haven't time to pick roads, for it will be dawn in another hour. If they come over here they are certain to see our footmarks, but no doubt we shall get on to grassy land soon, and that will throw them off the scent."

Standing up for a few moments, to make sure that no enemy was near, they plunged into the fields and walked steadily on for an hour; but still no house was in sight. Half an hour later, when they were almost in despair, and when a faint flush in the east and a waning of the pale, silvery gleams of the moon heralded the approach of dawn, they caught sight of some outbuildings on their left, and were hurrying towards them, when Phil suddenly saw some ghostly-looking horsemen issuing from behind them, and clutching hold of Tony, dragged him forcibly into a narrow ditch which he was in the act of crossing.

"What's up?" asked Tony, somewhat nettled; but Phil's whispered reply, "Cossacks! Hush!" appeased him.

The ditch was half-filled with water, but a thorough sousing is preferable to captivity, and the two companions squeezed still closer into it, wedging themselves into its slime and mud, and thrusting their bodies as far as possible beneath the long grass and reeds which sprang from its bank, for a hasty glance and approaching sounds told them that the Russians would probably pass close at hand. Five minutes later their voices were audible, and a series of splashes and thuds told them that they had leapt the ditch a few yards higher up.

"They are not there, and you have led us a fine goose-chase!" Phil heard one of the Russians angrily exclaim. "What made you take us on such a fool's errand, Petroff?"

"It is no fool's errand," another voice replied gruffly. "I distinctly saw two figures cross the land beyond. They are not at the farm, that is clear; but we shall catch them, and then they shall suffer. Pigs that all Englishmen are! I myself will tie them to a wheel and thrash them before their comrades. It will be a good example, and our master the Czar would approve of it."

The speakers passed on, and Phil hastily interpreted what he had overheard.

"Whack us, will they?" muttered Tony, gritting his teeth. "That's one more chalked up against these Cossack chaps. Pigs, indeed! Yah!" And his indignation being too great for words, he subsided into silence. Giving the patrol sufficient time to get well away, they sprang from the ditch, and hastily squeezing the water from their clothes, struck across to the outhouses. Beyond them and within fifty paces was a small farmhouse, standing in absolutely open fields, with not a sign of a vineyard or patch of cultivated ground, while fenced-in enclosures and distant bleating and lowing told that this was a grazing-farm, and that its owner did not trust to crops for his livelihood.

By this time the light was distinctly clearer and the night was rapidly drawing to a close; so that, if they were to escape observation, it was necessary that they should hide themselves away.

"The outhouses will be the best for us," said Phil, thinking aloud. "Come along, Tony; we must see which one will suit us best. If they are merely empty huts, meant for cattle, they will be of no use to us, and we shall have to try the house, or get into an empty pig-sty or something of the sort."

The first was simply an empty shed, and the second proved equally useless. The third was much larger than the others, and the big, closed doors showed it to be a coach-house.

"That will do, so we'll get inside at once," whispered Phil. "Just run round, Tony, and see if there's a window close to the ground."

While Phil knocked out the pin that held the hasp of the door, Tony went in search of a window, and returned to say that the only opening he could find was a trap-door high up, evidently leading to a hay-loft. But there was no ladder.

"Then we must find one," said Phil quickly. "It will never do to get in and leave the door open. If we cannot find a ladder, perhaps there will be a piece of rope inside, and we can manage it like that."

Tony disappeared again, while Phil, opening one of the huge doors, entered the shed. In it were several arabas and heavy carts run close together, while behind them, and pushed close against the wooden wall, was a dilapidated and old-fashioned four-wheeled carriage, completely covered in by an antiquated leather hood, and yet by its mere presence there proving that the owner was a moderately well-to-do person.

"Just the thing for us," muttered Phil. "Now for a rope or a ladder."

He hunted about in the dim light, and presently came across some harness, made of twisted hide, hanging close against the door. To take it down and buckle the traces together was only a few minutes' work, and by that time Tony had returned, to dolefully inform his friend that he had searched everywhere without discovering a ladder, and that, in addition, while prowling round the house, he had seen a light moving, showing that its occupants were already astir.

"How'll this do, Tony?" asked Phil, producing his improvised rope. "Now, who's to do the climbing? You—or shall I be the one?"

Tony settled the question by stepping outside and closing the door, having taken the precaution to leave his stick with Phil. Then he jammed the hasp to, and, having replaced the pin, ran round till he was beneath the trap-door.

A series of niches had been left in the planks which formed the wall, and up these Phil rapidly swarmed, and gained the loft. Throwing the trap-door open, he lowered his rope, and sitting on the floor, with both feet wedged against the wall, called softly to Tony to climb. Two minutes later they were together.

"Now, Tony," said Phil, "pick up a big armful of hay and toss it down. You will find an old coach in the corner of the shed. Take the hay there and make all comfortable, while I close and fasten the door, and put these traces back."

Working rapidly, for there was no saying when a hot search might be made for them, it was not long before they were both comfortably ensconced in the dilapidated coach, leaving the interior of the shed as they had found it.

"All we want now is a look-out," said Phil thoughtfully. "You stay where you are, Tony, while I search for one. In any case I shall have plenty of time to get back to you, for no one could get in here without giving us plenty of warning."

"Search away, old horse—search till yer find it. I'm as comfortable here as a prince in his palace," exclaimed Tony, with a broad grin of contentment, throwing himself back upon the hay which filled the roomy carriage.

Phil opened the door and stepped out. Then he searched the walls thoroughly, finding many cracks and apertures by which he was able to obtain a clear view of his surroundings. Better than all, he discovered a long crevice between two planks directly behind their hiding-place.

Stepping into the carriage he closed the door, and, opening his knife, cut a large triangular slit in the leather covering. Through this, to Tony's absolute bewilderment, he thrust his head, and stared through the aperture in the wall, to find that it commanded an excellent view of the farmhouse and surroundings.

"There you are, Tony," he laughed, withdrawing his head. "That is our look-out, and one of us must be stationed there all day. This slit I have made is never likely to be noticed. Have a look yourself."

Tony did so, but withdrew his head almost more quickly than he had thrust it out.

"Bust me! the Russians are already after us," he cried. "See for yourself, Phil. They are hammering at the door of the farmhouse."

Shouts, shrill hoots, and loud hangings reached their ears, and, glueing his eyes to the crevice, Phil saw that a party of horsemen had ridden up and halted before the farmhouse, and within a short distance of the outhouse in which he and his friend were hidden. A few moments later the door of the farmhouse was opened, and a man appeared looking somewhat startled.

"What do you want?" he asked angrily. "Am I to have no peace? It is scarcely an hour since you roused me in search of some of your beggarly prisoners who have escaped. Am I to be disturbed like this because you do not keep a careful watch?"

"Gently, old man, gently," a rough fellow with a rasping voice answered. "We are but doing the duty of our country and our master, and you had better keep a civil and obliging tongue in your head. We know of farms very near at hand that are farms no longer. Don't we, my comrades?" he asked with a brutal laugh. "They were burnt—by accident, perhaps—and their owner hangs to the nearest tree outside. Perchance—wretched man—of his own act, and perchance, my surly friend, because he was indiscreet."

"What do you want, then?" asked the farmer in a more civil tone, evidently overawed by the black and lowering looks of the Cossacks, and by the covert threats which their spokesman had uttered.

"Something good and of your beat, my friend, for we are hungry; and after that we will search the farm once more."

"Very well, come in if you will. Here, wife," he shouted, "prepare a meal for these good fellows."

"What's all the noise about," asked Tony impatiently, tugging at Phil's arm.

Then when he had learnt he grumbled. "Something to eat. That's what they're after now, is it? Young 'un, the very mention of a meal makes me as hollow as the drum of our Grenadier band. Just keep an eye upon them till they are out of the way, and then we'll fall to ourselves. We've only bread and water, but I feel like tackling anything."

A little later the Cossacks had entered the house, leaving their ponies outside, unsaddled, and tied by the halter to a long rope attached to a ring in the door-post. A plentiful supply of corn had been given them, and while their masters were busy with knife and fork, they ate it hungrily, and having finished it, promptly drooped their heads and fell asleep, for the Cossack pony, though hardy and full of strength, is a long-suffering animal, and never knows how soon he may be called upon for work. Therefore, having been on the move most of the night, one and all took immediate advantage of the moment's respite given them. As for Phil and Tony, stretching their legs and bunching a thick layer of hay beneath them, they set to work on the bread they had saved, and enjoyed their meal in spite of its being so simple.

An hour later there was a commotion outside, and Phil, who was on the watch, saw the Cossacks emerge from the farmhouse.

Then they separated, and in couples searched every corner of the house and its surroundings.

"This looks a likely kind of place," said one of them, approaching the shed in which Phil and Tony were hidden. "Come, Petroff, we will enter it together. I would not for the wealth of the Czar undertake the search alone, for these English fools, though unarmed, are capable of killing us. See how our unlucky comrade was damaged by a blow from one of their fists. He says he remembers only thrusting at them with his lance, and then a flash in his eyes as of a thousand stars. Truly they are brutes who learn to strike down men with their clenched hand alone."

"What is the good of entering there?" his companion answered surlily. "Can you not see, fool, that the door is pinned outside? There is no other entrance but the trap-door, so how can they be there, unless, indeed, they possess wings? For I know the ladder is within the farmhouse. Still, we will search the place, and then can honestly say that we have used every endeavour."

A grating sound accompanied by loud creaking followed this as both doors were thrown wide-open to afford a better light.

Crouching close between the seats of their refuge, the two comrades waited breathlessly, stick in hand, and with fast-beating hearts, while the two Cossacks searched every corner of the dwelling.

"They are not here, as I said," a voice cried from the loft. "This trap-door is bolted on the inside, and the big doors on the outside. It is clear that our trouble is for nothing. Still," he added, having scrambled down by means of the niches, "were I escaping from our enemies this is the place I should choose, and that carriage over there is the roost I should take possession of. From its size it should form most comfortable quarters;" and as if to prove the truth of this, he crept between the carts, and, turning the handle, attempted to open the door.

"Hang on for your life, Tony," whispered Phil, who had overheard all that passed. "This fellow is trying to pull the door open."

Both at once clung to it, Phil grasping the handle inside, while Tony dug his fingers into the window slits and pulled with all his strength.

"Bah!" muttered the Cossack, disappointed in his attempt. "What is the use of a carriage with a door that does not open?" and, turning away, he and his companion left the outhouse.

"That was a near go, Phil, old horse," whispered Tony excitedly. "I thought it was all up, and was ready to jump out and tackle the other beggar while you settled the fellow tugging at the door. We'd have downed 'em, too, but I suppose they'd have given warning to the others."

"Certain to have done so, Tony. You may not know it, but the man who was doing his best to break in here is the gentleman who proposes to thrash us when we are captured."

"Oh, he is, is he?" was Tony's grim reply. "Wait a little while and I'll settle the hash of that fine chap."

A quarter of an hour later Phil saw the horsemen collect together, and, having saddled their ponies, they rode away from the farm, evidently to the no small satisfaction of the farmer. In half an hour two of them returned, and having unsaddled they turned their horses into a shed, and, carrying their saddles, banged at the farmhouse door again.

"What now?" surlily asked the owner, appearing.

"Only a lodging for the two of us," one, a big burly fellow, the same that had attempted to open the carriage door, answered with an oath. "Come, master farmer, we want no trouble; accommodation for two, good feeding, and plenty of that vodka we have already tasted, are what we desire. We have been ordered here to keep a look-out for the runaways."

With a growl of displeasure the man bade them enter, and nothing more of them was seen till the evening, when they appeared, evidently in an intoxicated condition.

That night Phil was lowered from the trap-door by Tony, and when he returned he brought a loaf of bread and a joint of meat, which he had abstracted through an open window of the farmhouse, and in addition, a pocketful of apples from a tiny orchard growing near.

The following day passed uneventfully. The two Cossacks made a thorough search of the surroundings, and once more returned to their beloved vodka.

That night again Phil went out in search of provender, but, in endeavouring to reach a plate of provisions which stood upon a shelf within the window, he upset a dish which clattered to the ground and smashed into a thousand pieces. Instantly a window was thrown open and a head put out.

Phil crept into the shadow and crouched low.

"Who is there?" a drunken voice called. "Comrade, there are thieves about. Rouse yourself."

The window closed with a bang, and, darting across to the outhouse, Phil rapidly clambered up through the trap-door, and he and Tony having gained their hiding-place, once more waited anxiously for what was to follow. But the Cossacks evidently preferred the comfort of a warm room to searching for a thief who was, for all they knew, far away already. So, grumbling that they would see to it on the morrow, they turned in again, and soon all was quiet.

"We shall have to clear away from here, Tony," said Phil as they waited. "The disappearance of food is certain to lead to suspicion, and we shall be caught. To-morrow night we will make a bolt for it."

On the following morning it was evident that more than suspicion had been aroused, and a hot search was instituted, for, from what Phil overheard, none in the farmhouse doubted that the escaped prisoners were close at hand. Saddling up, the Cossacks searched every corner of the fields, and returned utterly baffled at mid-day. A feed of corn was tossed into the shed close at hand, and the ponies driven in ready for an instant start; then the Russians betook themselves to their favourite bottle, and when they reappeared were evidently the worse for its contents. But they were far from giving up the search.

"They must be close at hand," the man, whose voice Phil had heard so often, exclaimed with an oath. "We must find them too, comrade, and then we shall be rewarded. Where can the fools be? Ah! let us try the coach-house again. These English, I have heard, are dense and slow, but perhaps these two have more wits than their brothers."

"Tony, we're done for, I fear," said Phil, hastily withdrawing his head. "This shed is to be searched again."

"We must just chance it then," grunted Tony. "It's a bad scrape we're in, but we were lucky the other day. If this fellow does find us in here, why, we must just silence the two of them. It's their lives or our liberty, and I'm determined to get out of their hands. Lie low, old boy, and if these coves spot us it'll be the worse for them."

Tony shook his stick threateningly, and was on the point of launching into an elaborate explanation of the exact punishment he would mete out to the Cossack who had promised his friends to thrash the fugitives, when the door of the shed was thrown open with a bang, and the two Russians reeled in.

"Search the loft, comrade," said the big man authoritatively. "This spirit of our friend's is good and powerful stuff, and my legs are none too steady."

The man did as he was told, and, peeping through the window, Phil watched him laboriously climbing to the loft, looking as though he might lose his grip and fall at any moment.

The big man stood still for a second, stroking his beard. Then, evidently struck once more by the appearance of the covered carriage, he crept towards it.

"What is this?" he muttered loudly when a few paces away. "Is it the vodka, or did I turn that handle and leave it so?" With an effort he pulled himself together; suddenly remembering that he had indeed turned the handle and neglected to restore it to its usual position, and realising that it was now closed, he gave a drunken shout and rushed at the door.

135

Chapter Fourteen.

Almost Trapped.

The sight of a burly, black-bearded Russian of forbidding aspect, half-maddened moreover by drink, rushing at one's hiding-place, is calculated to inspire the bravest with trepidation, and in the case of Phil and Tony it can be recorded, without fear of their incurring the epithet of coward, that both were more than a little alarmed for their safety. But they were in a cage—in an extremely tight corner without doubt—and, rendered desperate by the knowledge, and that recapture meant, if not death, certainly ill-treatment, they determined to make a light for it.

"Silence him at all costs," Phil whispered rapidly. "Let him pull the door open, and then drag him in. I leave it to you to silence him, Tony."

"Ay, I'll do that, never fear," was the hurried answer in a tone which showed that though a handkerchief as a gag had possibly occurred to the gallant Tony as a method, yet he knew of other and surer means.

A second later the handle was wrenched open, and the door flew back with a bang, while the Cossack almost fell into the carriage.

There was a swish and a sounding crash, and he flopped into the hay limply, stunned by a heavy blow from Tony's club, which, had it not been for the thick astrakhan hat the Russian wore, would have settled his fate there and then.

His helpless body was instantly dragged into the corner and a hurried consultation held.

"We've got to fix up that other chap," said Tony grimly. "Now his pal's gone the fat's in the fire."

"No doubt about it, Tony," agreed Phil. "We must silence both. Let us get out and wait near the door for the other fellow. We can leave this man for the present, for that crack you gave him will keep him quiet for a time."

Tony chuckled.

"And he was the chap as was going to tie us up and whop us!" he said, with huge enjoyment. "He was going to give us a taste of the rope! He shall have some himself soon, but for the present the dose of stick will suit him."

м 845

"THE PURSUING COSSACKS HALTED"

Shaking his club at the unconscious man, he followed Phil out of the carriage and closed the door. Both crawled beneath the cart till close to the niches down which the Russian must climb, and waited eagerly for his appearance. But there was not a sound above, and nothing but the certainty that he had ascended to the loft to convince them that he was there still.

"What has happened to him?" asked Phil. "Do you think he heard the noise below, and has escaped through the trap-door?"

"Not he," Tony answered with assurance. "He's up there, p'r'aps hiding, but most like dead asleep. Listen. Perhaps we'll hear him."

There was a minute's silence, when both heard heavy snoring from the loft, and looked at one another, uncertain how to proceed.

"We're in a fix," said Phil shortly. "We dare not move out of this till nightfall, for the surrounding country is open; and we cannot leave this fellow asleep up there. He may pull himself together at any moment and search for his friend. Also if we climb up to him we are likely to rouse him, and he will give the alarm before he can be silenced."

"Yes, it's a real fix, Phil; but we've got to get out of it," muttered Tony, scratching his head in bewilderment. "Why not sing out to him in his own lingo and tell him to come down?" he suddenly suggested. "Then as he gets close to the ground we can nobble him."

"Of course; just the thing;" and Phil, who had heard Petroff address his friend as "Nicholas", called to him in a low voice.

At first there was no response; but presently the man above moved, and they heard him grumble something, and evidently turn over to sleep again.

"Nicholas, here are the English. Remember our reward," cried Phil in a harsh tone.

"Ah, what?" they heard the man say. Then there were sounds as if he had risen to his feet and fallen again. But he was evidently fully aroused, and soon his legs appeared through the opening above searching for the first of the niches. He found it, and commenced to descend, while Phil and Tony crept a little closer and prepared to dart out from beneath the shelter of the cart and overpower him. Suddenly there was an oath as one foot slipped from its hold, then a sharp cry of fear, and before either Phil or Tony could utter an exclamation, the unhappy Cossack, overpowered by drink, had lost his hold and fallen like a sack to the ground, where he lay huddled in a heap, while a crimson stream ran from his ears and nose.

Phil crept to his side and found that he was dead.

"We are saved our trouble," he said sorrowfully. "The poor fellow has smashed his skull. What's to be done, Tony?"

His friend looked blankly round and shook his head.

"Blest if I know, Phil! Here we are with two Russian coves, one of them dead, and here we've got to stick for a matter of four hours and more. It beats me. The farmer chap saw them both come in here, and it won't take long for him to search. It's a regular fixer."

"And the worst of it is too, Tony, that if we are found with this dead man we shall be accused of having killed him. I have it. We'll hoist him to the loft again, and place the other fellow alongside him. Then we'll take up our quarters there. If we are discovered we can make a good fight for it, and if the farmer comes in search he may think his unwelcome visitors have left the shed to investigate some other spot and will return to his house."

Tony looked at his friend as if to say, "Well, you're a good 'un," and, without venturing on a remark, stepped to the wall and returned with the traces which had already served as a rope. One of these was buckled round the dead man, and the other trace attached. Then both climbed into the loft and hoisted their burden after them. Another trip and the still unconscious figure of their enemy Petroff was dragged up beside them. The harness was returned to its peg, and with a hasty glance round to make sure that there was nothing about the shed to show that a struggle had taken place within it, Phil and Tony climbed into the hay-loft and sat down to regain their breath and rest after their exertions.

Two hours passed almost in silence, when Phil suddenly slapped his knee and gave a sharp exclamation of delight.

"We'll reach our friends yet, old man," he said enthusiastically. "I've thought the whole thing over and have decided what to do. At first I imagined that our best way would be to relieve these gentlemen of their clothing in exchange for ours. But it would not do. If we were captured it would mean a file of muskets at six in the morning, for we should certainly be condemned as spies."

Tony grunted hoarsely, showing that he had a decided dislike to this arrangement.

"But though we do not take their clothes, we will make free with their swords and ponies," continued Phil, "and so soon as it is dark we will get away from this. By riding at night, and making allowances for the wide détours we shall be compelled to undertake, we should reach our friends in three days at most. We have still a large piece of meat left, and with that and the bread that remains, and an occasional drink of water, we must be satisfied. Now we'll secure this fellow. Slip down and get some of that harness, like a brick, will you, Tony?"

That evening, soon after dusk had fallen, two stealthy figures crept from the shed, and stole towards the outhouse in which the Cossack ponies were kept. The door was only latched, and, waiting merely to slip on the bridles and tighten the girths, the two adventurous Englishmen vaulted into the saddle and rode out into the night. They were not gone many minutes when the farmer, wondering at the prolonged absence of the Cossacks, and having seen them turn their ponies into the shed, came to see if the animals were still there, and, finding them gone, returned in anything but a pleasant mood to his house.

"Those two brutes are gone, wife," he said testily. "They have not even thanked us for our hospitality, nor paid for the vodka which they drank. May it kill them then is all that I wish!"

Had he but known it, his unkind thought had already been partially accomplished, for in his hay-loft one of the Cossacks lay dead, a victim indeed to the fiery spirit, while the second, destined for many days to be sick in his house, and demand careful nursing and feeding at his expense, reclined, unconscious, in a heap of straw, bound hand and foot, but left ungagged, a circumstance of which he took advantage early in the morning by screaming for help at the top of his voice.

Once more returning to the post-road, Phil and Tony rode along it quietly, only the jangle of their Cossack swords breaking the silence. Three hours later a line of watch-fires in the distance told them that they were approaching the Russian field-army, and warned them to find some safe hiding-place.

"They are seven or eight miles away at least," said Tony, "and we are lucky to have spotted them so soon."

"Yes, Tony, we are," Phil remarked thoughtfully. "We are still more lucky, for this side they will have only a few pickets and outposts, and we must be far outside their circle. Also they will not be expecting anything. I fancy our best course will be to ride to our left, keeping the lights at the same distance as now. Then we will choose some sort of a shelter, on high ground if possible, so that to-morrow we can see what direction to take. Once past those troops, Tony, and safely through the scouts who are certain to be watching our fellows, we shall be back in the British camp."

"Safe in the British camp. Yes," echoed Tony, "and I hopes stowing away the first decent feed for many a long day now. Coffee and bread's all right, but my strength is just going for the want of meat."

More than two hours later, and just before the dawn broke, they rode their ponies into a big vineyard situated on the slope of a hill which seemed to command the camp.

Daylight discovered a splendid panorama spread out before them, for they had been unconsciously but steadily ascending all night, and now were at such an elevation that they could see, beyond the Chersonese heights, Sebastopol in the far-off distance, merged in a haze of sea and land, and only distinguishable by the whiteness of its masonry; while directly beneath them, as it seemed, lay the Russian camp, seething with horses and troops, which were very soon to try the fortunes of war with their adversaries.

To the right of the Chersonese heights another line of rugged hills stretched as far as the river Tchernaya, which could be seen winding here and there, and flashing back the sun. Along these heights ran the Woronzoff road, branching off before it reached the river, and, running parallel and at some distance from it, deflected by other heights, known as the Kamara. To the right of these was a deep valley, the ever-memorable "Valley of the Shadow of Death", opposite which, by straining their eyes and shading them with their hands, the broad folds of the grand flag of England could be distinguished flaunting in the breeze, even at that distance, so clear was the atmosphere.

Phil pointed it out to Tony.

"That's the place for us," he said shortly, "and we must manage to get into that valley. After that all will be plain sailing. But it's a big job. I fancy I can make out earthworks along that road you see upon the heights, and, if I am not mistaken, there is a large camp to the right, resting by a collection of houses close to the river."

Tony followed the direction of Phil's finger, and gazed long and earnestly.

"It's a camp, Phil," he agreed, "and I suppose it ain't likely to lie British. Tothers is earthworks, I think, and manned with guns, or I'm a wrong 'un. Look! you can see one against the sky-line. If they are our batteries, all the better. But in any case I am for steering clear of them, and cutting into the valley."

"Yes, I think so too, Tony; and now, how to get there. We are well to the left of the Russian camp below us. By keeping still more so, we ought to reach that big clump of houses and vineyards you see over there before the morning, and next time the night falls I hope we shall be able to answer an English challenge."

Had they but known it, Phil and Tony were to meet with more than one adventure before the well-known "Halt! Who goes there?" struck upon their ears, for this was the 23rd of October, and on the 25th that small camp down by the river Tchernaya was to be swollen by the emptying of the one directly below them, and the Russians were to try conclusions with the Allies.

It was destined to be a brilliant spectacle, and brimful of gallant deeds—one more striking than all the rest, and to find a lasting place in the history of our race, a deed of dare-devilry and sheer disregard of life and limb which Phil and Tony were never to forget, and the honour of their having taken part in it will ever be cherished by their descendants.

141

Having made a thorough survey of the scene below them, Phil and his friend removed the saddles and bridles from their ponies, and replaced the latter with a halter attached to the saddle. Then, finding a stream near at hand, Tony watered them and led them back to the vineyard, where he secured them in a part completely obscured from view. Meanwhile Phil crept out to a shed at the end of the vines, and returned with a large armful of hay. That done they ate some of their bread and meat, and, flinging themselves down in the shadow of the vines, were soon fast asleep.

The sun was low down in the heavens and fast sinking when Phil awoke, and, rubbing his eyes, kicked Tony playfully.

"Up you get, old chap," he cried cheerfully. "We'll have a meal, and then make for that clump of trees. Let us have one more good look at it before the night falls. See! by striking a little to the left we shall get into that narrow valley, and by keeping to it shall be going directly for our goal."

Tony sprang to his feet, and, thrusting his stout stick through his belt, joined Phil in an open spot, from which, unseen, they could look down towards Sebastopol.

A curious figure he was too—more like a scarecrow than a British soldier. A short stubbly beard covered his chin, while a flaming red handkerchief was tied round his head in place of his bearskin, lost long ago now at the Alma. His red tunic was tattered and stained with mud, and his trousers hung in rags round his boots.

As for Phil, he was in no better plight; but still, strange to say, he looked spruce and neat beside his rough companion, the short fair down upon his cheeks scarcely showing, and contrasting most favourably with Tony's spiky beard.

"Right again, young 'un!" agreed the latter, evidently in the highest spirits. "We'll lie up over there to-night, and then make a dash for it. That sleep has just put new life into me, and now I'm ready for anything; and I tell yer, Phil, it's got to be five to one afore I gives in to the Russians. Let's have a look at this here toothpick;" and he dragged his sword, a heavy cavalry sabre, from its sheath. "Sharp as a razor," he remarked, with a grim smile, feeling the edge. "All the better. It's got plenty of weight too, and once I wants to use it, blest if I don't make it cut clean through the head of one of our Cossack friends."

He swished the sword round in the air, narrowly missing Phil in his eagerness. Then, thrusting it back into the sheath, he stalked across to the ponies and commenced to saddle up.

That night they reached the vineyard close against the heights bearing the Woronzoff road, and in it they passed the following day, devouring an abundance of grapes, which were perfectly ripe, and served to keep off the pangs of hunger, now that their bread and meat had disappeared.

When darkness fell again they were fully prepared for the last dash. A nek between two stunted hills forming the ridge of heights had been chosen, and through this they were to ride into the valley, and from there into the British camp. Crowning the heights they could discern three batteries, but no flag flew above them, though the fact that the guns, which were now clearly distinguishable, were turned towards the opposite Kamara heights, in occupation by the Russians, pointed conclusively to the fact that they were manned by the Allies.

"They are our batteries undoubtedly," said Phil when discussing the question with his friend, "but for all that, I propose we slip between them, and make for our own camp. They may be occupied by the French or Turks, and as we could not answer their challenge, and our speech is as likely to be taken for Russian as for English, we should run a great chance of being shot or bayoneted before they discovered which side we belonged to. No, decidedly, I am for slipping through."

Tony expressed his approval, and indeed it was the wisest course to take, for as it turned out the batteries were manned by Turks, who, on the following day, were to defend them valiantly, and the majority of whom were to lose their lives in doing so.

At last the moment for setting forth arrived, and the state of excitement into which Phil and Tony had worked themselves may be imagined. This was the last struggle for freedom, the trump card upon which their fortunes depended. If they failed to pass unnoticed through the ground intervening between themselves and the batteries no doubt a hoard of Cossack scouts would be quickly on their track, like vultures on their prey, for the waning light had shown numbers of these shaggy horsemen dotting the plain below. Still, the risk was no greater than that which they had already run, and, buoyed with the hope of liberty on the morrow, and, as Tony did not forget to mention again, a substantial meal for the first time for many a long day, they vaulted into their saddles and commenced to ride from the vineyard.

"Hark! What is that?" asked Phil suddenly, in a subdued tone of alarm. "I am certain I heard something over there;" and he pointed towards the Kamara heights.

Both listened intently, and distinctly heard the rumble of distant wheels, and a dull, heavy sound as though of a large force of men approaching.

"Back for our lives!" cried Phil excitedly. "It must be the Russian troops coming this way. We must watch them, Tony."

"Ay, it's the enemy right enough," muttered Tony angrily. "Phil, them chaps is always coming up against us and spoiling our fun. First they stopped us from carrying that colour back, and then blest if a Cossack cove didn't try for to keep us when we was bolting from the camp. He paid for that, he did, and I expect he'll be more careful in the future. Then them drunken swabs turned us out of what was house and home, if yer can call an old rickety carriage such. Law! what a jolly time we give them too! And now they are after us again, the brutes!" and with a grunt of disgust Tony dragged the club from his belt, silently determining to fight the whole Russian army, if need be, and to help his comrade back to liberty.

"Hush! Can't you keep quiet?" whispered Phil sharply. "Follow me through the vineyard. The road runs close beside the farther end, and we must hide there and watch."

Somewhat abashed, Tony followed, and soon both were crouching within, a few yards of the road. A few minutes later a front guard of Cossacks passed like so many silent ghosts. Then field-guns and ammunition-wagons rumbled by, followed by battalions of infantry, and by regiments of Cossack horse. It was an impressive sight, especially when the Russian horsemen filed by, for in front of each regiment rode the commander, superbly mounted, and chanting a song, while behind him came other horsemen, clashing cymbals, to the accompaniment of which the whole regiment took up the refrain, and sang with voices far more melodious than could be expected from rough soldiers.

"There is some big movement on," whispered Phil, "and I fear our difficulties in getting through will be vastly increased. Still, I am for trying to-night. To-morrow we might be hunted out of this. What do you say to our joining the stragglers, who are certain to follow the main body? The night is too dark for them to recognise us except when close at hand."

"Seems to me a likely way out of the fix," agreed Tony, after a moment's consideration. "There won't be many of them, and if one happens to spot us, why—it'll be his own fault, Phil. Yes, we'll follow, and by keeping reasonably near we shall see where these fellows bivouac, and have a better chance of slipping through."

Accordingly they waited till the army had got a quarter of a mile away, and then fell in behind. Occasionally stragglers passed them, and once a squadron of horsemen galloped by; but, taking the two solitary figures for scouts, they swept on without a word. An hour later they were beyond the Russian camp and ascending the nek. No one seemed to be about, and they were not challenged. Once over the summit they turned abruptly to the left, and rode down into the valley, keeping close to the heights. But here again another difficulty faced them. Watch-fires twinkled in every direction, some undoubtedly being Russian, and, fearful of falling into the enemy's hands, or what would perhaps be equally bad, stumbling against a French or Turkish outpost, and being shot before an explanation could be given, they once more selected a vineyard and bivouacked there till the day broke, hoping to be able then to make a dash for the British camp.

Chapter Fifteen.

Balaclava.

The dawn of October 25th broke dull and chill. Banks of fog hung over the heights, and the "Valley of the Shadow of Death" lay hidden in mist, as if cloaked already with a funeral pall. Blades of grass and leaves drooped with the added weight of the moisture, and Phil and Tony, crouching in their vineyard, shivered and longed for the sun to rise and bring warmth and cheerfulness.

A gentle breeze was blowing, and, freshening, it soon cleared the fog away, while the mist in the valley disappeared mysteriously a little later. It had scarcely done so when the boom of guns on the Russian side of the heights which the two friends had crossed during the night broke on their ears, while flashes from four points on the summit, and still louder reports, showed that the Turkish batteries, between which they had passed, were hotly engaged.

Situated as they were, close to the end of the Causeway heights, along which ran the Woronzoff road, Phil and his friend were in an excellent position to view a large portion of the historical battle which was now commencing. Facing across the valley, with the Chersonese height on their left, they looked towards the river Tchernaya, and a group of low hills, known as the Fedioukine heights, already manned by Russian guns and infantry. And now they gazed upon a wonderful sight. A Russian army of 25,000 infantry, 34 squadrons of cavalry, and 78 guns was commencing its march, intending to cross the Causeway heights, descend into the valley south of that ridge, and capture the harbour of Balaclava and all our stores of food and military equipment. And between them and their goal were interposed 4 Turkish batteries with 9 guns in all, the foremost being two miles in advance of its nearest infantry support, which consisted of some 500 of the 93rd Highlanders under command of the famous Sir Colin Campbell, a few Turks, and a battery of horse artillery. In addition, some 600 horsemen, belonging to Scarlett's Heavy Brigade, lay in the valley south of the Causeway heights, while 600 sabres, composing the Light Brigade, sat on their horses at the opening of the Tchernaya valley—the valley now better known as that of the Shadow of Death, and within a short mile of Phil and Tony.

"What can be happening?" asked Phil, in a voice scarcely above a whisper. "The guns we hear must be those belonging to the army that marched past us last night, and the cavalry are certainly the same who sang while they filed by in the darkness. What does it all mean, Tony? There must be some huge movement afoot, for I have never seen so many men marching together, save when the Allies advanced on the Alma."

"And now it's the Russians advancing towards the camp of the Allies," Tony answered thoughtfully. "What's their game? you're asking, Phil. Why shouldn't it be Balaclava? The harbour is just chock-full of British shipping, and, if that was captured, where should we be without our stores of grub and ammunition? Nowhere. That's their plan, I can tell you. Depend upon it, that is what they're up to; but you'll see how it will end. I give them a couple of hours to play about in, and after that our chaps will drive 'em off the field."

"Then I hope we shall have a chance of joining friends soon, Tony, for to be compelled to sit here and watch the battle would be harder luck than we bargained for. But look at the Russian army. What a grand sight it makes!"

And indeed the greatest enemy of Russia, with mind morbidly awry with jealousy and dislike, could not look upon that advancing army and fail to admire.

Steadily, and with a swing which told of long practice in marching, the infantry advanced in thick columns, rifles at the slope and caps well set back upon their heads. And between them and on either flank rumbled heavy cannon, the drivers holding in their horses as yet, while they turned eager eyes to the left to watch their more fortunate companions who at the moment were engaging the Turkish redoubts. Beyond the guns, and away in front of all, rode the huge force of cavalry, squadron upon squadron, riding knee to knee and listening to the music of the guns and the jingle of their own equipment.

Amidst the cavalry the flash of polished brass would occasionally be seen, while sometimes, as the squadrons moved apart for the moment, a battery of small field-guns came to view, the bright metal sparkling in the sun. But though a casual glance might suggest the idea that these were merely toys, given to the cavalry to play with, yet the day was not to pass before the men who manned these tiny field-guns were to show that, protected by horsemen and capable of an extremely rapid advance and retreat, these same batteries became a formidable item when fired at moderately-close range.

"Yes, they make a very fine sight," Phil admitted, to himself again, "and I only wish I thought that we could beat them as easily as Tony suggests. I wonder what our troops are doing!"

Turning his eyes to the left he swept them along the Chersonese heights, and saw a long line of infantry there hurrying towards Balaclava, while on an eminence to the left a brilliantly-dressed group suddenly appeared, and, lifting telescopes, fixed them upon the Russians. It was Lord Raglan and his staff.

Lowering his eyes still more, Phil swept them along the valley, and soon hit upon the Heavy Brigade, looking, even at that distance, a most formidable body of men, while their horses, laden with cavalry saddles of great weight and a considerable amount of kit, seemed huge when compared to the Cossack animals.

Passing from Scarlett's famous "Heavies", Phil's eyes then lit upon the 600 troopers of the Light Brigade. Bright, gallant fellows they looked as they sat there jauntily upon their saddles and slowly rode up the valley. And little did Phil and Tony, and for the matter of that hundreds more who looked upon them in the early hours of that morning, imagine that, long ere the sun set again and the grey mist fell upon hill and valley, more than half of those fine horsemen would be silent and still for ever.

Slowly, and as if careless of the huge mass of the enemy, they rode up the valley till the mile which separated them from Phil and Tony was considerably decreased.

There were friends close at hand, and, saddling up hurriedly, the two prepared to gallop across to them. But now a turn in the fortune of battle changed their plans, for, gallantly clinging to their position, the Turks holding the battery on the extreme left nearest the Russians had been decimated by a storm of shell, while, before they could think of retiring, 11,000 grey-coated infantry came rushing up at them. What could a mere handful of men do in the circumstances? They broke and fled, and, seeing this, their comrades in the other redoubts also took to their heels. Instantly a cloud of Russian horse burst from their ranks, and, sweeping into the plain, made short work of the flying gunners.

Phil and Tony looked on, disconcerted, for to ride across to the Light Brigade now would mean almost certain destruction.

"Done again by those Cossacks!" grumbled Tony, who took all the enemy's horsemen to be Cossacks. "Done brown this time, Phil!"

"We'll have to wait, that's all," said Phil, with a sigh of resignation. "We are safe here, and it won't be long before those fellows ride back. See! they are already riding up the heights on our right after the Turks who bolted into the other valley."

This was the case, and to follow the movement we must for the moment leave the valley into which Phil looked, and ride with the Russian horsemen over the Causeway heights.

Scarcely heard upon the springy turf, the horses' feet strike hard and ring with a sound of iron upon the beaten path, and then the thunder of a thousand hoofs dies down again as if by magic, and he who rides with the fiery Cossack horsemen hears only the dull stamp upon the yielding grass, and the clatter and jangle of sabres and accoutrements. And when the summit is topped, another valley comes into view, running almost parallel with that just left behind, and merely separated from it by the Causeway heights, the slopes of which gently fall in rolling stretches of green till the bottom is reached. From there the grass runs on, undulating in big waves, sometimes falling and sometimes rising, till at last an upward sweep brings the rider to a crest from which the narrow basin of Balaclava can be seen.

Yes, there it is, a fairy pool set in this wide stretch of green, and bearing upon its flashing surface a host of vessels, anchored and crowded close together. There, too, is its narrow entrance, scarcely wide enough to pass in two vessels side by side, and there, close beside its shores, is an array of huts already filled with stores, while outside, boxes of biscuit and barrels of salt pork are piled in huge stacks which overtop and completely swamp the dwellings.

And where is the defending force? Where are the men told off to protect this most important harbour and its valuable contents? The rider stares and gasps with astonishment when all he sees is a handful of kilted men standing to arms upon the sloping grass leading to the harbour. Long ago their paucity of numbers was known to the enemy, and now the Russian commander sends his Cossacks against them, hoping to sweep them aside and capture the harbour.

Rallying to their comrades, a thousand lances swept down against the thin line of 93rd Highlanders. It was a sufficiently imposing array to have scattered a stronger body of troops, but the brawny kilted warriors were maddened by the sight of the unhappy Turks being cut down in their flight, and moreover, at that moment a ludicrous affair set them roaring with laughter. They had received as supports some Turkish troops, and these, having no stomach for a cavalry encounter, fled from the ranks.

"Let 'em go," muttered one Highlander, with a laugh. "We come out here to fight for those chaps, and see how they help us. We'll turn the cowards into servants."

But one at least was roused to indignation. One of the women of the regiment struggled amongst the Turks, belabouring them with a club, and, catching one big fellow at this moment, thrashed him soundly, ordering him between every stroke, and in shrill falsetto, to return to the fighting-line.

Roars of laughter and cheers ascended from the thin line of Highlanders, and laughing still they were, and bandying jokes with one another, when the Russians swept down upon them.

"Back, lads! back!" shouted Sir Colin, waving his sword, and having to do his utmost to keep his eager men from rushing down upon the enemy. Then came the sharp command to fire, and, a second discharge following, the Russians broke and fled.

And meanwhile the widely-separated regiments composing the heavy brigade of cavalry were quietly riding along the valley, keeping the Causeway heights on their left. Suddenly Scarlett, who was in advance with 300 of the Greys and Inniskillings, saw a perfect forest of lances upon the summit of the heights, and not more than 600 yards away. Three thousand Russian cavalry had just come into view, and, seeing the British horse, their trumpets rang out shrill, and like an avalanche they dashed down the slopes. Scarlett's decision was taken in a moment. "In any case it must mean death and destruction," he thought. "Better to meet the enemy face to face than ride across their front and be cut to pieces."

"Left wheel into line," the gallant old fellow shouted, and as calmly as if manoeuvring at home the squadrons took up their new position. And then— think of the audacity and coolness of the action—they were halted, while the officers, facing round, dressed the line, which had been somewhat broken by rough ground. And a stubborn line it proved to dress, for not a man but leaned forward in his saddle, cursing the delay, and eager to fly forward. Hoarse growls arose from the ranks, and troopers snatched angrily at their bridles, pulling their horses back upon their haunches, well knowing all the while that it was themselves and not the willing animals they bestrode that needed curbing at that moment.

"Had not Greys and Inniskillings led the field, charging side by side at Waterloo?" each man asked himself. "Yes, their ancestors were on that glorious battle-ground; and were they, their descendants, to be kept back now? 300 against 3000 charging down upon them. What mattered the odds?"

Well was it that Scarlett delayed no longer, for his men were out of hand. "Charge!" he roared, his eyes blazing with excitement.

His trumpeter sounded the call, and away went the gallant band, their fine old colonel fifty yards in advance of them, mounted on a remarkably big horse.

And the Russians, seeing this spectacle, halted. Three thousand of them halted and pondered—almost wavered with doubt.

Crash! The gallant old colonel had struck the mass and cleft into its very heart, and following him, with a fierce shout of exultation, 300 men rushed in, and were instantly lost to view, nothing but plunging horses and flashing swords being visible. Truly it was a marvellous sight, and the 93rd, together with the First and Fourth Divisions, who were marching down in support, held their breath and halted to see what next would happen. They had not long to wait. Gathering pace as they advanced, the 4th Dragoons, who were some way in rear of Scarlett's 300, thundered down upon the Russian flank, and with never a pause swept right through the mass of cavalry from flank to flank, leaving a lane of wounded and killed and frantically struggling horses in its path.

Ah! it was grand work that Britain's sons were doing for their Queen that day, but more was yet to follow, for with hoarse shouts and the fierce lust for battle in their eyes, the Royals, the 5th Dragoons, and another squadron of Inniskillings burst upon the Russians, cut their way to join their gallant colonel, and, crumpling the enemy on every side, finally put them to flight. Three thousand flying for their lives from a sixth of their numbers! Truly it was a great day for Britain, and at the final act a perfect torrent of hoarse cheers burst from the onlookers, head-gear was tossed into the air, and men turned and shook each other heartily by the hand, blessing the fact that these fine cavalry fellows were their brothers, and that they had the fortune to be their countrymen.

And now let us return to the valley on the right slope of which Phil and Tony lay in hiding. Unconscious of what had happened, and yet aware by the rattle of distant musketry and the heavy booming of guns that a battle of large proportions was in progress, they itched to be moving so as to rejoin the battalion of Grenadier Guards and take their share in the fight.

"Bother those fellows! When will they clear off and give us a chance?" exclaimed Phil impatiently, anathematising the Cossack skirmishers who still galloped about on the plain beneath in search of more fugitives.

"Why do not our horse attack them? The Light Brigade might easily sweep the whole lot up and give us the opportunity of joining them as they rode by. And we'd take it, Tony," he added enthusiastically. "We have some scores to settle, and once the chance comes we'll have a smack at those Cossacks."

"Never fear, Phil. Take it easy, old horse. The day is only just beginning, and our chance will come. Do yer think all them cavalry of ours will sit still and do nothing? Bet yer life they'll be sweeping up here soon. Ah! Glad we stuck here so long. Look at them fellers returning."

Tony pointed to a horde of mounted Russians, the flower of their cavalry, which at this moment swarmed in disorder over the Causeway heights, and swept down into the Tchernaya valley, still too much unnerved to draw rein after their defeat by the Heavy Brigade.

"That looks well," muttered Phil. "We saw those fellows ride over half an hour ago as cocksure of victory as possible. They've evidently had rough handling. Why on earth does not the commander of our Light Brigade charge them? He could take them in flank, and, broken as they are, he could cut them to pieces. Charge! Why don't you charge?" he shouted excitedly, standing up and raising his voice to the highest pitch as though it could possibly reach right across to the Light Brigade.

"Come down," cried Tony fiercely, dragging his friend to the ground. "I'm ashamed of yer, young 'un. You'll be giving the whole show away, and one of them Cossack chaps will be riding for us. Wait and we'll have a go at 'em yet. Yah! why don't yer charge?" he said bitterly, shaking his fist at the distant British cavalry.

But though the Light Brigade were ready enough for anything, as was yet to be shown, their colonel still held them back. Posted as they were, at the mouth of the valley and on some rising ground, they too had witnessed every incident of the battle. They had seen the gallant charge of the 'Heavies', and they bit their lips and swore beneath their breath, itching to be let loose, and show their comrades that they too could ride straight, ay, and fight too, till death settled their account if need be. As the Russian cavalry came flying in clouds over the Causeway heights, their eagerness made them almost unmanageable, and loud growls of anger and vexation came from the ranks. But Lord Cardigan, who was in command, had orders to defend his position, and to strike at anything that came within distance of him. Undoubtedly this was the opportunity he should have taken, but he chose to forego it, and thereby allowed the Russians to escape, while his men looked on and fumed with rage and disappointment, and Tony and Phil hid in the vineyard and thought all manner of awful things.

But now the enemy commenced to remove the guns from the captured Turkish redoubt, and an order reached Lord Lucan—who commanded the combined brigades of cavalry, heavy and light—to recapture the Causeway heights. Lord Raglan had, however, omitted to provide the necessary infantry supports, and in consequence the movement was delayed. Then a second and more peremptory order was sent to Lord Lucan, by means of Nolan, a noted cavalry officer, who believed that all things were possible with that arm of the service.

Lord Raglan wishes the cavalry to advance rapidly to the front, it ran, *and try to prevent the enemy carrying away the guns.*

"To the front? What front? Surely not right up the valley and into the very jaws of the Russian army!" everyone will mutter.

Lord Lucan also was bewildered. Long ago the captured Turkish redoubts had sunk into insignificance, and the guns now most in evidence were those right up the valley. That too was "front" to Lord Lucan. Then what could be the meaning of this message? "Attack what? What guns are we to attack?" he asked anxiously, fixing his eyes upon the batteries on the Causeway heights, and then upon those at the tip of the valley.

"There," replied Captain Nolan, with something akin to a sneer, and in tones which angered Lord Lucan. "There, my lord, is your enemy, and there your guns." And he pointed away up the valley to the Russian batteries occupying a commanding position nearly two miles away.

It was a monstrous error, for how could horsemen hope to live and be effective after such a ride, when cannon fired directly into their front, while the heights on either side, converging to the apex occupied by the battery, were lined by more guns and by infantry in huge numbers. On whose shoulders rests the onus of the terrible error it is almost impossible to state. Had less ambiguous orders been issued it would never have occurred, and a deed of daring, unparalleled in war, would never have been recorded in the annals of heroic struggles to which England is ever adding.

Lord Lucan transmitted the order to Lord Cardigan in person. The latter saluted, and pointed out the desperate nature of the undertaking, but being told that there was no choice but to obey, turned and gave the command, "The brigade will advance!"

"By George! They are off," cried Phil, who had been watching the Light Brigade intently. "Get ready, Tony. You were right; our chance has come at last."

Both tightened their girths and prepared to dash out, for the direction the cavalry were taking would bring them close at hand.

"It's a charge right enough," cried Tony excitedly, "and I'm going to be one of 'em! Come out!" and with a whirr he dragged his sabre out of the sheath.

"Good heavens! look at what is happening!" cried Phil aghast. For the Light Brigade had suddenly swerved away from the Causeway heights. "I thought they were to attack the Turkish redoubts, but they are heading right up to the centre of the Russian army. It is madness! sheer suicide!"

At this moment they saw a horseman, the unhappy Nolan, gallop transversely across the now fast-galloping Light Brigade. He had discovered the terrible mistake, and attempted to set it right, but a shell from the battery in front burst with a roar in front of him, and killed him instantly.

"Now for it, Tony," shouted Phil, kicking the ribs of his pony. "We'll join our friends at all costs, and see more fighting before we die."

"Hurrah! I'm with yer, young 'un! Who-hoop! at 'em for all we're worth!"

Fortunately both ponies were fast and sturdy animals, and, still move fortunately, Phil and Tony had had good practice on horseback when with the menagerie. They thrashed the animals with the flat of their sabres, and, dashing down the hill, fell in beside the 4th light Dragoons, who, with the 11th and 8th Hussars, formed the second attacking line, the first being composed of the 17th Lancers and the 13th Light Dragoons.

Faster grew the pace, and still faster. Men sat close down on their saddles, and jerking their sword lanyards higher up their wrists, clutched the hilts, and stared straight before them with a look of enthusiasm in their eyes. The blood of the British cavalry was up, for as yet they rode silently, a warning sign to those whom they might come against, for your Englishman does not shriek aloud. He says things beneath his breath till the moment comes, and then what a shout he gives!

And as they charged, from either side and from the front, flame and smoke belched out, and the valley echoed with the sound of exploding cannon. Shells shrieked overhead, rolled like huge cricket-balls along the turf, and burst in the midst of the gallant horsemen, sweeping scores to the ground. And yet they did not flinch. Instead they dug their spurs still deeper, till they were actually racing for the Russian enemy.

What a sight! A green-clad valley, cloaked in eddying smoke, which was rent asunder every second by a blinding flash; and through it, all that remained of that galloping 600 now clearly visible, and a moment later plunging deep into the reek and smoke of the cannon.

Suddenly the guns in front ceased to fire. The first line, or rather what was left of it, rode over them and dashed pell-mell into the cavalry behind, breaking them and scattering them like chaff. And now came the moment for the second line, and for Phil and his friend. It was indeed a race, men and officers doing their utmost to outdistance the others. Long ago Phil had lost sight of his companion in the smoke, but now a riderless horse, frenzied by fear, came up and thundered along on either side of him. Suddenly a ringing "Tally-ho!" came from some officer in front, and with a roar of furious excitement the line rode over the smoking guns and dashed full into a huge mass of Russian cavalry.

Phil found himself still with the riderless horses alongside, amidst the men of the 11th Hussars. Standing in his stirrups, he leant over and cut savagely at the grey-coats which seemed to rise up on either side of him, while a loud hissing sound, produced by the excited Russians, filled the air around. There was a rush and a crash, and the horse on his right was swept away. He scarcely noticed it, but, seeing a comrade at that moment fall in front of him, he pulled his pony in with a jerk, and made such good play with his weapon that for a moment he kept the long Cossack lances from the fallen man.

Whack! A tremendous blow on his shoulder sent him flying from his saddle to the ground, where, looking up, he was just in time to see Tony standing in his stirrups with sabre raised on high. Down it came on the head of the man who had just struck him from his pony, and with a groan the Russian flopped upon his horse's neck.

"Up! Up yer get!" shouted Tony, laying about him with a will. "Full yourself together, old man."

Phil sprang to his feet, and, holding his sabre in his mouth, lifted the prostrate form of the trooper.

"Hold on here, Tony," he cried. "That's it. Now wait a minute. Those horsemen have cleared away."

Rent asunder by the terrible British horse, the Russians had in fact opened out and retired, disclosing the bulk of their army forming into square close at hand. Phil took advantage of the lull.

A riderless horse stood close at hand, and in a few seconds he was in the saddle. Then he sheathed his sabre, and, riding up to Tony, said:

"Now, hand him up here. He's stunned by the fall."

"And what about getting back, mate?" asked Tony, still holding the man. "It'll spoil yer chance. They are certain to come after us."

"I'll run the risk of that. Now, up with him, Tony," answered Phil abruptly.

"Look here, old pal, this is my job," said Tony stubbornly. "I owe yer a score, and I'll take this fellow for yer."

It was a generous impulse which prompted the gallant fellow, for to hamper one's retreat with the body of a comrade was practically certain to lead to a fatal result. But Phil ended the matter promptly. His eyes gleamed savagely, and though, when all was over, he thanked Tony with tears in his eyes, yet now that his wishes were opposed, and he had set his heart on the matter, his temper got the better of him.

"Hand him over," he hissed angrily. "Come, there is no time to waste; the men are falling-in again."

Tony looked as though he could have wept, but he helped to pull the trooper up, and, having seen him into Phil's arms, fell in behind, determined to bring his friend through or perish in the attempt.

"Rally, men! rally!" the officers were shouting, and at the sound the troopers came hurrying up. There was a short pause to allow stragglers to regain the ranks, and then, setting their heads down the valley, the remnant of that gallant 600 retreated at full gallop.

Bang! bang! The guns were blazing at them again; from behind and on either side grape and shell came shrieking at them. Then suddenly came the gleam of lances in front, and there stood a body of cavalry prepared to hedge them in and make them prisoners. As well set a mouse to catch a lion! These were the men who had ridden into the very "jaws of death", into "the gates of hell"; and was one single regiment of cavalry to bar their retreat when they had fearlessly attacked an immense army? Ridiculous! And bracing themselves once more, the British horsemen swept them on either side as if with a broom, and torn, shattered, bleeding, and exhausted, returned, still exulting, to their friends.

Heroes indeed! Well has it been said of them, "Honour the Light Brigade, noble six hundred!"

Chapter Sixteen.

Honour for the Brave.

Balaclava was saved, and the historical battle, which had, seen two memorable cavalry charges, ended with the return of the Light Brigade. But the redoubts on the Causeway heights still remained in the enemy's hands, and Liprandi at once set about strengthening them, while battalions of grey-coated infantry bivouacked, there, ready for instant attack or defence. The Allies therefore found themselves confronted by a series of defences of formidable character, and barring their inlet to Sebastopol, while within the town was an army greater in number than their own, and from whom a sortie in force might be expected at any moment, thus pinching them between two bodies of troops, both within easy striking distance. And of no less importance to the invaders was the fact that winter was at hand, to be spent by them—and particularly by the British, who were to suffer all the torments of starvation and exposure, and amongst whom disease was destined to find many victims—in one long struggle with privation and misery.

But to return to Phil and his friend. Almost falling from their saddles with fatigue, they rode slowly towards the Chersonese heights when once they were out of range of the Russian guns. By a miracle neither had been hurt during the retreat, but already Phil felt the effects of the blow across his shoulder. His arm was stiff and almost powerless, while the sabre with which he had been struck had cut through his clothing and inflicted a nasty slash which had bled freely. However the blood had long since congealed, and a plentiful supply of strapping later on in the day did all that was necessary.

At the mouth of the valley an officer dressed in the same uniform, as the man Phil carried in his arms and accompanied by two troopers rode up to him.

"You can hand over our comrade to these men," he said. "Now, corporal, what is your name and corps. By your tunics you should be Guardsmen; but how on earth you came to be with us in that glorious charge is more than I can understand."

"We were taken prisoners at the Alma, sir," Phil answered, "and were escaping and hoping to ride into the British lines upon two ponies which we captured, when the battle commenced. We both belong to the Grenadier Guards."

The officer stared at Phil.

"Corporal Western by any chance?" he asked, with a lift of his eyebrows.

"Yes, sir," that is my name, "and this is the friend who was captured with me."

To the absolute astonishment of the two young soldiers the officer shook each in turn eagerly by the hand.

"Ah, my lads!" he said gaily, "we have heard of you already, and your friends, I guarantee, will give you a lively welcome. Let me tell you that the affair of the flag has gone through the allied camp. Lieutenant McNeil wrote a letter with all the particulars, and had it passed through to as by the courtesy of the Russian general I expect that there will be something waiting for you, and you thoroughly deserve it. As for this other matter, I shall take it in hand. You are a gallant fellow, Corporal Western, and saved that man's liberty if not his life. Now I must be off, but some day I shall hope to hear all about the escape."

"Can you tell us where the Guards are?" asked Phil, after having thanked the officer.

"Over there, Corporal;" and he pointed to a force of men returning along the Chersonese heights. "The First Division marched out early in the morning, and by cutting across here you will reach camp almost as soon as they do."

The officer rode off, and Phil and his friend turned their tired animals to the heights and rode for the Guards' camp in silence, their thoughts too much occupied by what they had heard to allow of speech. Sundry deep chuckles, however, told that Tony at least was immensely pleased at something that had occurred.

Half an hour later, looking more like beggars than Guardsmen, they rode into the camp.

"Let's ride straight up to our own mess and get something to eat," suggested Tony. "I am fairly empty, and longing for some grub."

But the sight of two tattered Guardsmen riding through their lines was too much for their comrades.

"Why, who are they?" they shouted, rushing forward to meet them. Then, recognising them, a man in Phil's company cried at the top of his voice, "Hi, come along, mates! Blow'd if Corporal Western and his pal ain't come back to us. Where do yer come from, Corporal? And what's happened to yer both since yer was taken?"

Men rushed forward and plied them with questions, and then, becoming enthusiastic, they lifted the two young fellows from their saddles and carried them shoulder-high through the camp.

It was a hearty greeting, for the men were anxious to do full honour to their two comrades who had gained distinction at the Alma. Very soon the babel had roused the officers, and before Phil and his friends could well collect their scattered senses, they were standing stiffly in front of the colonel and his adjutant, war-worn, weary and bedraggled, but for all that holding their heads erect, and quivering with excitement.

"What's this? What is all this noise about? Who are these two men?" the former asked abruptly, gazing at them searchingly and failing to recognise them.

"They are the corporal and man who helped to rescue Lieutenant McNeil's colours, sir," the adjutant replied, looking at them proudly. "They belong to the regiment."

"Ah!" and the colonel's face beamed. "Two of our brave fellows! Yes, I recognise them now. My lads," he continued earnestly, "many a brave act was done by our men at the Alma, but of all yours was the most conspicuous. We are proud to own you. You, Corporal, are promoted to full sergeant, and you," addressing Tony, "to full corporal."

Flushing with pleasure, Phil and his friend thanked the colonel and retired to their comrades, who had prepared a sumptuous feast for them.

"Here yer are, Corporal!" said one enthusiastic fellow, addressing Tony, and emphasising the corporal, "take a bite at this;" and he offered him a helping of a wonderful pie.

Tony blushed, and looked upon the point of exploding, for he was unused to his new title. But he took the helping and quickly caused it to disappear.

"Look here, mates," he said, after a long pause, "I'm promoted corporal, and yer can call me that as much as yer like to-day, but after that it's off. Remember that;" and he glowered round at them. "This here pal of mine," he continued, pointing to Phil, "is a full sergeant, but that ain't all—he's a gent, and this very day he's done what'll bring him the gold lace of an officer. I tell yer all he saved a chap right up there by the Russian guns, when the Light Brigade charged, and brought him safely out. That's what he did, and mind what I say, to-morrow or next day will see him an officer. Then I chucks the stripe and takes on as his servant."

The honest fellow's face shone with pleasure, while his comrades looked on in astonishment. Phil reached over and grasped his gallant old friend by the hand.

"Tony," he said with a gulp, "you're talking bosh. Of course I sha'n't be an officer; besides, you helped to bring that wounded man out as well. But if ever I do get a commission I'd have you as my servant and true friend sooner than anyone."

The men cheered eagerly.

"Hallo!" said one of them, recovering from his momentary excitement, "what's this here about bringing a pal out? Yer talk about the Light Brigade. Spin us the yarn, mates, and don't forget to tell us how you was taken, and how you gave them Russians the slip."

Late that night, when all turned in, Phil and his friend were the heroes of the camp, and Tony, whose admiration for his friend had increased, if possible, during the past few trying days, blurted out to the man lying by his side that Phil would make as fine an officer as ever wore queen's uniform, and that if anyone dared to gainsay this he would smash him to pieces. A loud snore was his only answer; but, relieved to some extent by this outburst, the noble-hearted fellow fell peacefully asleep.

When the orders for the army were published two days later, there was one portion which particularly attracted the attention of the Brigade of Guards.

Corporal Western, the paragraph ran, *is promoted to sergeant for gallantry at the Alma in helping to save a colour.*

Then it continued:

Sergeant Western, who was captured at the Alma, escaped from the enemy, and, taking part with his comrade in the memorable charge of the Light Brigade, rescued and brought out a wounded trooper. For this act of bravery he has been appointed an ensign in the 30th Foot.

The paragraph ended:

Lieutenant Western's comrade, who was promoted to corporal, resigns that rank.

In a state of huge excitement Tony managed to secure a copy of the order, and rushing up to Phil, presented it with an elaborate salute and a face which worked with emotion.

"Congratulations, sir," he said hoarsely. "You're ensign in the 30th Foot."

Phil hastily glanced at the order, and for the moment felt dizzy, for here, long before he could have expected it, was a commission.

Clutching Tony by the hand, he shook it warmly, while tears rose to his eyes.

"Thanks, my dear old friend!" he murmured, with a catch in his voice. "At length I have obtained what I wanted. But it will make no difference to us. Promise me that, Tony. We have been comrades so long, let us continue so, and if you still wish to be my servant, as you have often declared, why, come, by all means; I shall be more than glad to have you."

"Spoken like a true 'un, mate," growled Tony, sniffing suspiciously, and glaring round as much as to say that if anyone were even to suggest that emotion had got the better of him, he would do unutterable things.

"Beg pardon, sir, Colonel's compliments, and will you go over and see him now," said a stalwart orderly, approaching at this moment and saluting with such smartness that Phil nearly jumped out of his skin.

It was a moment of intense pleasure to all the fine fellows standing round. Here was a comrade who by his own bravery had obtained a commission from the ranks. They were intent on doing full honour to him, and though the strange anomaly of seeing an old friend, bearing sergeant's stripes, saluted as an officer caused many to indulge in a secret grin, yet it was his right now, and they were determined upon seeing he had it.

Utterly bewildered, Phil made his way to the colonel's quarters, where he received more congratulations.

"There now, we won't worry you any more," said the colonel kindly. "The adjutant will tell you what to do in the way of uniform, and, Western, my lad, remember this, the Grenadier Guards will always welcome a visit from you."

At this moment the adjutant took Phil into his tent.

"Of course you must get some kind of uniform," he said. "I dare say there will be no difficulty in obtaining the kit of one of the officers of the 30th killed at the Alma. I will send over and enquire. Meanwhile you can do as you like: mess with us, or go back to your old comrades for the night."

Phil looked at his tattered and mud-stained garments.

"I think I'd rather do that," he said. "Once I have the proper kit I shall feel more like an officer. At present I can scarcely believe it."

Accordingly he returned to his messmates, who did full honour to him that night. An extra tot of rum had been secured, pipes were set going, and a pleasant evening was passed with songs round a blazing camp-fire.

The next day he was fortunate enough to obtain a complete kit of an officer of the 30th, and, buckling on his sword, strode over to their camp, where he was expected. His new comrades gave him a cordial welcome, and recognising that he was a gentleman, and, moreover, one whose pluck had already been tried, they made the most of him.

From that day Phil was kept remarkably busy. He had his share of outpost duty to do, and when not engaged in that he was in the trenches under continual fire, for the batteries on either side thundered all day long. Already the French had recovered from the explosion at Mount Rudolph, and, increasing their guns, were now ready to rejoin their allies in another attempt to reduce the fortress. Once the redoubts were destroyed, and the enemy's cannon put out of action, there would be a general combined assault. November the 5th was settled upon as the date for the bombardment.

"How it will succeed I scarcely like to guess," remarked Phil to Tony one afternoon as they trudged back to the camp after a long spell of duty in the trenches. "On the last occasion the fire we poured upon Sebastopol was simply terrific, and one would have thought that not a living being could have survived. And yet, though some of the Russian guns were silenced, the majority hammered away at us in return, and did no little damage. Look at the French battery. Mount Rudolph, as our allies called it, was simply blown to pieces."

"Yes, sir, it was that," Tony agreed. "And it was just that fact that prevented our capturing this place we're sitting down in front of. That night we should have assaulted, but the explosion took the heart out of the Froggies, and when next morning came, and they were feeling a little more like themselves, why, the fortifications which our guns had knocked to pieces had been rebuilt. They're hard-working chaps over there, and plucky too; but this time it's going to be a case of 'all up' with them. You'll see our guns smash them to pieces. Why, it was bad enough when we were prisoners in there, so what will it be how when the Allies have any number of guns in addition. Depend upon it, mate, we'll do no end of damage with shot and shell, and then we'll assault and capture the place."

"I wish I thought so, Tony," Phil answered doubtfully. "I cannot forget that the Russians are at least two to our one, which is just the opposite of what it should be, for a force assaulting a fortified place should always be of greater proportions than that defending. Then look at our trenches and the distance which intervenes between them and the Russian earthworks. Long before we can race across, it seems to me that the guns, which will be trained to sweep the open, will blow us to pieces. Still, we'll have a good try if the orders come for an attack. But I shall be happier about our success if we can sap still closer, until little more than two hundred yards separate us from the Russians."

Now the fear that the fortress might be taken at the next attempt had not failed to rouse the Russians. They recognised the necessity of diverting the attention of the Allies, and, moreover, receiving on November 4th large reinforcements from Odessa, they determined to march against the positions held by French and English, and if possible annihilate them, or at least drive them still farther south towards Balaclava, and so render the causeway leading from Sebastopol over the Tchernaya river less open to attack. By means of this causeway they replenished their garrison, which was daily diminished by the severe losses it suffered. This time the wily enemy chose a different field for their operations. At dawn on the 5th a huge force left the fortress and formed up on the Inkermann heights, beyond the Tchernaya. These heights, filled with caves, littered by massive boulders, and capped by grey battlemented walls, formed a background, bounded on the west by the Careenage ravine leading almost south, and on the north by the great harbour. Directly in front of the heights, and separated by a wide stretch of valley, was a horseshoe-shaped crest, behind which lay the Second Division. On its extreme right was the sandbag battery, without guns, and composed merely of a bank of earth, while between it and the Russian position was a conical hill, known as Shell Hill, which was very soon to be manned by some 100 Russian guns.

Combining with another force, the total numbers reaching nearly 40,000, the enemy advanced against our position, hoping to capture it, while the remainder of the field-army threatened the French from the Causeway heights and made a feint of attacking. The huge garrison within the fortress, too, were to take a part, for their orders were to fire steadily at the trenches, and if much confusion was noticed, to make a sortie and capture them. Thus it will be seen that nothing short of a complete and overwhelming defeat of the Allies was aimed at. Had it not failed, England's reputation would have gone for ever, but November 5th was destined to be a glorious day. Scarcely 4000 were to keep at bay and cause awful losses to an enemy vastly outnumbering them, and that 4000 was composed of British infantry; alone, almost unaided, they were to beat back the enemy, and to their dogged pluck, their fierce lust for battle and disregard of death, and the fortunate assistance of a thick fog which obscured them and hid from the Russians the thinness of their ranks, they were to owe this glorious victory. There was no order, no scheme of defence. It was impossible in the circumstances. It was essentially a soldiers' battle. Broken into knots and groups of anything from 200 to 20, our gallant fellows fought on, at first with a furious valour, white-hot in its intensity, and later, when almost dropping with fatigue, with a grim, undaunted firmness of purpose which stamped them as men—true men—of an unconquerable bull-dog breed.

Phil and Tony bore no small share in the battle, for, on the very evening before, it fell to the former's lot to be on outpost duty.

"Take your men well up the valley and post them at wide intervals," said the colonel before he started. "There is no saying when we may be attacked by the enemy, and, to tell the truth, I am uneasy. The Russians have tried to take Balaclava and failed; but they captured the Causeway heights, and from there they are constantly menacing the French. Supposing they were to take it into their heads to advance from Inkermann against this ridge here, there is only the Second Division to bar their progress, and what could we do against a horde when we barely number 4000? No, I tell you, Western, I am troubled and uneasy, and that is why I am so particular as to my orders. Post your men at wide intervals, and before leaving them settle upon some rallying-spot. I would suggest the barrier at the neck of the valley. In any case, if you notice any movement in the enemy's camp, send me word and fall back slowly. The longer the delay the better."

"Very well, sir. I understand perfectly," Phil answered, and, raising his sword in salute, he turned and strode away to his tent.

"Bring along a rifle for me, Tony," he said. "We may have trouble this evening, and if we do I'd rather return to my old friend. I know it well, and feel better able, to fight with a bayonet in front of me."

"Right, sir!" was the cheerful answer. "Glad to hear that you wish to return to it. It's won England's battles, I reckon, and, compared to a sword, why, it's— it's worth a hundred of 'em. Look at yours. A regular toothpick to go out and fight with!"

With a disdainful toss of his head Tony picked up Phil's latest weapon and drew it from the scabbard. Then, wiping its blade upon the tail of his tunic, he thrust it back and set about getting other matters ready. A handful of dry chips enclosed in a sack were placed in the middle of a small collection of sauce-pans and cups. Over these a couple of blankets and a small sheet of oiled canvas were laid and then rolled tightly. That done, the faithful fellow went across, to another tent, and returned with an extra rifle and bayonet. A large ammunition-pouch accompanied it, and in addition Tony provided his master with a haversack, into which a piece of bread and some half-cooked pork were thrust, so that, if by chance he were separated from his men and the bivouac, he would yet have something with which to keep away the pangs of hunger.

An hour later twenty-five men of the 30th foot fell in, their blankets over their shoulders, and canteens slung from their belts. Then Phil emerged from his tent, looking smart and soldier-like in his new uniform. A hasty inspection having satisfied him that each man was provided with ample ammunition, and prepared for a night's outpost duty, he gave the order to march, and, slinging his rifle across his shoulder with a freedom and ease which told his men that he was well used to it, and had lately been one of themselves, he strode down the hill, and, crossing a wall of stone known as the "barrier", which practically shut the mouth of the valley, he led his small command straight on towards the Russian camp.

"Halt!" he cried as soon as he had reached a spot much broken by boulders and overgrown by brushwood. "Now, my men, you will go on duty every two hours, one half relieving the other at the end of that time. You will post yourselves in a wide circle, some twenty paces apart from one another, and stretching well across the valley. If anyone hears a noise, he will inform those on his right and left and then come and let me know. I may tell you that trouble is expected. If it comes, stick to your positions to the last, and then fall back upon the barrier. That will be our rallying-place. Now, let the rear rank fall out and choose a good site on which to bivouac I will take the front rank on and post the sentries."

Leaving the others to select some comfortable spot, Phil strode on with the front rank of his command, and only halted them when the brushwood showed signs of becoming too scanty to act as cover. Then he took each man individually, and, repeating his orders to him, placed him in the position he was to occupy.

That done to his satisfaction, he returned to the camp, to find that Tony had spread the blankets beneath an overhanging rock, and was already engaged preparing supper.

But Phil had other matters than his own comfort to think about.

"I am sure the colonel expects an attack," he murmured, as he sat upon a boulder and gazed at the flames. "Something is about to happen. I have been put in the responsible position of commander of the outposts. If I fail in my duty the result might be terrible to the Allies, for if only the Russians could reach the camp of the Second Division without observation, nothing could stop them from driving the remaining troops from their camps and trenches down to Balaclava. Well, at any rate I am warned, and to make sure that my sentries are alert I will go round every hour."

Accordingly, Phil spent a restless and watchful night, constantly passing from man to man and listening for movements of the enemy. But nothing seemed to disturb the silence save the moaning of the wind and the splash of rain as it beat upon the boulders.

Towards dawn, however, he fancied he heard sounds from the heights of Inkermann, and, posting himself amongst his men, he waited anxiously, vainly endeavouring to pierce the thick, white mist which had replaced the rain, and now filled the valley from end to end.

M 845

"THE REMNANT OF THAT GALLANT SIX HUNDRED RETREATED
AT FULL GALLOP"

Tramp, tramp, tramp! What was that? The sound rolled dull and muffled along the valley. Scarcely had Phil time to ask the question when a battery of Russian guns, placed on an elevation in front, fired a perfect salvo, the shells shrieking overhead, and bunting near the camp of the Second Division; while at the same moment columns of grey-coated infantry loomed up in front and to either side, marching rapidly towards him.

Hastily lifting his rifle, Phil sighted for the central one and pulled the trigger. There was a flash, a sharp report, and the rattle of other rifles answering the Russian fire, and telling those in the English camp that the enemy was upon them, and that the battle of Inkermann had commenced.

Chapter Seventeen.

Against Overwhelming Odds.

Huge indeed was the Russian army which Phil and his outposts saw advancing upon them through the mists of the valley. Thousands of infantrymen were in each of the thick columns, while far behind were others, resting on their arms and waiting in reserve. To attempt to keep back such a force was ridiculous, but much could be done by resolute men to delay its march, and Phil decided to attempt this with the handful at his command.

"The columns to right and left I must leave to themselves," he said hurriedly. "In any case they will march on and overlap me. But the central column is the biggest and most important, and, therefore, I will concentrate all my fire upon it. Pass the word along there for the men to close," he shouted. Then, turning to his sergeant, he said: "Hurry back to the camp at once and warn them that three Russian columns are advancing. Say I will hold them in check as long as possible."

Saluting hurriedly, the sergeant turned and ran back towards the barrier, leaving Phil and his handful of men face to face with the Russians.

Nothing daunted, and well knowing that much depended upon his exertions, for a long delay would enable the Second Division to get under arms and take up good positions, Phil concentrated his men, and with a rapid order formed them into line, the ends of which he swung backwards till they were in a semicircular formation.

"Now," he said, standing in front of them with rifle at the slope over his shoulder, "about turn; retire ten yards, and when you are well in among the bushes, lie down and wait for the order to fire."

Steadied by the example of coolness and determination shown them, the outpost-party swung about and retired into a thick belt of scrub, which, with the aid of the dense morning mist and numerous boulders, completely hid them. Each man at once threw himself upon the ground and waited, with rifle resting upon a stone.

Standing in their midst, Phil directed the greater part to pour their volleys into the central column, while a few files on the flanks engaged those on either side. Tingling with excitement, and filled with dogged determination to harass the

Russians to the last, the men levelled their rifles and waited eagerly for the word.

And as they waited, the tramp of thousands of feet grew nearer and still nearer, while the low and buzzing hiss of excitement, which Russian soldiery indulge in when about to attack, seemed already to have passed beyond them. Suddenly, however, a puff of wind blew the mist away in long trailing flakes, and the central column appeared, marching at a rapid pace, and already within thirty yards of the outpost. Almost at the same moment the lateral columns came into sight, but separated by a little wider interval.

"Fire!" cried Phil in a loud voice.

Instantly a rattling volley was poured into the dense masses of men, who came to an abrupt halt, while confusion and alarm spread through their ranks. Then officers rushed to the front, sword in hand, and called upon them to charge.

Flash! Another volley was poured into the struggling ranks, and men were seen to drop on either side.

Bending down so that the scrub just concealed them, Phil and his men rapidly reloaded, and had emptied their rifles again before the mist fell once more and hid the enemy from sight.

"Load again," cried Phil. "Now, are you ready? Then follow me to the right. We will change our position before these fellows recover sufficiently to open fire."

Running through the dense growth of bushes, the outpost-party soon took up a new position in front of one of the other columns, where, spreading out so as to pour their volleys into all three columns, they waited again for the command to fire.

Meanwhile shouts and oaths came in a perfect storm from the Russians, and their hiss of excitement rose to deafening pitch.

Then the mist was suddenly rent asunder by a flash of flame which ran along their front, and a hail of bullets was poured into the bushes where Phil and his party had lain not a minute before, sending a shower of twigs and leaves pattering to the ground, and striking the boulders with a series of sharp thuds, which told that but for the fortunate change of position, the outpost-party would have been decimated.

"Now we'll give them another taste," said Phil aloud. "Then we'll retire some fifty yards and wait for them again."

The movement proved even more successful than he could have hoped, for, bewildered by the mist, and fearful that they had stumbled upon a strong force of the Allies, the Russians still stood rooted to the spot, while the bullets tore remorselessly through their crowded ranks, doing awful execution at such close quarters. Standing in front of them, officers waved their swords gallantly and called upon them to advance, but, stricken by the fire and in dread of the British bayonet, the grey-coated host stood there doubtful and hesitating, and kept from flying only by the press of men behind, unaware as yet of the trouble which had befallen their comrades in advance.

"We'll play the same game again, my men," cried Phil coolly, as soon as the retirement had been carried out. "Then we'll make for the barrier and rejoin our friends. The 80th is there by now, and will be ready to help us if we are in difficulties."

"What's that there, sir?" asked Tony suddenly, standing by his master's side and pointing to the left. "That's a column of Russians, I reckon, and if we're to get back to friends alive we'd best be quick about it. See, they're already behind us."

Staring through the mist, Phil recognised with a start that the force of Russians to the left, suffering less from the galling fire of the British outposts, had recovered their wits, and, advancing up the valley, were tramping past him and already deploying between himself and the "barrier."

"Get together, men," he cried hastily. "Now, in two lines, and bayonets to the front! Keep your fire till at close quarters!"

Springing to their feet, the outpost-party hastily fell in, and, following Phil, who went some paces in front, retired at a ran, darting round boulders and clumps of brushwood, and keeping as much under cover as possible. But though they retired rapidly, the Russian ranks deployed even more quickly, and while those to the far left pushed on directly in their front, taking the course of a narrow ravine, others spread towards the centre, hoping there to join hands with their comrades.

And now an additional element of danger presented itself to Phil and his comrades. Behind them they had left the bulk of the enemy hesitating and uncertain how to act, and pouring an aimless and useless fire into the cover which had concealed those who had done them so great a mischief. At first firing independently and wildly, they had soon taken to well-ordered volleys, and, there being no answer to these and no more missiles of death flying through their ranks, they took courage and, coaxed by their officers, advanced. Arrived at the brushwood cover, they found not a single British soldier. Only deep footprints in the mud, and the litter of twigs brought down by their own bullets, could be seen, and recognising that they had been duped, they broke from a hiss of excitement into a roar of fury, and, breaking from control, dashed forward over boulder and scrub towards the British lines.

"Hark! What is that?" said Phil, holding up his hand to arrest his men. "What do those cries mean?"

"It's the Russians coming," answered Tony. "Listen: you can hear them tearing through the wood. Quick, or we'll be taken. Look, there are men in front of us." A hasty glance told Phil that Tony was speaking only the truth, for at this moment a swarm of grey-coats could be seen between themselves and the barrier, and one of these, turning round at the moment, caught sight of the British outposts, and with a shout attracted his comrades' attention.

"Get together, lads!" said Phil, with coolness and decision. "There, that will do. Now let me take my place on the right. Remember, keep your fire till the muzzles almost touch their coats, and then pull the triggers. Are you ready? Then charge!"

In a close and compact mass, and with bayonets well to the front, the little party dashed forward, and, directed by Phil, charged where the Russian ranks seemed thinnest. With eyes flashing, and courage roused to the highest, the men behaved with a coolness and disregard of danger which was magnificent. Waiting till the whites of the Russians' eyes were distinct, they poured in a terrible volley, and then threw themselves upon the enemy with a shout. For five minutes a furious mêlée raged. Bayonets thrust the air wildly on every side, and death seemed in store for Phil and his small command. Struck by bullets, or thrust through by the steel, some of his gallant men fell before a minute had passed, but, undismayed, and filled only with an enthusiasm and fury which made them forget all else, the remainder wielded their weapons unceasingly, and, plunging ever forward, cut their way to the heart of the enemy, and then through its crowded ranks, until not a Russian lay between them and the barrier. Then turning fiercely they waited only to cast off a few who still clung to them, and, dashing them to the ground, took to their heels, and within a minute were over the barrier and lying full length upon the ground, panting and endeavouring to regain their breath ere the enemy were upon them.

As for Phil, he cast his rifle to the ground, and, seating himself upon a boulder, waved his arms at the officers surrounding him, and endeavoured to tell them how vast was the force about to attack the British camp.

"There, sit still and say nothing," said the colonel who had spoken to him on the previous evening. "Thanks to the timely warning you sent by the sergeant, we are as prepared as it is possible to be, though our numbers are dangerously small. Still, we are ready, and we must thank you, Western, for delaying the enemy and so giving us time. Let me tell you you have done a gallant and most useful service for the army. Now, I see you are better. Take a small nip from this flask. It will help you to pull round."

Phil did as he was directed, and just as the enemy reached the barrier had recovered his breath and strength sufficiently to snatch up his rifle again and join his company.

And now commenced a battle upon the fortunes of which depended the fate of the Allies. Here was an immense army marching in three columns upon a ridge held only by a division scarcely 4000 strong. In rear of it lay the French, at present wholly unable to help or reinforce, for, though not attacked, they sat in their trenches, menaced by Liprandi's large force from the Causeway heights, captured on "Balaclava" day. And on their left the roar of cannon from the fortress could already be heard as they thundered at the British, while behind the masonry thousands of Russians were massed in preparation for a gigantic sortie upon the investing trenches.

No one could help that gallant 4000, for everywhere troops were urgently needed against threatened attack. But lack of numbers was fully compensated for by a courage which becomes even more remarkable as one thinks of it— courage sufficient to urge them to march over that crest, and, leaving their tents, amongst which cannon-shot were already hurtling, to descend the slope and advance against an army of huge proportions. Fortune favours the brave, indeed, for where can history show a brighter example? Eager for the fight, and reckless of the consequences, the British troops descended the ridge and threw themselves upon the enemy. The mist opened, and the Russians saw a double line of red, and faces furious with excitement and lust of battle, charging upon them, but next moment the British ranks were hidden. A breath of wind to dispel the vapour would have turned the fortunes of the battle, and changed glorious victory for the British into disastrous defeat. But there was no breeze, no puff of wind to clear the atmosphere, and, ignorant of the thinness of the opposing lines, and feeling sure that they were already face to face with the bulk of the allied army, the Russians came forward slowly and carefully. There was none of that dash and recklessness which would have brought them victory; instead, they paused, swayed this way and that, torn incessantly by volleys from rifles which, far superior to their own, caused ghastly slaughter in their ranks; and gave way whenever a company of England's soldiers fell upon them.

Meanwhile what had happened at the barrier? Two hundred of the 30th Foot lay behind it, and alone met the central column with their bayonets. Rushing at the low wall of stones, swarms of grey-coated warriors attempted to climb it, only to be hurled back from the bayonets. Time and again did they renew the assault, but always with the same result. And all the while bullets pelted amongst them, so that at length, despairing of surmounting the barrier, they turned to the left and joined one of the lateral columns. All day long did that gallant handful of the 80th cling to their position, and almost incessantly were they called upon to oppose other bodies of Russian troops, who came to renew the combat. Worn out with their exertions, with blackened faces and blood-stained clothing, they threw themselves upon the miry ground and slept the sleep of exhaustion till another alarm was given, when, shaking off their drowsiness by an effort of will, they sprang to their feet once more, and, grasping rifles, again flung themselves upon the enemy. Gallant souls indeed they were, but not more brave and determined than their comrades upon that memorable battle-field. Sweeping by them on the right one Russian column fell upon the flank of the British and hurled it aside by sheer weight of numbers. Then, advancing rapidly, they wheeled to the left, and were within an ace of taking the division in rear. But again fortune favoured the British. Buller hurried up with reinforcements at this moment, and, falling upon them with bull-dog ferocity, pushed them back, then rent them in pieces, and sent them hurrying away in disorder.

And on the British right events of no small moment were taking place. Pushing past the barrier, with the 200 of the 30th growling on their flank, and constantly hurling volleys at them, an enormous column closed with the soldiers in red and pressed them up and up the hill till the crest and the sandbag battery were reached.

And now commenced a stage in the battle that is memorable, that stands out amongst all the glorious deeds of that splendid day as more glorious than all the rest. As if at school and struggling for the possession of some imaginary castle, British and Russians fought fiercely for the sandbag battery. A mere mound of earth, and having no guns, it was but a mark, a ridge upon the rolling crest, which attracted the eye. Foiled in their main attempt to force the enemy back and march on towards Balaclava, the Russians forgot the object of the day, and those in the neighbourhood of the battery straggled furiously for its possession. Frantic with rage and disappointment, and with noble courage, they hurled themselves upon it time and again, only to be as bravely met and dashed down the hill once more. Grim, bareheaded, and full of valour the Guards clustered round that battery and disputed its ownership with the Russians. Undaunted by the numbers advancing, time and again they hurled them back, and then stood leaning upon their rifles, and between their gasps for breath called to the Russians to come again, to mount the slope and capture the position. And the grey-coated host glared up at them across a stretch of beautiful green turf now

173

piled high with poor lads who had fought their last fight. Yes, hundreds of fine men lay there, some barely more than boys, others in the prime of life, gaunt, raw-boned Russian linesmen, with ugly red streaks upon their faces, or big patches of like colour growing ever larger upon the grey cloth of their uniforms. Amongst them, too, still clutching rifles, and some even with hands clenched and tightly grasping their enemies, lay fine stalwart Guardsmen, young men in the pride of youth and strength, and veterans. Death had called them away, and just as many an eye would dim, and cheeks be moistened, in far-away Russian cabins for those near and dear who had gone, so in good old England women and lasses would soon be weeping for those gallant sons and brothers who had died for the country's good.

For long hours the conflict raged round the battery, but though the Russians were in far greater numbers than the British, the Guardsmen budged not an inch; and when the day was done, stood victorious and proud owners of the position.

Meanwhile the orderly lines of the Second Division had been broken by sheer weight of numbers, and pushed back here and there; in other parts they pressed forward with irresistible valour into the enemy's columns, and fought on in parties of two hundred, and often less—as few even as twenty,—with desperate courage and determination, and with a lust of battle and ferocity that was truly marvellous. Not once, but many times, these small groups flung themselves upon the enemy, and, thrusting and slashing on every side, cut their way to the very centre of the mass of grey, pushed on with assailants surrounding them, and at length passed to the other side, only to turn and bury themselves once more in the Russian ranks.

Late in the day, too, when the fate of the battle still hung in the balance, more artillery arrived, and, engaging the batteries on Gun Hill, caused them to retire. Then slowly and grudgingly the Russian infantry turned round and retreated in disorder to the heights of Inkermann, leaving an enormous number of killed and wounded behind them.

Oh for Scarlett's Heavy Brigade, or the remainder even of that glorious 600 horse who had charged into "the gates of hell" on Balaclava day! One dash, one fierce charge amidst those retreating soldiers, and defeat would have been a rout, a decisive victory, which even at this date might well have led to the surrender of the fortress and the humbling of Russian pride.

But no horse were there, and the retreating forces of the Czar reached their bivouacs sullen and dispirited at their crushing defeat, but without suffering further injury save from the shell and plunging shot as the British guns opened upon the flying mass.

But that deep valley and the slopes leading to the ridge were piled with dead and wounded innumerable, for both sides had lost heavily, the Russian casualties amounting to many thousands.

Phil took his full share in the battle, while Tony hovered like a guardian angel near him, many a time turning aside a flashing bayonet meant for his friend.

One thrust, indeed, got home, the bayonet transfixing Phil's thigh and bringing him to the ground.

With a roar Tony was upon the man and had knocked him senseless with a tremendous blow on the head from the stock of his rifle. Then, lifting Phil, he carried him into a safer position behind the barrier of stones.

"It's nothing," exclaimed Phil, with a smile. "Slit up my trousers and just tie your handkerchief round. That's it. Now I think I shall be all right. The pain made me feel a little faint."

Taking a pull at his flask, which contained weak brandy and water, he was soon on his feet again, and had taken his place in the fighting-line. When all was over, Tony helped him back to his tent, and fetched the regimental doctor, who bandaged the wound.

"It's a simple flesh wound," the latter said encouragingly, "and, if you rest a little, will give you no trouble beyond a little stiffness. The difficulty is to get you young fellows to sit still for a moment. But you must rest, and as there happens to be a convoy going to Balaclava in an hour's time I'll send you with it and have you put on one of the ships."

"I'd rather stay here and get well," said Phil eagerly. "After all, it's only a scratch, and will be right in a week."

"Now, I'm treating you, my boy," the doctor exclaimed shortly, "and for your own good I shall send you on board ship, so there is an end of the matter."

Phil resigned himself to what he thought was a hard fate, for he was anxious to stay with his regiment. But no doubt rest for a few days was required, and the doctor was right in insisting upon it.

"Pack up my things, Tony, and we'll see whether I cannot get a lift in an araba," he said. "The convoy is to start from the crest, so you might slip up and see what can be done."

Tony did as he was told, and was able to secure a place for his master. Phil was then carried to the top of the hill, and, being lifted into the cart, was driven off. The convoy reached Balaclava at dawn, and Phil, with Tony in attendance, and some fifty other wounded men was sent on board a small schooner, which at once weighed anchor, and sailed out of the harbour.

"Nasty place that," said the captain, a rough-faced, genial old sea-dog, jerking his thumb towards the harbour. "Safe as a house so long as the wind's off shore; but once it begins to blow the other way, God help those aboard ship. There'll be only bare rocky cliffs to welcome them if the vessels go ashore, and how could they help doing that, for the anchorage is notoriously unsafe? Can't imagine why they stick there! There's many a safer harbour hereabouts."

The captain looked anxiously at the fine transports swinging to their cables, and then muttering "Thank heavens I shall be at sea and have a better chance than they!" nodded to Phil and dived below.

He was a knowing man, this sailor, and, being accustomed to the Black Sea, was well aware that the season for violent gales and storms of rain and snow had now arrived. That night indeed, and all the following day, it blew so fiercely that the vessel's bowsprit carried away, and she was obliged to put back into Balaclava for repairs. A few days later she once more set sail.

"Don't like the look of things," muttered the captain, looking round anxiously as they sailed from the mouth of the harbour. "If it comes on to blow on-shore to-night it'll be bad for them ships in there. But it isn't my affair. The chap as is in command has been warned more than once already."

"Do you think we are going to catch it again?" asked Phil.

"Can't say for certain, but it looks precious like it; I wonder what the glass is doing?" and with an anxious expression the captain went to consult his barometer.

"Falling fast," he said shortly, "and it's getting much colder. We're in for a dusting, I think. Mr King, get those sails taken off her, and make all taut. I'll go my rounds in half an hour and see how things are." He crossed the deck and fell into earnest conversation with his mate, leaving Phil to make his way aft and talk matters over with Tony.

The captain's fears were not unfounded. That evening, November 14th, a gale of wind sprang up, blowing dead on-shore, and soon a terrific storm was raging. With her head jammed close up into it, the *Columbine* seemed to make fair progress; but soon darkness had obscured the cliffs, and there was nothing by which to judge their position.

"We're far closer to those cliffs than I like," Phil shouted in Tony's ear. "Still, we seem to be getting well out to sea, and if only we can manage that we ought to be safe."

"I'd rather be fighting the whole Russian army than knocking about here," Tony roared back. "'Tain't that only neither. This sea puts a chap off his grub, and we ain't had such a lot of late as to let us afford it. Look what a rat I'm getting;" and with a comical air of despair he clutched the tunic he wore, to show that it was too large for him.

An hour passed, and it was very evident that the fury of the storm increased rather than diminished. Phil struggled on to the poop and found his way to the captain's side.

"We're in the hands of Providence, I reckon," cried the old sailor reverently. "Every foot we make we lose to leeward, and away over in that direction are the cliffs. We're running a trifle more along the coast now, for there's not a ship that's built that could face this gale. God help us, young man! We can do nothing more for ourselves."

Three hours later a tremendous sea struck the ill-fated ship and smashed her rudder to pieces. Instantly she commenced to broach to.

"Get a grip of something to hold you up," shouted the captain. "That'll finish her. Good-bye, lad!"

Phil grasped his hand for the moment and looked into his face. It showed more clearly than a book could how desperate the situation was.

Leaving him, he crawled along to Tony.

"Get hold of a rope, old man," he screamed in his ear. "She's going fast towards the rocks."

Whipping out their knives, they soon obtained two long pieces of stout cordage. With these they tied two of the large wooden gratings at the hatchway together, and obtaining some more rope, secured themselves to the woodwork, so that if the ship went down the hatchings would float away and support them.

Meanwhile huge billows of green water poured on board, thumping the ship till every timber quivered. Then one immense wave curled right over her and smashed her decks like an egg-shell. Immediately all was confusion. Shouts occasionally reached Phil's ear, and he once caught sight of the grey-headed old captain kneeling in prayer. A moment later another wave turned the unfortunate *Columbine* completely over, and, filling at once, she sank like a stone.

Phil felt as though he was being smothered. The din of rushing water rang in his ears, and intense darkness surrounded him. He fought and kicked madly. Then something struck him sharply on the head, and he grasped the grating to which he was tied, and with an effort dragged himself upon it. Close alongside was the other grating, and upon it, clinging with all his might, was Tony. And thus, side by side, one now dancing on the summit of a wave, while the other hung in the trough, drenched with water of icy coldness and almost smothered by the surf and rain, they drifted fast towards those inhospitable black cliffs against which the tempest thundered.

Chapter Eighteen.

Saved from the Deep.

More than an hour of misery and terror passed as Tony and Phil clung, half-submerged, to their gratings, and as they held on, the sound of huge waves, breaking upon the iron-bound coast to which they were fast approaching, grew louder. Phil pulled upon the rope which kept their fragile rafts together and shortened it, bringing them close alongside one another.

"Good-bye, old man!" he shouted, between two gusts of wind.

Tony's mouth opened and he bellowed something, but the words were carried away on the gale. Conversation, even by shouting, being hopeless, they once more fell into despairing silence.

"What has happened?" cried Phil half an hour later. "We seem to have left the crash of waves on the cliff behind us, and already the sea seems to be going down."

Tony crept closer. "The wind ain't going down," he shouted hoarsely. "It's blowing stronger if anything, and though we lies low in the water, we're bowling along in fine style. Can't make it out, mate; this sea going down looks as if we'd been washed into some sheltered cove. Anyway we shall know soon," and he jerked his arm to the right, where already the black clouds were lifting.

Half an hour passed, when Phil suddenly caught sight of high cliffs to right and left, while on the summit of one of them seemed to be a fort, for the white masonry was distinctly visible. He stared through the gloom and sweeping sheets of spray, and thought he detected another fort on the opposite side. A few minutes later they were washed through a large opening in the cliffs, and the forts flashed by on either side; at the same moment the sea became still quieter, and the roar of the wind seemed left behind them.

"I think I saw a fort on either side," cried Phil, "and as I know there is only one harbour on this coast with high cliffs and forts, I feel certain that we are drifting into Sebastopol. Great Scott! We shall be made prisoners again."

Tony groaned. "Can't be helped," he shouted, suddenly brightening. "If we are, why, it'll just give us the fun and excitement of escaping again. But, old friend, this here's an escape from sudden and horrible death, and if it hadn't been that the Almighty up there, above them black clouds, had been keeping His eye on us, we'd have been washing about amongst the fishes hours ago."

Tony looked upwards to the sky, and his lips moved. Phil watched him curiously, and there, tossing on the storm-troubled water, offered up a prayer for his safety so far. Nor could he help contrasting Tony's condition of mind as it was at that moment with what it had been when first he made his acquaintance in the menagerie many months before.

"Hallo! What's that over there?" he suddenly shouted, catching sight of a dark mass in the water. "It looks like a piece of wreckage. Perhaps there is someone on it."

Both stared at the object which, being much larger and higher out of the water, bore down upon them quickly. There was no doubt now that it was a portion of a ship, perhaps of the wrecked *Columbine*, and in the hope that it was, Phil and his friend dipped their hands in the water and slowly propelled themselves so as to lie in its path.

"I can see something red on it," said Phil, shading his eyes. "Can you make anything out, Tony?"

"There's a chap there in red breeches, or I'm an idiot, Phil. Yes, I can see him plainly. He's tied to the wreckage, and as far as I make out there isn't a move in him. Tell yer what, old man, that would be a safer place than these here gratings, and I advise that we swop."

When the floating mass reached them, Phil and Tony sprang on to it, securing their gratings to it, and casting off the ropes with which they had fastened themselves. Lashed to a ring-bolt was a little, red-breeched French linesman, apparently dead.

Phil cut his lashings free, and turning him on to his back, tore his coat open. "Not dead yet," he cried eagerly. "Lend a hand here, Tony. We'll pull this fellow round. He is as cold as ice, so we'll take his shirt off and rub his chest and arms. That ought to restore the circulation."

Setting to work with a will they tore the clothing from the unconscious Frenchman, and chafed his body and limbs with such energy that soon there were obvious signs of returning consciousness, and moreover their exertions had made both of them thoroughly warm, whereas before they had been numbed with cold.

Suddenly their ally opened his eyes and stared round wildly.

"Mon Dieu!" he groaned, and seemed to relapse into unconsciousness. Once more opening his eyes he stared at Phil, and, recognising him as an English officer, stretched out his hand, while a look of relief and gladness overspread his face.

179

M 845
"A RATTLING VOLLEY WAS POURED INTO THE DENSE MASSES
OF MEN"

"Mon cher, mon cher!" he cried joyfully. "Ah, zis is ze grand plaisir. Ah!"

"Cheer up, my good fellow," said Phil kindly, patting him on the shoulder, for, overcome by emotion, the little man had burst into tears. "Come, tell us how you came to be wrecked like us. You speak our language, so we shall be able to understand."

"Oui, monsieur, I speak ze language of ze English. Ah, I speak 'im well!" laughed the Frenchman, with some pride. "Once I live in England three months and act as a waiter. You wish to know how I came here. Ah, c'est terrible!" And he covered his face with his hands.

"Now then, pull yerself together, little 'un!" exclaimed Tony encouragingly. "We're all in the same box. Fire away and let's have the yarn."

"Eh, bien," said the little man, sitting up. "I leave my beloved France six months ago, and sail for to fight ze perfide Russian. Then after ze battle for Balaclava,—monsieur, what horsemen terrible are yours—I get ze malade; ze—what you call 'im—ah, ze water and ze cold do catch me here;" and placing his hands on his stomach, he rolled his eyes till the whites alone showed, and groaned dismally. "Ze officer say, 'mon pauvre garçon!'" he continued, "and send me on the ship *Henri Cinq*."

"What! you don't mean to say that that fine boat has gone down?" interrupted Phil.

"Alas, monsieur, it is true!" the Frenchman answered, lifting his hands. "Behold, all is peace; ze sun 'e shine so brightly. Then ze tempest come, ze ship fight bravely, and then rush on the land. 'Sauve qui peut', ze captain shout, and I tie myself here. Then I think of my country, and all is dark. I wake, and you are here, mon cher. Aha! what does he matter? Mais—ah, monsieur, mes pauvres camarades!" and once more the little man relapsed into tears.

Meanwhile the wreckage had been rapidly drifting, and as the darkness lifted it became perfectly evident that the harbour into which the gale had swept them was indeed that on the shore of which Sebastopol was built. Soon sentries noticed the wreckage, and before long boats had put off to secure it, for wood was of value for fires. To offer any opposition was hopeless; the three were lifted into one of the boats, and were rowed swiftly into the inner harbour, where they were handed over to a guard.

"Our second visit to this place," said Tony disgustedly. "Blow'd if it ain't the hardest luck as ever was. But I sha'n't grumble no more. We've come safe through when other lads have gone to their last. I say we was saved by a miracle."

"Yes, indeed," agreed Phil. "We have much to be thankful for."

"Then you have been prisonaire before?" asked the Frenchman, astonished.

"We only escaped a matter of three weeks ago," answered Phil.

"You make ze escape, monsieur?" the little man repeated, lifting his eyebrows in his amazement. "Truly, you Englishmen are brave. Ha, ha!" he went on, clapping his hands, "what need I, Pierre Moutard, fear? We will make ze escape with each others, and we will snap ze fingers at our perfide enemy;" and, putting his arms akimbo and throwing his chin proudly in the air, he frowned at the nearest sentry as though he would eat him. The man answered with a hoarse growl, causing the Frenchman to start and take his place between Phil and Tony rather hurriedly.

"Aha, ze perfide!" they heard him mutter beneath his breath. "He think 'e frighten me."

"I wonder where they will take us!" mused Phil. "If only they will be good enough to put us in the same prison as last time, I think we can guarantee that we will get out somehow."

"That we will," answered Tony with emphasis. "But what about this here Froggy with the red legs?" he asked in a cautious whisper. "He's kind of tied himself on to us—made pals of us, yer see,—so I suppose he'll have to escape with us too?"

He asked the question as though an escape had been already arranged.

"Heaps of time to think of that," said Phil, with a laugh. "But I must say the little man seems rather nervous."

"Pah! nervous! Just fancy getting frightened when one of these surly-looking guards growls at him. It's disgusting, that's what it is."

"Well, we won't worry about it now, Tony. Look out. Here come our orders."

An officer joined the group at this moment, and closely inspected the prisoners.

"What has happened?" he asked, less gruffly than usual.

"We were wrecked by the storm and blown into the harbour," answered Phil in his best Russian.

"Ah, you speak our language, sir! Good! You were wrecked, you say, and must therefore be cold and exhausted. Sergeant, take the prisoners into the guard-room, and bring this officer to my quarters. See that coffee and a glass of vodka are given to the other two. In half an hour you will call for my guest and march them all three to the prison-hall."

The man saluted, and led Tony and Pierre away, while, taking Phil's arm, the Russian led him on one side and asked how he happened to have the little Frenchman in his company.

A few minutes later he strode away, but rejoined Phil when the latter had been taken to the quarters set aside for officers.

"Sit down there, sir," said the Russian, politely motioning Phil to a chair.

"Now we will have breakfast, and I am sure you must be in great need of food. You look quite exhausted."

He struck a bell, and a meal of steaming hot fish and coffee was brought in, to which Phil did ample justice. Then a cigar was handed him, and he puffed at it with the greatest pleasure.

"It has been a terrible night, a truly awful gale," remarked the officer after a few moments' silence. "Even here we have suffered. Vessels have sunk in the harbour, and roofs have been torn from the houses, and many people killed in consequence. But at sea the unhappy English have met with a shocking disaster. It is said that along our coast and within the harbour of Balaclava no fewer than twenty-two fine transports have gone ashore, including the French ship*Henri Cinq*. Few lives have been saved, I fear, and how you and your comrades managed to escape is past belief. It is the fiercest storm we have experienced for years."

Phil was struck dumb with consternation. "Twenty-two ships ashore!" he murmured in a broken voice. "How awful! All those lives lost, not to mention the stores."

It was only too true. Twenty-two vessels had been wrecked, and of these the majority were filled with valuable stores of warm clothing and food, the former being urgently needed at that moment, for the cold weather had set in in earnest, and snow and sleet were falling.

"I grieve for you, sir," said the officer kindly. "It is ill fortune indeed. But, if you feel so inclined, tell me how you came to be washed into our harbour? It must have been a terrible experience."

Phil described the foundering of the *Columbine* and their miraculous escape.

"To be taken prisoner is always painful, Englishman," the officer said consolingly, "but to be dashed upon the cliffs is to meet with a reception compared to which your comfort here will be perfect luxury. It is unfortunate for you, but war is always filled with misfortunes. I will see that you and the two men with you are given blankets, and I will speak to the prison official for you. For myself, I leave for the field-army to-night. Ah, I hear the sergeant! Farewell, sir, and the best of fortune!"

Phil thanked him suitably, and half an hour later found himself in his old prison. As before, there were a number of other soldiers present, who greeted them enthusiastically, and eagerly asked for news.

"Some of us have been here since a day or two after the Alma," said their spokesman, "and we are dying for news. These Russian beggars won't even give us a hint. But we keep our spirits up, and when there's an extra heavy bombardment, we shout and sing till the guards get angry and come in and threaten to shoot. But we only laugh at them. It is the same if the food is bad; we kick up as much noise as possible, and in the end get what we want, for these fellows seem almost afraid of us."

"Is there no chance of escape then?" asked Phil.

"Not a morsel, sir. We've had a try all round, but always failed. There was an officer here named McNeil. He was wounded, and in trying to escape got stuck again with a bayonet. Then an ugly little brute they call an inspector of the prison came in and struck him with his whip. He seemed to know him, too, and accused him of inciting us to escape. That afternoon the lieutenant was dragged away, and we have never seen him since."

"Hum! that looks bad for us, Tony," muttered Phil. "If it is Stackanoff, and he recognises us, it will be a bad business. He is sure to pay off old scores if possible."

"Trust the brute," growled Tony. "But if he tries to come any of his larks on us he'll be getting a tap over the head like that fellow who found us hidden in the carriage."

At this moment the door of the prison was thrown open, and some blankets were given to the new prisoners.

"Prepare for a visit from the inspector," said the jailer curtly, "and see that everything is clean and straight, so that you do not disgrace me. It will mean evil for you if his excellency is not pleased."

A yell of derision met this speech, for the English prisoners had already met with such poor entertainment that they could scarcely receive worse, and, moreover, finding that a noisy, mutinous line of conduct overawed their guards, they had long ago got quite out of hand.

"Don't you go for to worry yerself, Whiskers," cried one sturdy linesman. "This place ain't no palace, so the cove who expects to find it such will be a fool. But it's clean, and always will be, 'cos us chaps ain't the sort to live in a pig-sty. Now hop away, Whiskers, and don't fret. We'll put it right with the inspector."

The Russian looked round at the grinning faces, while Phil, who had translated his message, put the last speaker's into Russian, taking the liberty, however, of making it more polite.

"Very well, do not fail me," growled the jailer, showing his teeth. "It will be the worse for you if you do."

"He will discover us as sure as we are alive!" remarked Phil as soon as the man had gone. "I mean Stackanoff, of course, for I suppose he is inspector. We must try to disguise ourselves."

Accordingly he and Tony ruffled their hair and disarranged their clothing. Then they took a place amongst the prisoners, taking care to keep well in the background.

Suddenly the door was thrown open with a crash, and Stackanoff stalked in majestically, his little pig-like eyes glaring at the prisoners.

"Line them up," he said, with an angry snap. "I wish to see if all are here."

The prisoners fell into line, and Stackanoff slowly inspected them.

"Who is this?" he asked, as he came opposite Pierre. "This is a Frenchman."

"He came with two other prisoners this morning, Excellency," answered the jailer. "They were wrecked and washed into the harbour."

"Fool! What do I care about their method of reaching here?" snarled Stackanoff, turning on the trembling man. "They are prisoners. That is good enough. Bring them before me."

"It's all up, Tony," whispered Phil. "We are to be brought before him."

"Let him take care, that's all!" muttered Tony, looking daggers at the Russian. "I'll down the fellow yet."

Stackanoff stared at them spitefully when they were marched in front of him, but for the moment did not recognise them.

"Ha! what is this?" he suddenly exclaimed, gazing at Phil. "Your face I know. Who are you? Ah!—villain!" And suddenly realising that Phil was the Englishman who had thrown him from his saddle and brought him into disgrace, he drew his sword, and, mad with rage, threw himself upon him with tigerish fury.

Phil was helpless. Another moment and he would have been cut down, when Tony grappled with the angry Russian, and, picking him up like a child, turned him upside-down, and, using all his strength, held him there, cursing and screaming with rage, and with his head resting on the floor.

"Get hold of his sword, Phil," he shouted. "Now I'll let him up if he promises to behave."

Phil snatched up the weapon, while Tony, now aided by a second prisoner, clung to the legs of the frantic Stackanoff, while the remainder looked on and laughed at the ridiculous scene till they were doubled up with merriment.

"You can let him go now," said Phil quietly. "If he rushes at me again I shall set to work with my fists and give the brute a thrashing."

Tony and his helper promptly released the inspector, and he doubled up in a heap on the floor. A second later he was on his feet, glaring savagely at Phil, his lips curling away from his teeth, and his hair and beard bristling with fury. But the steady stare with which Phil greeted him, and his air of preparation, caused the Russian to pause and think before attacking him again.

"Viper! Wretched Englishman!" he hissed. "You shall pay bitterly for this insult. Ah, you are dressed now as an officer! You were a private before. Your friend too has different uniform. You are spies—spies!" he shrieked, with a hideous laugh. "Yes, the tale of the shipwreck is a lie, and you two have been sent here to learn our plans. Take them away. They shall be severely dealt with."

"Where to?" asked the jailer, who had looked on anxiously at the scene, not knowing how to act.

"Fool! To the cells, of course," Stackanoff cried. "We have an empty one. Place them there, and take this Frenchman too. He also is a spy;" and he glared at poor Pierre as though he would kill him.

"What is it, monsieur?" the little man asked tremulously. "What are they about to do to ze prisonaires?"

"He says we are spies," answered Phil.

"Ah, spies! He make ze lie. Pierre is no spy. But they will not believe, and we shall all die!" The poor little man threw himself on the floor and howled dismally.

"Come up, won't yer?" exclaimed Tony with disgust, clutching him by the seat of his red breeches and hoisting him to his feet. "Ain't it enough to know as you're to come along with us? Ain't that bad enough? Shout when you're hurt, but till yer are hold yer tongue, or it'll be the worse for yer."

Pierre wept softly, his narrow shoulders and baggy breeches shaking with convulsive sobs. His chin was bowed upon his breast, and altogether the unhappy little Frenchman looked the very picture of despair.

"Pshaw! At least the Englishmen have courage!" scowled Stackanoff disdainfully. "Call the guard."

Half a dozen armed Russians marched in and surrounded the prisoners. Then, followed by shouts of farewell and encouragement from their comrades, the three prisoners were taken to the opposite side of the town, close to the fortifications facing the British guns, which could be heard booming in the distance, while an occasional shell passed overhead.

"You see that," said Stackanoff maliciously, drawing Phil's attention to a group of low buildings which in parts were tumbled into ruins. "The cells are there, and perhaps a friendly message from your comrades on the heights may find you out. It would be best for you, for no man has yet insulted me and lived to boast of it."

Phil did not deign to answer, but, looking closely at the buildings, noticed that they had indeed suffered heavily from the British fire. Walls were lying flat, roofs were broken, and a large brick chimney had been shorn off like a stick struck by a sword.

The escort halted opposite it, and a door was thrown open by a jailer.

"Place these three in number five cell, and come to me when you have done so," said Stackanoff. "I have special instructions to give you as to their comfort," he added cynically.

He turned on his heel and was gone, while Phil and his comrades followed the jailer down a steep flight of stone steps and entered a gallery. They stopped opposite a door studded with big nails. It was thrown open, and half a minute later had closed behind them with a harsh clang.

Chapter Nineteen.

You are Spies.

"We are properly bottled this time," exclaimed Phil, with some concern, closely examining the cell into which they had been thrust. "Look at these walls, all of thick stone, and pierced by two tiny windows with grilles. It is a regular cage, and after a first look at it I should imagine escape will be impossible."

"We was in a worse hole before," cried Tony encouragingly. "And yer must remember there's lots of ways of getting out besides digging holes in the wall. For instance, we might collar that surly-faced jailer and make a bolt for it. But it wants a bit of thinking out."

"Consider now, monsieur," chimed in Pierre in a plaintive voice. "To make ze escape from this—ah—I do not know 'is name, mais—maison—oui, maison—comprenez-vous, monsieur? To make ze escape will bring ze death to us, ze bang and ze bullet. Alas, it will be for ze no good!"

"Nonsense!" said Phil shortly. "If we want to get out we must chance that."

"Mais, monsieur, we are so happy. Why should we make ze escape? See, ze wall is strong, and ze cannon will not reach us," Pierre answered, with a shrug of his shoulders.

"Bah! thought you was for getting out?" cried Tony in disgust. "Look here, little 'un, if we tries the game you're welcome to this here cell to yourself."

Pierre subsided into silence, and commenced to make beds of the blankets, while Phil and Tony made a thorough inspection of the cell.

"Not a loophole for escape," growled Tony. "I suppose we'll have to dig our way out, for get away from here I will."

"And I too, Tony," Phil answered quietly. "There must be a way. What is this?" and he pointed to an open grate, upon the hearthstone of which were the long-cold embers of a fire. He put his head into it and looked up the chimney, but all was black as night. Suddenly a familiar voice, sounding a long way off, reached his ear.

"What can it be?" he cried, withdrawing his head. "I can hear that brute Stackanoff distinctly. Hush! I will get higher up into the chimney. Pierre, if you hear footsteps warn me in good time." Phil crawled beneath the overhanging lip of the grate, and stood up in the chimney. Then, finding a rest for his feet, he gradually ascended. Suddenly his head struck against some brickwork, and by stretching out his hands he found that the chimney bent upward at an easy slope. Surmounting the corner he crept up with some difficulty. The voice now sounded much nearer, so he lay still and listened.

"Know, then, that I have set hands on your comrades, beggarly Englishman!" he heard Stackanoff cry in a cruel voice. "They have been taken as spies, and I hope will be shot. I promise you that you shall see the fun."

"Wretch!" a weak voice replied, in tones which sounded like Lieutenant McNeil's, "have you not already ill-treated me sufficiently, and must you now persecute my poor countrymen? Were it not for this wound, which lames me, I would spring upon you and crush the life from your miserable carcass. Leave me, you coward!"

A derisive laugh was the only answer, and, having waited in vain to hear more, Phil slipped back into the cell, looking more like a sweep than a British officer. He was greatly excited, and that, together with the fact that he was partially choked by soot, made it difficult to answer Tony's eager question.

"What luck!" he cried at last. "This cell must communicate in some way with the next one, and in that is Lieutenant McNeil. Listen, and I will tell you what happened."

Sitting on his blankets he rapidly communicated the words he had overheard.

"I'm going up there again," he said, when some ten minutes had elapsed. "If this chimney allows us to reach the other cell, it will allow us, perhaps, to escape. Evidently our pleasant Stackanoff knows nothing about it. At any rate, if I can get into McNeil's prison, and can find some way out for both of us, he comes with me. Poor chap! See how long he has been shut up."

"What, another!" exclaimed Tony aghast. "Ain't it bad enough to have this here Froggy? ain't that hard enough? And now yer wants to take on another pal?"

Phil glared at him.

"Very well," he said curtly, "we'll not make the attempt. I am sorry, for I did not know you were a coward."

"Call me a coward, me a funk!" cried the gallant Tony, springing from his blanket-bed and striking himself on the chest. "Me, yer old pal too!" He looked half-sorrowfully and half-angrily at Phil. Then his face suddenly flushed.

"So I am," he cried hoarsely. "Ain't the poor young officer in distress, and me wanting to desert him? Phil, old friend, here's my hand. I won't say another word against it."

"That's right," said Phil, with a smile of relief. "I knew I had only to call you names to make you give way. Now I'll go up again. Come and give me a lift."

Climbing into the chimney he worked his way up laboriously. Soon his hand caught upon a sharp ridge of brick, and happening to look up at that moment, he saw a square patch of light with somewhat rugged margins.

"By George," he muttered, "that must be the broken chimney."

He turned over so as to be able to inspect it the better, and, with an exclamation of annoyance, noticed that several bars crossed the chimney some eight feet up.

"That will be our greatest difficulty," he thought. "Still, they are only built into brick, and we ought to be able to loosen them. Now for the other cell."

He felt the brickwork with his hands, and was delighted to find that it descended suddenly at an angle, showing that it corresponded to the part in which he was lying, and that two fireplaces were evidently arranged to pour their smoke through one common chimney. The flue down which he was looking then must communicate with the other cell.

"McNeil!" he cried softly. "McNeil!"

"Hallo! Who's that?" came a muffled answer.

Phil repeated his name again more loudly.

"Come to the chimney!" he cried. "I am up here."

A minute passed, and then the small patch of light which he could just discern beneath was suddenly obscured.

"Who are you? Whatever is happening?" McNeil asked in an eager whisper.

"Hush! Speak low. The jailer lives close outside my cell."

"Do you remember Corporal Western and his friend? The two who helped you with the flag?" asked Phil, making a funnel of his hands.

"Yes, of course I do. But who are you?"

"I am Corporal Western, or rather I was," said Phil. "I am now a lieutenant in the 30th. But I will explain later. My friend and I, together with a Frenchman, were wrecked and blown ashore this morning. That brute Stackanoff recognised us, and has put us in the cell next to yours, with the accusation that we are spies."

"Stackanoff! That man must die, Western," the stern answer came. "He has treated me with the foulest brutality. I am half-starved, and altogether lame, for the second wound I received while trying to escape has festered, and I am racked with fever. For God's sake get me out of this, old chap!"

"I mean to," Phil cried cheerfully. "We have no idea how we shall get out yet, but we gave the Russians the slip once before, and will do so now. Be ready at any moment. But I will try to warn you in good time. Now I will slip back, but to-morrow I will come right down into your prison."

Carefully lowering himself, it was not long before he was back in his own cell, and telling Tony all that had happened and what chances there were of escape.

"Speak low, mate," said Tony cautiously. "Tell yer what it is. This 'ere Froggy"—and he nodded contemptuously at Pierre—"ain't worth a bag of salt. My advice is, don't tell him what we're up to. You can see he ain't got the pluck to get out of this, and he's bound to know he'll catch it if we get away and leave him. So he'll round on us if we're not careful."

"Impossible!" exclaimed Phil.

"Look at the fellow then, and perhaps you'll change your mind," replied Tony in a whisper.

Pierre was lying disconsolately in his corner, and when Phil glanced at him the Frenchman's eyes were shifty. He looked ill at ease, and was evidently deeply curious as to his fellow-prisoners' movements.

"What for does monsieur mount ze chimney?" he asked peevishly. "Eef ze door open, what happen? Vraiment, ze bang;" and he shuddered at the thought that all would be shot.

"Look here," said Phil sternly, and with hardly repressed anger and contempt, "that man Stackanoff has got us in his clutches, and if we are to live we must escape. I went up the chimney for that purpose, but could see no way out in that direction. If we find a loophole, you must decide whether to accompany us; but mind me, do not attempt to betray us, or we will break your neck!"

"Betray monsieur! Ah, non!" the little man cried, lifting his hands in expostulation. "Surely I will come with you. I will brave ze death."

"Mind yer do then," grunted Tony, looking searchingly at him.

But the incident, small as it was, was sufficient to put Phil and his friend on their guard, and after that they kept their counsels to themselves.

At dusk, the sour-faced jailer brought in some bread and a jug of water, and without answering Phil's remarks that the cell was not fitted for officer or men, banged the door and locked it. Before he did so, Tony caught sight of six Russian soldiers standing in the doorway.

"No chance of rushing that when the jailer comes in," he said shortly. "Never mind, the chimney's good enough for me."

The bread was now divided up, and they fell to hungrily. Then, when his wound had been dressed, Phil and his friends lay down. Fortunately for the former, the bayonet had made a clean thrust through the muscles, and though he suffered some pain, and was stiff, the wound was too slight to incommode him greatly.

The following morning, just as dawn was breaking, Phil slipped off his coat, climbed up the chimney, and slid down into the other cell, where he found McNeil sleeping soundly. He was shocked at the poor fellow's appearance. He was greatly emaciated and intensely pallid. Phil woke him gently.

"Hush, keep quiet!" he said. "Here I am, come to have a chat with you."

McNeil sat up with difficulty.

"Ah, Western!" he cried, grasping Phil by both hands, while his lips quivered, "yours is the first friendly grasp I have felt since I was taken prisoner. So you are now a subaltern, and have been taken prisoner for the second time? How did you escape? I sent a letter to say how gallantly you and your friend fought by my side for the flag."

"Yes, and it reached the camp safely," said Phil, "and I was promoted to sergeant, and my friend to corporal. But I will tell you all about it later. Now let me know about this brute Stackanoff."

"Ah, he is a brute! See here, Western! He has refused me the help and advice of a doctor, and my wound daily gets worse and cripples me."

Phil looked at it, and going to a basin in the corner of the cell, filled it with water and returned.

"I'll set you right in a minute," he said. "I was for a little while in the cholera hospital, and know a little about wounds too."

Some linen lay at hand, and with this he cleaned the wound and dressed it carefully.

"Thank you, Western!" said McNeil gratefully. "You are my good Samaritan. Now what about this escape? I can just limp along, and shall be ready at any moment."

"The door is out of the question," Phil replied thoughtfully. "It is too strong to break, and a guard accompanies the jailer. Then the windows are too small and too high up, while the floor is impossible. The only way is up the chimney."

"Good heavens! up the chimney?"

"Yes; listen! Our cells communicate by slanting flues, and above the junction rises a brick chimney, which is amply wide enough for our bodies. At present it has bars across it, but my friend—who, by the way, is now my servant—will help me to remove them. Fortunately, a shot has cut the chimney off short, and I noticed before coming in that the drop from the top to the roof is not very great."

"And what do you intend doing once you get out?" asked the wounded officer. "Remember you are in the fortifications, and the Russians are as thick as peas all round."

"We must make for the harbour, if possible, and in any case we must chance it. I have been thinking it over this morning; and that is the only way out that I can see. Of course if we cannot get down to the shore and secure a boat, we must creep out between the forts and bolt for our lives. That would be a desperate undertaking."

Both were thoughtful and silent for a moment.

"Now I think I had better return," said Phil. "Be prepared at any time, for the sooner we are away the better. Our lives are never safe while Stackanoff has us in his power."

He grasped McNeil's hand and crept into the chimney.

That night, when all was quiet in the cells, and only the distant booming of the English mortars, and the louder crash of their exploding shells, broke the silence, Phil and Tony crept into the chimney, leaving Pierre breathing heavily on his bed.

Phil climbed to the angle and helped Tony to reach his side. Then, taking it in turn, they stood on one another's shoulders, and wrenched at the bars.

They were more solidly-wedged than had at first seemed likely, but the shell which had struck the stack had cracked the brickwork below, and this lessened the difficulty of their task. It was terribly hot work, however, and by the time two heavy bars had been wrenched free they were exhausted.

"We'll jam the loose bars here," said Phil in a whisper. "Who knows when we shall want weapons with which to defend ourselves!"

Tony chuckled. "You're a cool hand," he laughed. "Who'd have thought of all this if it hadn't been for you. Now all's plain sailing, and I prophesies complete success. Ah, if only that chap Stackanoff would get in my way I'd smash him into a jelly!"

Cautioning him to keep quiet, for both were by now still more doubtful of the cringing Pierre, they slipped down to the cell, and were soon sunk in deep sleep, as though nothing out of the ordinary had occurred.

On the following afternoon the cell door was thrown open, and Stackanoff stalked in with his guard. He glared at his prisoners in a manner that showed his temper had not improved since they saw him last.

"Ah!" he said at last, glancing at the trembling Pierre,—who thought his last hour had come,—and gloating over his terror, "the whole plot is discovered. You are all spies."

With a sob the little Frenchman fell on his knees, and with clasped hands cried, "Mercy, Monsieur ze Russian, je suis innocent!"

"Get up, you little funk," said Phil bitterly, while Tony clasped him by the collar and jerked him to his feet.

"Yes," continued Stackanoff, "you are all spies. The tale that you were washed ashore is exploded. Confess now, and I will promise to deal leniently with you."

"Confess!" shouted Phil, roused to anger. "You know well that we are no spies. And let me tell you, you are merely an inspector, and have no right to punish us. Is this fit treatment for a British officer? Wait," and he shook his finger at the Russian, "I will yet communicate with the gentleman who dismissed you, and probably he will be less pleased with your conduct than before."

"You will! then I will give you little time, you Englishman," snarled Stackanoff, beside himself with rage at the mention of his disgrace. "To-morrow I will have you brought before the military court, and I myself will swear that you are spies who escaped me once before. Then you will be shot. After all, it is an easy death," he laughed sardonically.

Phil felt inclined to fly at him, but he kept his temper.

"After all," he answered quietly, "it is more easy than death by the bayonet, and that perhaps is why so many of your comrades chose death by the bullet in the fight at Inkermann."

"Ha, you would remind me of our disgrace!" hissed the Russian. "Listen, you stubborn English pig. Once you disgraced me and pulled me, Stackanoff, leader of a regiment of Cossacks, to the ground. I did not forget, and I will repay in full measure. You shall come before the military tribunal, as I told you, and that officer for whom you did that foolish deed shall be evidence against you. You will be condemned, and at early dawn, when the cold fog still lies on the ground, you shall be led out to your doom. I shall be there. Do you hear? I, Stackanoff, who hate you worse than any, shall be there, and I myself will shoot you. You shall hear the word, my brave Englishman; you shall see the musket raised, and you shall wait. Ah, yes! you shall have time to think over and regret your folly. Then, when your knees give way like those of this cur of a Frenchman, I will shoot you, and your body shall be flung into the sea. Thus you will learn that it is ill to bring disgrace on the head of a Stackanoff."

Phil laughed in the man's face and looked at him with steady gaze, before which the fiery Russian's eyes lowered.

"You call this man a cur," said Phil with a smile, nodding his head at Pierre. "Believe me, you Russian dog, he is a brave man compared with you, for he would not murder his fellow-being. If that time comes of which you have spoken, I will do my best to bear it; and should your time to face death come first, I trust you may set me an example. I doubt it though. Bullies, such as you, are ever cowards, and vengeance, when followed too far, is apt to bring disaster to the avenger. My only wish is that I could reach your comrades. They have proved themselves brave and honourable men, and would spit on you."

The Russian's face was an ugly picture. Flushed with hate and rage, he looked as though he would repeat his former assault. But, standing upright and sturdy as he did, his head proudly held in air, Phil did not look a young man to be trifled with, even by one with weapons in his hands. Moreover, Tony was close alongside, his eyes fixed upon the Russian's face, and clearly showing that at the slightest attempt he would treat him less gently than before.

"You defy me and laugh at me," said Stackanoff wrathfully. "Very well, I will leave you now and visit your friend. But you shall see me again very soon."

With a snarl of rage he turned on his heel and left the cell.

"What's it all about?" asked Tony eagerly. "This lingo's too much for me, and how you ever picked it up beats me altogether. Get up, you sniveller;" and with an angry growl he hoisted Pierre to his feet once more, for the Frenchman had given way to his fears.

"He's off to McNeil's cell, Tony," Phil answered hurriedly. "I'll tell you all that passed in good time, but give me a lift into the chimney. I must hear all that happens."

He sprang to the grate, and, helped by Tony, was soon at the angle. Breathless with his exertions, he climbed still higher, leaning his body well over the sharp edge of brickwork, and listened eagerly. Suddenly there was a clash, the dull hollow echo of which came rushing up the chimney, followed by Stackanoff's voice.

"I shall be with this prisoner some time," he said, evidently addressing the jailer. "You and the guards can withdraw. I will hammer on the woodwork when I require you to let me out. Now close the door and dismiss the guard."

"Now, sir," he continued, harshly addressing McNeil, when the door had banged. "I have a proposition to make to you, and consider well before you answer it. Liberty is dear to every man, and more so to you, who are sick and wounded. You can buy yours at the price of that man's life who dragged me from my saddle. Swear that he was a spy then, and that that is his regular employment, and I will set you free. I will myself hand you over to the English sentries."

An inarticulate cry of rage burst from McNeil's throat. What followed Phil did not hear, for, suddenly overbalancing in his eagerness, he lost his hold and slipped headlong into the opposite cell, arriving with a crash into the open grate and rolling on to the floor before the astonished eyes of the prisoner and his Russian tempter.

Chapter Twenty.

From the Mouth of the Lion's Den.

Never before had our hero so much need of courage and quick resolution as on that occasion, when, helpless to save himself, he slid like a sack down the chimney, and plumped into the very presence of his bitter enemy. But he was the kind of lad to make the best of a difficult situation. It was not for nothing that he had joined heart and soul in cricket and football, and in every manly game. He had gone through a schooling indeed which no English lad should neglect, and which no one ever regrets; for even in later days, when the cares and duties of life prevent one from indulging in the old games, the quickness and sureness of eye and the presence of mind still remain, and may at any moment extricate one from danger or difficulty.

Phil was a young man whose muscles had been hardened in every game, and whose judgment could be relied on to count the chances of victory in each. Here was a game—one, indeed, of life and death—and instantly recovering from his surprise, and recognising that immediate action was necessary, he sprang to his feet and hurled himself upon the astonished Russian before the latter could grasp his sword. Linked together in a close embrace they swayed from side to side, but Phil had the advantage of size, and squeezing his adversary till the breath was driven from his body, he lifted him in his strong arms and dashed him to the floor.

"Great heavens! you've done for him," cried McNeil, kneeling by the Russian's side. "Look, his neck is broken."

"Then his death be on his own head," gasped Phil. "If I had not killed him, he would soon have had me shot, and besides, my tumbling down that chimney would have spoilt all our chances of escape. Now he's dead, and if we are to get away, it must be done to-night, for should the guards discover what has happened it will mean little mercy. As likely as not we should be taken out and shot before half an hour had passed."

"But what about the jailer?" asked McNeil. "We can be sure that he has heard nothing suspicious or he would have been in here by this. He is aware, though, that Stackanoff is with me, and he will be waiting impatiently for his return?"

"Yes, he will be getting impatient before long," mused Phil. "There is nothing else to be done at present. We will wait till his patience is exhausted, then my friend and I will knock, and as soon as he comes in we will collar him."

"It seems desperately risky, but I suppose it is the only way, Western. If you get hold of him, though, it will save the trouble of climbing through the chimney, an acrobatic feat which, in my present condition, I shall not be sorry to be spared."

"Quite so. I had not thought of that, McNeil," said Phil. "Now I will call Tony. I shall only be gone a few minutes."

Slipping into the chimney, Phil soon regained his own cell.

"Did you hear anything, Tony?" he asked shortly.

"Nothing, mate; but what's been keeping yer so long. You look flurried too. What's happened?"

Phil explained that Stackanoff was dead.

"We must get away to-night, Tony," he said, with decision, "and first of all we must capture the jailer. He is to open the door at Stackanoffs knock, and I propose that we throw ourselves upon him. Now, listen. After knocking, I will stand behind the door so that he cannot see me, and will call to him to come in. You will crouch behind me, and bang the door to. Then we will pull him down and gag him. Bring your blanket with you."

Meanwhile Pierre had listened anxiously, his ferrety little eyes shifting from face to face.

"What is this that happens?" he asked eagerly. "Monsieur makes ze disappearance up ze chimney, then he come back again."

"We must get away to-night, do you understand?" Phil replied, looking searchingly at him. "Are you willing to come?"

"Vraiment, I will accompany you, monsieur," answered Pierre hesitatingly. "Mais—ah, what will ze Russian with ze face severe do to us? Surely he will make ze bang."

"Oh, you little coward!" murmured Phil bitterly, "you will spoil everything yet. I tell you, Pierre," he added, clutching him by both shoulders, "if you wish to stay, do so; but you will probably be shot as a spy. That will be your bad luck in having been washed ashore with us. If you attempt the escape with us, beware how you behave, for should you make a sound to betray us, I will kill you. Now, stay here, and prepare to accompany us. We shall be back in half an hour. Come, Tony, it is already dark, and we must capture that fellow."

"Then in a half of the hour you make ze return," said the little Frenchman, looking as though he had smothered his fears. "Bien, I shall be prepared.

"Aha, my good fellows!" he muttered in his own language a few moments later, with quivering lips. "You have gone up the chimney, and will be back in half an hour. Why should I die for your foolishness? It would be suicide."

Creeping to the chimney, the crafty little coward listened while Phil and Tony slid into the other cell. Then he stepped to the door, and prepared to give the alarm, hoping thereby to escape the fate which would certainly befall the others if discovered. But, overcome by terror of the consequences, he remained irresolute for more than ten minutes ere he dared to shout, for he had a wholesome terror of the fair-haired young Englishman who had brought him back to consciousness when lashed to the wreckage, and moreover there was an ominous look in Tony's eyes as that burly young giant looked at him for the last time before entering the chimney.

Meanwhile Phil and Tony had entered the other cell.

"Now for it," said Phil. "McNeil, you are too lame to help us, so had better lie down on your blankets. Tony, tear up the blanket and get the gag ready. You quite understand?" he went on, when all was finished. "You crouch behind me, and slam the door as soon as the fellow comes in. Then we jump on him. It is dark enough now, so we'll knock."

Taking the precaution to drag Stackanoff's body into the corner behind the door, Phil knocked loudly, and, hearing footsteps outside, cried out in a feigned voice and in the fierce manner in which the dead Russian seemed to have been in the habit of addressing his subordinates, "Hi, you, fool that you are! Why do you not listen, and let me out?"

A second later there was the sound of a key in the lock, and almost at the same moment a most unearthly scream.

The escaping prisoners looked at one another with doubting eyes, but before a question could be asked the door was pushed open cautiously. Phil clutched its edge, so that it could not easily be closed, and waited. Then again came the scream, this time more clearly heard, while the voice of Pierre could be distinguished crying at the top of his voice, and still in broken English, as if that would be better understood by the Russians, "Help! help! Ze English prisonaire make ze escape!"

"Ah! treachery!" gasped the jailer, stepping back and attempting to close the door.

Phil darted out and made a grab at the man, but with a cry of terror the Russian took to his heels, and raced up the steep flight of steps, where he turned towards the town.

Phil followed him to the top of the stairway, and then returned hurriedly.

"He has got away, and has gone to call the nearest guard," he cried in hurried tones. "Tumble out, you fellows. They will be back here in a quarter of an hour or less, and if we are to give them the slip, it must be now. What are you doing, Tony? Come here, you idiot!"

Tony crept from the chimney, into which he was in the act of climbing, and slunk back to his friend's side abashed, and yet full of indignation.

"Going to leave that cabbage-eating French monkey?" he asked angrily. "What's he done? Why, just spoilt all our chances; that's all."

"It is the very thing you will be doing, old man," answered Phil. "Now, give me one of those bars, and keep one yourself. McNeil, I'm ready, if you are. Here is Stackanoff's sword for you. As for that little coward, he has done all the harm he can possibly do us, so we will leave him to his own devices."

They grasped their weapons, and Phil and Tony, placing themselves on either side of the wounded lieutenant to help him along, hurried out of the cell, up the stairs, and ran for a deep ditch which they had noticed as they were marched to prison. It seemed to be a trench constructed to command the rear of some of the fortifications, and for the moment would prove an excellent shelter.

"Listen, I hear the guard returning!" whispered McNeil, "and the bell that is ringing must be a warning to announce that prisoners have escaped. Whew! that was a nasty one!" he exclaimed a moment later, for the guard had advanced with a blazing torch to assist in the search, and, the street being visible from the British trenches, and the range known to a nicety, a shell had been pitched with precision just in front of the group. The torch was instantly extinguished and all was darkness again, but the sound of distant marching, and an occasional order sharply given, proved that troops were being hastened from their quarters to patrol the streets and cut off the escaping prisoners.

"They know that the harbour is our only chance," said Phil bitterly. "I fear it looks like failure this time, McNeil."

"It does look bad," agreed the latter sadly. "What hard luck, when we had all set our hearts so much upon it!"

"Are you game to try the other way?" asked Phil eagerly.

"Game!" answered McNeil enthusiastically; "just you try me. I've had enough of Russian prisons for a lifetime, and I tell you I would rather die than go back."

"Then we go forward," said Phil shortly. "Keep close together and steer between the forts. If anyone challenges, leave me to answer."

Climbing from the ditch, they set their faces for the British camp and crept forward cautiously till they recognised the Malakoff looming big and shadowy in front. Phil led the way and attempted to make out the position of the earthworks and trenches. "There—there they are, only a few yards in front of us!" he whispered eagerly. "Hush! down for your lives!"

A figure suddenly rose up in front of them and listened. Evidently the man was a sentry, and had heard something suspicious, for next moment he challenged loudly.

Long ere this Phil had learnt that polite words are not usually wasted on Russian privates, and he determined to take advantage of the fact.

"Idiot!" he answered roughly. "Cannot you see that I am your officer, and can I not give instructions to my lieutenant without your challenging?"

"My orders are to challenge everyone," the sentry answered humbly. "Excellency, give the countersign and I shall know you better. Some dogs of prisoners have recently escaped, for I heard the bell, therefore I must be cautious."

"My word, we're done again!" groaned Phil. Then taking the bull by the horns, he advanced a pace and said roughly, "How can I remember the word every night after all these weeks? Wait, though—ah, was not the first letter 'N'?"

"That is right, excellency; and our master the Czar's name also commences with that letter," the sentry replied encouragingly.

"Nicolas!" cried Phil boldly.

"Excellency, your pardon on my insisting; pass whither you will. All is well."

"That is good, fellow," Phil cried. "Come, comrades, we have business with the Malakoff."

Another fire minutes, and the sentry and trench were passed. Skirting by the great fortress, they bore up for the British trenches, crossing as they did so several rows of ditches and earthworks. Then they lay down and listened. Close at hand there was a hum of voices, while away on the left a sharp musketry fire was being maintained, the flicker of the exploding powder cutting the darkness at every second. In front all was pitch blackness in the valley in which they stood, but higher up on the elopes beyond fires were burning, and dark figures were occasionally silhouetted against them as they passed.

"Now for it!" whispered Phil. "If there is any firing lie on your faces. We don't want to be killed by our own side."

Sneaking through the mud and mire on hands and knees the three crept forward in absolute silence. Soon the last trench was passed, and the British earthworks loomed in the distance. At last they were close to liberty and friends. Not more than sixty yards separated them, and already the murmur of the men's voices could be heard, when, with a sharp exclamation, Phil disappeared.

There was a scuffle, a startled cry of astonishment and fear, and the loud report of a musket.

"Quick, help me!" Phil cried from the rifle-pit into which he had fallen. Then there was a choked cry, and all was silence for a few moments.

With a growl of rage Tony threw himself into the pit, almost smashing Phil as he fell.

"That you, Tony?" the latter asked coolly.

"Yes, it's me sure enough, mate. Are yer hurt, old man?"

"Not a bit, but it was a hard struggle. I fancy the Russian is dead, for I gave him a tremendous blow on the head with my iron bar. Now, let us push on, for the alarm has been given, and it will mean capture if we stay."

But the Russian sharpshooters had taken the alarm. Occupying a row of pits, each of which was sufficiently large to hold one man, they had orders to worry the besiegers by their fire, and to be always on the look-out for an assault. At the report of their comrade's weapon they imagined that they were about to be attacked, and poured volley after volley at the British earthworks. Instantly the sharp crackle of Minié rifles broke out, and Phil and his friends found themselves in the awkward position of receiving fire from their friends.

"Down in here for your lives," cried Phil; and within half a minute they were wedged in the pit, while a perfect hail of bullets swept overhead. Both sides imagined that a sortie was taking place, and the alarm spreading, the guns on either side opened fire, and a perfect torrent of shell hummed in the air and burst with deafening crashes in the darkness. A loud scuffling was then heard in the British trenches, there was a sharp order, and a host of dark figures sprang over the earthworks and dashed at the Russians.

Phil and his friends lay flat upon their faces, while the Russians in the other pits for the most part fled for their lives. Those who did not were bayoneted.

"Hallo, come out of it, you skulkers!" a voice cried; and, looking up, Phil caught sight of the figures of English soldiers at the mouth of the pit.

"Don't fire," he shouted, "we are friends. We are escaping prisoners."

"Now, then, none of yer sauce," the same voice answered wrathfully. "Most like you're deserters. Out yer come and let's take a look at yer."

In a trice they were dragged ignominiously from the pit.

"Why, what's this?" the sergeant, who had charge of the party, exclaimed. "The light's bad, but blow me if there ain't two British officers here. Get round 'em, boys, and bring 'em along."

With a rush the group of soldiers returned, bearing Phil and his friends with them.

"Now, send along that lamp," cried the sergeant, as soon as they were safely sheltered by the earthworks. "Blow me, but I'm right. They're Britishers or I'm a wrong 'un," he cried, lifting the lantern to their faces. "Hi, pass the word to Mr Ellis there."

A moment later an officer came hurrying along.

"What is all this commotion about?" he asked sharply. "The whole camp is disturbed, and you seem to have made a sortie, Sergeant."

"Quite right, sir! There was a bit of a ruction over in them rifle-pits, and as I knew you was anxious to teach them Russians a lesson, and the boys was mad to get at 'em, why, we did a rush and cleared 'em out like rats. We found these three there. They said they were escaping prisoners, so we brought 'em along."

"Who are you, then?" asked the officer, examining them by the aid of his lantern.

"Why, bless my life if it isn't Western, reported drowned at sea!" he exclaimed with a start. "You're like a jack-in-the-box, Western. Who are your friends?"

Phil mentioned their names.

"We had a near squeak for it," he said faintly. "By the way, Ellis, is there a doctor near? McNeil is in need of dressing, and I fear I have got a bullet in my ribs."

That was the case. At the first outburst of firing, a bullet had struck him in the side like a sledge-hammer, but Phil kept his groans to himself. Now, however, when all need for further silence and exertion had passed, he sat down suddenly, and went off into a dead faint, frightening poor Tony almost out of his life. A few drops of brandy were forced between his teeth, and by the time he had been placed on a blanket he was conscious again. Then he was carried with great gentleness up to the field-hospital.

"Another bullet wound, my lad," said the surgeon kindly. "That makes the fifth I have seen already to-night. Let me have a look at it;" and with the greatest sympathy and gentleness he removed Phil's clothing and examined the wound.

"Ah! a nasty one," he said gravely. "Two ribs badly smashed, and the lung injured. Not fatal, though. Oh, no! not by any means. We'll dress it carefully and get you out of this."

Phil gave an exclamation of disgust.

"It's awfully bad luck, doctor," he said testily. "Here I am, scarcely landed on the Crimea, and already I have been captured twice. And now I am to be sent away for the second time. Couldn't I possibly stay? I am very anxious to serve to the end of the campaign with my regiment."

"Yes, I know you are, my lad, but Scutari is where you are going," the doctor answered firmly. "Twice captured since you landed! Yes, but you forget to mention that in the short time that has elapsed, you have escaped twice from the Russians, taken part in two pitched battles, and joined in a famous cavalry charge, not to mention having been promoted to a commission for distinguished gallantry. Now, no more talking. To-morrow you go, and your friend too."

Expostulations were unavailing, and on the following day Phil and Lieutenant McNeil were carried to Balaclava and hoisted on board a ship bound for the great hospital at Scutari, with her decks full of sick and wounded soldiers. As was only natural, Tony accompanied them.

Before the convoy set out from camp the news of their reappearance had got wind, and many officers of the 30th, besides friends from the battalion of Grenadier Guards and Lieutenant McNeil's regiment, came flocking to see them. Phil was scarcely in a condition to talk, and Tony, who had, as it were, mounted guard over him, insisted that the doctor's orders should be obeyed. But he himself was quite ready to dilate on their adventures, and he did so in a manner which would have made the bashful Phil blush. At length they were on the sea *en route* for Scutari, and within two days, thanks to the cold and bracing air, and an excellent constitution, Phil was able to lie in a hammock, on deck, suspended between the mast and the top of the saloon skylight.

Douglas McNeil had taken the greatest liking for his young friend, and to the latter's secret astonishment, spent hours in gazing at him thoughtfully, as though he were trying to recollect something. Very soon both were on the closest terms of intimacy.

"What are you troubling about?" asked Phil with a wan smile one day, noticing the look of perplexity on his friend's face.

Douglas was silent for a few minutes. "I will tell you," he said at last. "From the very first there has been something about you that has struck me; some strong resemblance to my dear mother. Sometimes I think, too, that you and I have features much in common. You never speak of your parents, Phil, and I have never liked to ask you, but if you care to tell me I should be glad to hear."

"Parents!" said Phil, with a short and somewhat bitter laugh. "I never knew my real father and mother. I was sold at the age of two, and that's a good long time ago."

"Sold! Who sold you? Where did it take place, and who paid the money?" Douglas asked excitedly, coming closer to Phil.

"As far as I have been able to learn from my adopted father, a poor woman, with many children, sold me. Where, though, I do not recollect I was sold to Mr Western, at one time an officer in the army, but for many years a clergyman."

Douglas McNeil stared at him with wide-open eyes, and seemed strangely excited.

"Listen, Phil," he said earnestly. "About twenty years ago my aunt, my mother's younger sister, fell in love with a poor officer in the navy. She married him against the wishes of her parents, and my grandfather, who was a stubborn hard-hearted man, refused to have anything more to do with her, refused even to hear of her or help her in any way. A year later Frank Davidson, the husband, was drowned at sea, and my aunt brought a boy into the world. For five years her relatives heard nothing. But the old grandfather had already repented of his harshness, and enquiries were set on foot. It is an odd story, Phil, and is full of sadness. That unhappy aunt of mine was friendless, and to obtain a post as governess was compelled to part with her child. You can imagine the poor thing's grief and loneliness. She placed the child with a certain woman who kept a kind of baby-farm in the midlands. For a year all went well, but my aunt died very suddenly of fever, and we learnt afterwards, from people who lived near the baby-farm, that the boy we were in search of was disposed of to a clergyman. The neighbours remembered having seen him. I suppose one cannot blame the woman in charge, though the thing sounds hateful and impossible in our free England. But, finding there was no yearly instalment coming for the child's keep, she answered an advertisement and handed him over to a clergyman. Unfortunately she herself died a few months before we instituted the search, and although we advertised widely we never obtained any more information. Tell me now, Phil, what you think of that?"

There was a long silence.

"Could it be possible that, after all, he was indeed the lost child?" Phil asked himself. "Was it possible that the story just narrated was his own, and referred to his father and mother. Was the vicar's test to be a useless one, for he had trained an adopted son for one purpose only? What joy it would be to have relations of his own?" The thoughts crowded through his brain, and his lips trembled with hope and eagerness.

"Douglas," he said at last, in a voice that was weak and broken with emotion, "I believe I am your cousin I believe that that unhappy lady you have spoken of was my dear mother, the mother I never knew. We cannot settle the question here, but my adopted father can do so as soon as we get back to England. Something tells me that you have helped me to discover the secret of my birth, and if so, then all I can say is, that I greet you as a cousin with all my heart. Providence has thrown us together, and let us hope that the same guiding hand will keep us good friends till the last."

The lads shook hands silently, while Tony looked on with a grin of pleasure on his face.

"Such a one as Phil is for making pals I never see," he muttered. "Lor', if it was girls around he would be turning their heads, and getting failed in love with by every one on 'em;" and with a loud guffaw he dived down the companion ladder. As for Phil and Douglas McNeil, they sat discussing the question of their relationship for more than an hour, and when they retired, it was with the mutual and hearty agreement that it was one of the happiest days in their lives when the fortune of war brought them together to fight side by side for the honour of England's flag.

Chapter Twenty One.

A Welcome Discovery.

It was a new thing indeed for our hero to have real relatives, and those who may happen to have read these chapters, and are placed in a position similar to his, will realise with what eagerness he hoped that it should turn out that he and Douglas McNeil were cousins.

True, Phil had had an adopted father and mother who, if not indulgent, were at least kind after their own way. But home life for him had always lacked that sympathy and that geniality which are the makings of a happy family circle. Where all was austerity, Joe Sweetman's ruddy, smiling face had come like the sun to lighten the gloomy house. No wonder that Phil took to him from the first, and no wonder that, now that the real secret of his birth seemed to be on the point of discovery, in which case he would have friends, aunts, uncles, and cousins like others he met every day of his life, he was more than a little excited. He and Douglas had many a chat over the possibility of their being relations, and before Scutari was reached the latter had written a long letter of explanation to his parents, while Phil wrote to Joe and to Mr Western, telling of his new life and fortunes, and asking for particulars of the place and the woman from whose house he had been brought many years before. Then, as nothing further could be done to settle the matter, they dropped the subject by mutual consent.

A week after they left Balaclava the huge barracks which now served as a hospital for the sick and wounded British hove in sight, and by evening Phil and his new friend were comfortably quartered in a small ward in which were three other officers. Fortunately neither was dangerously or seriously ill, though their wounds were sufficiently grave to make them incapable of active service for some time to come. Thanks, however, to healthy constitutions they were rapidly recovering strength, and therefore not in much need of attention. And it was well for them that matters were in such a satisfactory state, for the huge hospital, built on the quadrangular system, and with sides a quarter of a mile long, had some two miles and more of corridors and wards, all packed to overflowing.

"I never saw such a thing," remarked Phil sadly, after he and Douglas had been placed in their cots. "The men are almost lying on top of one another, and it cannot possibly be good for them. This overcrowding must have a harmful influence on their wounds."

"You are right there," answered one of the other officers bitterly. "I am a doctor, and I can tell you that the overcrowding and bad ventilation are killing the men in scores, and when to that trouble is added the lamentable fact that the hospital staff is quite inadequate, and attendants are too few and far between, you can imagine what suffering there is."

"But surely there should be sufficient orderlies to nurse and look after the men?" exclaimed Douglas indignantly.

"Undoubtedly there should be," answered the doctor, a man of some fifty years of age; "but the fact remains that there are not nearly enough. Who is to blame I do not know. Probably the lack of system is the chief cause of all our troubles, for without a regular system everything goes to the wall. It must be the case, especially when the strain comes, and it has come now with a vengeance. Men are simply falling sick in hundreds, and really you cannot be surprised, for as Balaclava is eight miles from the trenches, it is almost impossible to keep up supplies, and in consequence the men are nearly starved. Then the storm destroyed all their warm clothing, and as the rains have now set in, and many hours have to be spent in the earthworks, it means that our poor fellows are nearly always wet through. I can tell you that, after serving in many parts of the world, I have come to the conclusion that where an Englishman cannot live it is not worth the while of others to go. He can put up with most things in the way of heat or cold, providing he is well fed and clothed. But starve the strongest man, and see how quickly he will succumb to cold and exposure."

That this was true could not be doubted, for, continually drenched as our soldiers were, cut by icy blasts of wind, and almost starved, they fell ill in vast numbers. Overworked by long hours in the damp trenches, and continually harassed by a musketry fire from the rifle-pits, they flung themselves down upon the mud and greasy mire at night, and snatched a few fitful moments of repose, wrapped in a blanket as worn out as themselves, and almost certainly dripping with moisture.

It was no one's fault, this lack of clothing and supplies. It was the absence of a commissariat system of wide teaching power and with ample funds at its command. Given a base in England, with men there to choose and forward the necessary supplies in hired transports, there must still be others at the base in the invaded country to distribute what is sent, and yet again there must be more with clear brains and ready hands to bring those stores of food and clothing, and a thousand-and-one other things, to the very outskirts of the camp. Otherwise another burden is thrown upon your already hardly-taxed fighting regiments. And to distribute stores in this thorough manner, horses and carts are required, and, since the former cannot live on air, forage with which to feed them. Horses, too, like men, are apt to sicken and die, especially if ill-fed and exposed to bitter winds; and therefore remounts are always required, and these must often be sent for from far-off countries, and brought in big transports specially fitted for the purpose.

All this was admirably carried out in the Boer War of 1899-1900. A perfect system of transport and supply had long before been arranged, and officers and men trained to carry it out. Those who have seen will give unstinted praise, for supplies, remounts, clothing, every conceivable thing, were obtainable, often brought to the front at the cost of no small amount of labour and forethought by those responsible for the work.

In the days of the Crimea there was no such system, and, to add to everything, horses were extremely scarce, while eight long miles of mud intervened between the harbour of Balaclava and the trenches. Daily, men made beasts of burden of themselves, waded through the mud to Balaclava, and struggled back with food, which, when distributed, had too often to be eaten in an uncooked state, for fuel was at a premium.

It is no wonder, then, that men were incessantly falling ill, and that the hospital at Scutari was thronged with soldiers, who died at an alarming rate. Up to and during that November, one poor wretch died out of every two, for if there was no transport or supply system, there was likewise no hospital organisation worthy of the name. Surgeons were few and far between, and too much occupied in their work of mercy to be able to give time to other matters. Thus, the hospital at Scutari, never noted for cleanliness, became a hovel of filth and insanitation, to which the alarming death-rate gave ample, if painful, evidence.

Well was it for our poor soldiers that correspondents accompanied that army. By their publications, and by aid of the telegraph, the cry of the dying soldier smote the heart of the British nation, and roused it to wrath and pity. A fund was raised, and, better than all, those sent out by whose aid it should be rapidly and systematically distributed.

Florence Nightingale, that grand lady of undying fame, instituted her band of nurses, and by her untiring energy and ready brain brought for the first time some system and order into the management of the hospital at Scutari.

With a glance she conquered the whole working staff, doctors readily gave over the conduct of affairs to her, and in a wonderfully short space of time the death-rate had fallen vastly, dirt was hustled from the buildings, unhealthy sanitary arrangements were swept away and more suitable ones introduced, and last, but not least, a kitchen was built by means of which a thousand special diets could be prepared.

"YOU'VE DONE FOR HIM!" CRIED M'NEIL

Those who have fallen ill at home, and never ceased to fill the air with praises and thanks to the attentive nurse who cared for them so devotedly, can perhaps imagine what it means to some poor ailing soldier, sick almost to death, and with only the rough surroundings of war about him, to have some gentle hand to nurse him. It is better than all the delicacies under the sun, for where the womanly mind comes the material comforts will follow to a certainty.

Phil and Douglas did not stay long at Scutari. A consultation was held on their cases, and it was declared that months must pass before they could be fit for hard work again. Accordingly they were sent on board a transport returning to England.

"I'm jolly glad to get away, Phil," exclaimed Douglas with a sigh of relief. "Of course I'd rather have been with the regiment, but I fully realise that our advisers are right, and that we both require a long rest and change. To tell you the truth, too, I am not altogether sorry. All the big affairs in the campaign seem to be over, and now our fellows are having a miserable time in the trenches, waiting for the fortress to surrender. Besides, since we met, that little matter of your birth has puzzled me, and you can't tell, old fellow, how anxious I am to have it settled, though I feel quite sure now that you are my cousin. Every time I look at you I see the resemblance to my mother and aunt and to myself."

"I agree with you there," answered Phil. "I've looked at myself more attentively in the glass than ever before, and I think it is no fancy, but that there is in reality a similarity of feature. I trust it will be proved that I am your cousin. I shall be a lucky fellow if it turns out true."

"Perhaps you will be more fortunate than you imagine," said Douglas, with a gay laugh.

"Why? How?" asked Phil inquisitively.

"Oh! if you are my cousin, you will have little need to do hard work in the future."

"Why? I don't understand you, Douglas," Phil answered doubtfully.

"Great goodness! old man, you will be quite a Croesus," Douglas replied, with a laugh. "To tell you the whole truth, my grandfather was overcome with remorse, and, believing you would eventually be found, settled a large sum of money on you—larger than on any of his other children. My mother is one of the trustees of that fund, and I happen to know that it is now considerably swollen, having been most happily invested."

"It would be nice to have an independent income," Phil mused thoughtfully, "but I think, Douglas, that I would far rather have the new relations. See what an interest they would give me in the future."

"Yes, I think they would, Phil, particularly the cousins. I believe there are some fifteen of the latter, and ten at least are girls, one being my sister. Oh yes, old fellow! I've no doubt there would be a great amount of interest; for a young chap who wins his way from the ranks by a series of plucky acts, and who, moreover, is a gentleman and a cousin too, must necessarily be of absorbing interest to new relations."

Douglas laughed merrily, while Phil coloured hotly.

"I'm afraid I'm a shy fellow with girls," he stuttered, "but you'll stand by me, Douglas, won't you?"

"Rather, old man, and do my best to be of more interest than you," laughed his friend. "Cousins, particularly of the fair sex, are exceedingly charming company. It'll be a regular picnic, old man."

And now, before lowering the gangway and landing Phil, Douglas, and Tony on England's shore, let us briefly glance at the closing scenes of the Crimean war. In February, while our poor fellows were beginning to recover from their misery, and supplies, and even luxuries, were pouring into the trenches, the Russians attacked the town and port of Eupatoria, close to which the Allies had first disembarked, and which was now strongly held by the Turks and commanded by the guns of the fleet. The grey-coated battalions were driven back with considerable loss.

And meanwhile, through all the dreary weeks, Allies and Russians crept towards each other, cutting new trenches, sapping in all directions, and endeavouring to place their opponents at a disadvantage. On March 22nd a huge sortie was made from Sebastopol upon the French line of earthworks, while another column was launched at our right. Both failed, and the Russians retired with a loss of 1300.

Spring found the Allies in far better condition than they were earlier in the war, and particularly was this the case with the British. Supplies were now abundant, and, thanks to private enterprise, a railway extended from Balaclava to the camp, and so saved the labour of porterage.

Accordingly the siege was prosecuted with renewed energy, and on April 9th another general bombardment of the fortress took place and continued for ten days, ten awful days for the Russians, for a few hours had been sufficient to reduce many of the fortifications, and, fearful of an assault at any moment, large reserves had of necessity to be kept close at hand. Through the ranks of these unfortunate but truly devoted men the iron hail poured, tearing them here and there and toppling masses of masonry on to them. In those terrible days 6000 or more of the enemy were killed or wounded, and if Scutari had been a sight to bring tears to one's eyes, then the Assembly Rooms and other temporary hospitals in Sebastopol were perfect shambles, while the streets and the road from the fortress were lined with unburied dead.

Thankful indeed must we of more modern days be for the safety which the Geneva Convention gives. A red-cross flag over a hospital renders it sacred, and, once wounded, soldiers of all civilised nations can rely upon rest and freedom from further injury. Thus out of awful sufferings and loss of life we have seen that a new era of good has arisen. A Geneva Convention has sprung into being, and our army is provided with special departments for transport, supply, hospitals, and other matters, each ruled by a well-ordered system.

On May 22nd the French attempted to capture a new line of Russian works which commanded their own trenches, but were beaten back, though their losses were considerably less than the enemy's. On the same date a combined fleet sailed to the east, entered the sea of Azof, and took the town of Kertch. They also destroyed and captured many ships engaged in bringing supplies to the Russian field-army, and wound up their operations by taking other towns, and destroying huge depôts of supplies. On June 6th and 7th the fortress of Sebastopol was again subjected to a fearful bombardment from 544 guns, and its walls and forts reduced to masses of débris. In the evening of the second day the French attacked and took a position known as the "White" works. They then, with the aid of the Turks, captured a fort of great strength, and now for some time in existence, known as the Mamelon, while the English stormed and took others known as the "quarries". Thus the outer line of Russian forts and trenches was in the hands of the Allies. But still the stubborn and unyielding enemy clung to the fortress. The bombardment was resumed, and on the 18th the Allies assaulted the main works of the town, only to be driven back with heavy loss. After that, for many a day, they contented themselves with cutting their trenches and approaches, and slowly approaching to the fortress, the object being to get so close that their attacking-parties might rush across the open and reach the enemy before being swept away by the guns.

On 15th August a battle was fought close to the Mackenzie heights, in which the French proved victorious, the Russian field-army, with whom they were engaged, retiring with heavy loss. On the 17th the bombardment of the fortress commenced again, and continued for some days. It was renewed on September 5th, and continued till the 8th, when a gigantic and combined assault took place. At a terrible cost in killed and wounded the Malakoff was taken and held by the French. The remainder of the attack failed, the English being forced to retire from the Redan, while the French were driven from the little Redan and curtain bastion. Next morning, after a defence of which all Russia may well be proud, the enemy marched over a bridge built across the harbour, and retired in good order, leaving burning fuses to their magazines. Of these no fewer than thirty-five exploded with terrific noise and awful results, keeping the camp in a state of alarm for two whole days and nights, while fires blazed in every direction and lit the skies with their lurid flames.

And now a new phase of the campaign opened, for opposed to the Allies there was only a field-army. The two armies sat down facing one another, no battles of importance taking place; but in the meanwhile the docks and arsenals of Sebastopol were blown up by our engineers.

Russia had lost heavily in men and money, and, moreover, Europe was in conceit against her. Nicholas had died on March 2nd, and now the new czar was prevailed upon to listen to reason. A treaty was drawn up and signed in Paris on March 30th, by which, amongst other terms of peace, the Black Sea should be neutral in future, and no power should interfere between the Sultan and his subjects. On April 2nd a last salvo of artillery from the batteries on the upland slopes announced that the Crimean war was over.

Phil did not return to Russia, for his wound proved more severe than was at first imagined, while Douglas was still too lame to be fit for active service. They therefore remained in England.

There is little more to tell about them. Phil did not find Mr Western altered. Indeed he seemed more austere than ever, especially as his adopted son had risen instead of going to the dogs, as he had prophesied. But Joe was jubilant.

"Didn't I tell him you'd be no disgrace to him!" he cried, taking up his favourite position in front of the fireplace. "You've done well, Phil, my lad, and I am proud of you. Fancy, now! It seems to me only a year ago since you got into that scrape with the mayor. Ha, ha! what a mischievous young monkey you were! And now you're an ensign in the 30th, and have brave deeds to boast of. But there, you'll get conceited if I praise you. No, my dear boy, old Joe is right glad to witness your success, and still more pleased to find that your relatives have turned up. A year ago you were the adopted son of poor parents. Now you are the long-lost orphan, the offspring of gentlefolks, and heir to a tidy fortune when you come of age. Besides—I was forgetting—there are the cousins, the girl cousins, Phil;" and with a roar of laughter he pinched our hero's ear.

Phil had, indeed, to use a common expression, fallen on his feet. He had learnt that he was of no obscure parentage, and in addition, he had made some excellent friends amongst his relatives, in whose eyes he was now a young lion, covered with no small amount of glory.

Years rolled on in rapid succession, and in due time Phil reached the age of twenty-six, when he married his cousin Eva, Douglas McNeil's sister.

When one meets him now, as he follows the hounds or stalks through the streets of London, one unconsciously turns round and takes a second look, with the muttered remark, "What a fine, soldierly-looking fellow!" For he still stands as straight as an arrow, carrying his years easily, while his fine face and big, grey moustache give him a most distinguished appearance.

That Crimean veteran has many scenes to look back upon. He remembers his youth, his struggle to rise in the world, and the lifelong friends he made in achieving his object. He recollects with a happy smile his marriage, the toddlers who one by one made their appearance, only to grow up and flit away like fledglings to form nests of their own. Yes, he remembers all—that happy, gay old bachelor Joe, and his staunch, true-hearted Tony. Sometimes, too, when he sits in his chair and slumbers, he dreams that he is once again in the Crimea, and that his comrades, having heard of the laurels he has won, are still carrying him shoulder-high, and calling him "A Gallant Grenadier."

The End

www.ingramcontent.com/pod-product-compliance
Lightning Source LLC
Chambersburg PA
CBHW060618290526

45793CB00001B/74